Additional Praise for *Remaking Muslim Lives*

"Thanks to his curiosity and sensitivity to the lived experiences of religion, David Henig takes us beyond the clichéd images of Islam in Europe in this vivid ethnography of Muslim lives in postwar Bosnia and Herzegovina. As he explores small-town mosques, village houses, and communal graveyards, Henig pauses to reveal perceptive new insights and pose thoughtful questions that will resonate with historians, sociologists, anthropologists, and others interested in the layered meanings of Muslim religious practice today."

—Edin Hajdarpasic, author of *Whose Bosnia? Nationalism and Political Imagination in the Balkans, 1840–1914*

"Islam and the vital exchanges it creates—among people and with God—give Muslims in Bosnia and Herzegovina a tenacious grip on time and space. Henig traces these exchanges in amazing detail. He takes us beyond questions of whether Islam can be European to places where divinity and identity have already been woven into moral systems of incredible staying power. His analysis is driven by the sacred power of those places."

—Andrew Shryock, author of *Deep History: the Architecture of Past and Present*

Remaking Muslim Lives

INTERPRETATIONS OF CULTURE IN THE NEW MILLENNIUM

Norman E. Whitten Jr., General Editor

A list of books in the series appears at the end of the book.

Remaking Muslim Lives

Everyday Islam in Postwar Bosnia and Herzegovina

DAVID HENIG

UNIVERSITY OF ILLINOIS PRESS
Urbana, Chicago, and Springfield

1 2 3 4 5 C P 5 4 3 2 1
This book is printed on acid-free paper.

Library of Congress Cataloging-in-Publication Data
Names: Henig, David, author.
Title: Remaking Muslim lives : everyday Islam in postwar Bosnia and Herzegovina / David Henig.
Description: Urbana : University of Illinois Press, [2020] | Series: Interpretations of culture in the new millennium | Includes bibliographical references and index.
Identifiers: LCCN 2020008792 (print) | LCCN 2020008793 (ebook) | ISBN 9780252043291 (cloth) | ISBN 9780252085215 (paperback) | ISBN 9780252052170 (ebook)
Subjects: LCSH: Muslims—Bosnia and Herzegovina—Social conditions. | Islam—Bosnia and Herzegovina—History. | Bosnia and Herzegovina—Religious life and customs. | Bosnia and Herzegovina—Ethnic relations. | Bosnia and Herzegovina—Social conditions.
Classification: LCC DR1674.M87 H46 2020 (print) | LCC DR1674.M87 (ebook) | DDC 305.6/970949742—dc23
LC record available at https://lccn.loc.gov/2020008792
LC ebook record available at https://lccn.loc.gov/2020008793

For Emma

Contents

Acknowledgments

This book was a long time in the making. So many people have helped me over the years, and I would like to thank them all. My biggest debt is to the many people in Bosnia and Herzegovina who helped me in so many ways. To name them all would be an impossible task. I feel very lucky to have met so many great people during my time spent in Bosnia and Herzegovina who became real friends. In particular, I would like to thank all my friends in "Brdo" (pseudonym) and other villages for their generosity and hospitality. I cannot express in words my deep gratitude to my "adoptive family" who accepted me as their own—they know who they are. My friendship with Mujo's family was truly a gift. I am grateful to Azmir Muftić, his family, and all my friends in Vareš. Without Azmir's historical and ethnographic knowledge of the Zvijezda highlands, I would have never been able to complete this book. In Sarajevo, I always received support and help from the Zemaljski Muzej, as well as friendship from Samir and Ernis. Elvir Duranović, Hikmet Karčić, and Enes Karić always found time to meet with me and discuss my research. Tone Bringa was instrumental in setting up my research, and provided much-needed feedback and support over the years.

The research for this book was generously supported by the Wadsworth International Fellowship awarded by the Wenner-Gren Foundation. Durham University proved to be the perfect institution to pursue my anthropological training. I am grateful to my supervisors Stephen Lyon and Iain Edgar, and my teachers Michael Carrithers, Yulia Egorova, Robert Layton, and Bob Simpson for their inspiration, guidance, and support over the years. My colleagues and students at the University of Kent in Canterbury provided a stimulating environment for developing my ideas and pushed me to think more comparatively. I am grateful to Miguel Alexiades, Judith Bovensiepen, Glenn Bowman, Michael Fischer, Matt Hodges, Jon Mair, Daniela Peluso, Joao de Pina-Cabral, Mike Poltorak, Raj Puri, Andrew Sanchez (now at Cambridge), Dimitrios Theodossopoulos, and Anna Waldstein. In particular, Jon, Michael, Miguel, and Daniela were true friends and made Canterbury a real home for me for many years. My doctoral students at Kent and Utrecht—Ruth Auger, Marko Barišić, Tom Bell, Yana Bezirganova, Christopher de Coulon Berthoud, Jade Richards, and Ivana Ljuština—have been a tremendous source of inspiration and energy.

A major portion of the manuscript was completed during my Visiting Fellowship at the Centre for Southeast European Studies, University of Graz, in 2017. I am grateful to my hosts in Graz, Florian Bieber and Kerem Öktem for making my stay not only possible but also intellectually stimulating and productive. The final work on the book was made possible in my new academic home at Utrecht University. I would like to thank the Department of Cultural Anthropology for welcoming me so warmly and for supporting me in every possible way in the final legs of the journey. Throughout the process of finishing *Remaking Muslim Lives*, I have been fortunate to receive the enthusiastic support of the series editor, Norman Whitten. Marika Christofides and Dawn Durante from the University of Illinois Press, and my copyeditor Deborah Oliver, were extremely helpful and a real pleasure to work with. The insightful suggestions and careful reading of the manuscript offered by the anonymous reviewers were invaluable, as was the feedback I received during many workshops, conference panels, and departmental seminars over the years. I should like to mention the "Balkan Topologies" workshop organized by Nicolas Argenti in Athens, which was a turning point for many of the ideas discussed in the book.

For reading and providing invaluable feedback on portions of the book, and related arguments and thoughts I am grateful to Paul Anderson, Glenn Bowman, Matei Candea, Giovanni da Col, Chris Hann, Engseng Ho, Amira Mittermaier, Esra Özyurek, Madeleine Reeves, Jeremy F. Walton, Catherine Wanner, and Pnina Werbner. For many years I have been inspired by incredibly smart, creative, and generous scholars of the former Yugoslavia, who shaped my ideas in a profound way. I am grateful to Čarna Brković, Andrew Gilbert, Jessica Greenberg, Bob Hayden, Azra Hromadžić, Larisa Jašarević, Deana Jovanović, Larisa Kurtović, Darryl Li, Ivan Rajković, Maple Razsa, and Paul Stubbs. Stef Jansen has been always encouraging and available for a long discussion in Sarajevo. Sarah Wagner's support and generous input in the final stages of writing were critical. I owe a massive intellectual debt to three inspirational historians, Harun Buljina, Edin Hajdarpašić, and Dženita Karić. Over the years I have been fortunate to benefit from intellectual friendship, extended conversations, generous guidance, and critical reading from Andreas Bandak, Rebecca Bryant, Daniel Knight, Michael Lambek, Nicolette Makovicky, Magnus Marsden, Stavroula Pipyrou, Joel Robbins, Andrew Shryock, Daniel Sosna, and Charles Stewart. Their influence is obvious, but any shortcomings in the text remain entirely mine.

This book would have never been possible without the support of my family, despite never having got used to my nomadic way of life. My sister will always be a great source of inspiration, knowledge, and creativity. This book is dedicated to Emma O'Driscoll. It would have never been possible without her love, support, patience, inspiration, friendship, hugs, and smiles. Emma's belief in this project was unshakable from its inception. My wholehearted gratefulness to her is beyond any words. And finally there is our four-leg canine friend, Karenin, who always keeps me sane. The long walks provide not just much-needed exercise but also a welcome opportunity for thought and reflection.

Earlier versions of chapters 2, 3, and 6 appeared as, respectively, "'Knocking on My Neighbour's Door': On Metamorphoses of Sociality in Rural Bosnia," *Critique of Anthropology* 32, no. 1 (2012): 3–19; "Economic Theologies of Abundance: Halal Exchange and the Limits of Neoliberal Effects in Post-War Bosnia-Herzegovina," *Ethnos* 84, no. 2 (2019): 223–40; and "'This Is Our Little Hajj': Muslim Holy Sites and Reappropriation of the Sacred Landscape in Contemporary Bosnia," *American Ethnologist* 39, no. 4 (2012): 752–66.

Introduction

Late in the afternoon, on a warm autumn day in September 2008, I was sitting on a hillside just outside of the Muslim village of Brdo in the Zvijezda highlands, central Bosnia. My friend Raif, accompanied by his son Mensur, their neighbor Zakir and myself, were cleaning one of the fields that have belonged to Raif's family for generations.[1] Raif, who was sixty-five at the time, had recently undergone heart surgery and was taking regular breaks as he quickly got tired. When we finished the work, Mensur and Zakir laid their old military jackets out on the grass to sit on. It was time to relax. Mensur and Zakir took packets of Drina cigarettes out of their pockets and took turns smoking them. The sharing of cigarettes and the old military jackets were both reminders of the time they spent in the trenches in the surrounding hills while defending the village during the 1992–95 Bosnian war. The moment of sharing a cigarette was a testimony to the comradeship they had forged, cherished, and sustained ever since.

While Mensur and Zakir were absorbed in their conversation, Raif suggested that I accompany him on a stroll around the fields. He wanted to take the opportunity to check the fences, as the days were getting shorter and winter was slowly approaching. During the walk we talked rather haphazardly about politics and history, local and international, past and present. At one point Raif suddenly stopped walking and remained silent for about a minute, gazing at the verdant hilly horizon. Then he turned to me and said, "Bosnia is like a badly parked car, it has always obstructed somewhere or somebody. But what can we do? We must live and look ahead. *Inshallah* [God willing], everything will be fine." The metaphor prompted Raif to retrieve episodes from the past as these unfolded in village life over the course of history: the Ottomans, the World Wars, the repressive antireligious stance of the former socialist Yugoslav state, and repeated shelling of the village during the Bosnian war in the 1990s. These fragments of the past became inscribed into villagers' historical consciousness as well as the family fields we were walking on. For Raif, "the badly parked car" metaphor captured the widely shared sense among villagers of Bosnia as a constant frontier of clashing interests between geopolitical powers and realms. It simultaneously gestured toward the ambiguity and fragmented self-conceptions of what it means to be Muslim and live a Muslim life as a result of these geopolitical and historical entanglements. But, as he went on to say, one also needs to look ahead when reflecting on the past in the present, and situate these concerns in a larger realm, that of God's grace and destiny.

I had arrived a couple of months earlier to begin my fieldwork. My plan was to study Muslims' religious experience, and in particular ritual practices centered around the sacred landscape in the region. I therefore found this conversation rather intriguing. Since then, I have heard similar comments and stories from villagers of all walks of life. At the time I wondered why Raif was avoiding the themes I was trying to discuss with him. Why was he talking about a badly parked car? I was naive. It took me some time to realize that Raif was listening to me patiently and engaging with my questions very seriously. I was not yet able to recognize how historical consciousness underlay the everyday forms of Muslim religious experience I wanted to learn about.

By the time Raif expressed this thought in 2008, it had been sixteen years since the breakup of the Socialist Federal Republic of Yugoslavia, of which Bosnia and Herzegovina was part; and it had been thirteen years since the end of the ensuing Bosnian war (1992–95). When I visited Raif again during my return visits over the following years, he remembered our conversation. He was still convinced about the aptness of the metaphor. What was so evocative there, in the verdant hilly landscape, as to prompt Raif to make such a comment, in which history and religious experience became entwined? Was it the fields where we were walking? The fence? The military jackets laid on the grass? The nearby graves of unknown Ottoman soldiers-cum-martyrs, beside which villagers would pray when seeking blessing and protection? The forested hills on the horizon that were repeatedly used as a shelter while the villages were being plundered, ruined, and set alight over the course of the last century? The hazelnut tree in Raif's garden where the future leader of the Socialist Federal Republic of Yugoslavia, Josip Broz Tito, allegedly took a break with his Partisan

"A badly parked car"—the village landscape imbued with history.

brigade during World War II? Or was it an echo of the call to the evening prayer coming from the newly built mosque nearby, which was still a novel postsocialist sensory experience for elderly Muslim villagers like Raif, after decades of tightly controlled religious life?

Be that as it may, a badly parked car is a multilayered and potent metaphor that goes to the heart of the argument I make in this book. The metaphor gestures toward the everyday historical, social, and affective labor that people embark on in order to remake their lifeworlds in the wake of dramatic ruptures. Soon after our conversation, I realized that Raif was not alone in using such figurative expressions to make sense of past events that had transformed villagers' lives, influenced their pious sensibilities, and become sedimented layers of historical consciousness and religious experience in the postsocialist, postwar present. The past, articulated in vivid metaphors like a badly parked car, "offers itself up," as Michael Jackson observes, "to the living as a basis for creatively comprehending their present situation and making informed choices about how it is to be addressed and lived" (2007: 83). Now, a decade later, I hope to approach Raif's comment from a more nuanced perspective. What Raif was trying to convey in our conversations was that in order to understand Muslims' religious experience and practice in contemporary Bosnia and Herzegovina, one needs to take seriously the question of what living with the past entails, and how it shapes one's own prospective life trajectory.

Numerous scholars have pointed out how the debate about Islam and Muslims in Europe is often reduced to a contemporary immigration issue (Asad 2003, Özyürek 2015, Rexhepi 2017, Shryock 2010). The Muslim stories I follow in this book span generations and cut across thresholds of multiple national as well as global sociopolitical transformations. As stories of the past told in the present, they persistently "offer themselves up" amid a continuous reality of de-historicization, erasure, and omission. By tracing the entwinements of historical consciousness and religious experience embodied in the stories and actions of my Bosnian friends and interlocutors, this book paves the way for rethinking and writing against the historical silences that pervade popular and scholarly accounts of Muslim lives in Europe today.

The Focus of the Book

This book is a study of what it means to live a Muslim life amid the political breakdowns, economic deprivation, and transformation of religious institutions in postsocialist, postwar Bosnia and Herzegovina (hereafter BiH, after Bosna i Hercegovina). The book revolves around the question of how Muslim lives and cultural values have been reconfigured in the face of ruptures caused by political violence and cultural and economic dispossession ensuing from the violent disintegration of the Socialist Federal Republic of Yugoslavia in 1992 and its aftermaths. This is an ethnographic study about the "hard-to-name period after 'the postwar'" (Nelson 2015: 40), as well as the postsocialist condition, and about the role Muslim religious experience and everyday historical work play in shaping and making sense of it all in the present.

The end of socialism and the war were critical events that radically disrupted the lives of individuals, families, and polities. These two critical events now constitute a dominant frame of reference in public debates as well as in the scholarship. Although it is tempting to see them as the defining moments of the recent past, such a view of history, as Michael Jackson writes, "often downplays the ways in which past events are continually being transmuted into myth" (2007: 80) and embedded in nationalist narratives. Indeed, "critical events" is often itself a contested historical category detached from lived experience and memory (Das 2007, Feuchtwang 2011). For Jackson, the past is never one thing, a critical event for example, "but *many* and characterized less by necessity than by *potentiality*" (Jackson 2007: 81, original emphasis). Throughout the book I refer to this realization of the potentiality of a past that "offers itself up" in the present as *everyday historical work* to ethnographically elucidate what living with the past in the present entails and how it shapes temporal orientations toward the future (Bryant and Knight 2019). A focus on everyday historical work moves away from the idea, perpetuated in the nationalistic historiographies, that villagers like Raif are subjects who constantly confront—and are confronted by—a history of critical events. My ethnographic interest lies in elucidating the creative capacities of everyday historical work and how villagers act on these capacities to become historical subjects (Trouillot 1995: 24). Raif's evocative metaphor of "a badly parked car," coupled with the expression of divine grace (*inshallah*), captures how the everyday historical work villagers do is highly textured and encompasses critical events within other temporal orientations and moral frames, rather than being simply determined by the critical events.

In addressing these concerns, this book pursues the often surprising ways in which religious practice, materialities, experience and imagination are reconfiguring rural BiH in the wake of the violent disintegration of socialist Yugoslavia. Violent events and wars, as Heonik Kwon suggests, need to be situated within "the dimension of a social order and the spectrum of everyday life" (2008: 66). Failure to do so, Kwon continues, "makes understanding of the historical transition to a new era critically incomplete" (66). Kwon's argument is helpful because it invites us to elucidate the creative potential of the social and religious imaginings that emerge from transformative events (see also Mittermaier 2011). My chief interest is the question of how the materiality of social forms (such as house, family, and neighborhood) interacts in the present with the legacies of past ruptures and is thereby infused with religious imagination and experience. How do these entanglements shape, fracture, and reconfigure religious convictions and conduct? What is the role of religion in the processes of endurance, recuperation, restoration, and anticipation that constitute everyday historical work? By focusing ethnographically on how these issues are articulated and embodied in manifestations of care, mutuality, religious sensibilities, and rituals, my aim is to show how Muslim lives have been lived over generations, and what living with such history entails in the Zvijezda highlands in the present.

Living with the "Posts"

Friday is an important day for villagers in the highlands. The Friday sermon (*džuma*) takes place in the municipal mosque, and there is also a large weekly outdoor market. During my fieldwork I often joined villagers on their Friday visits to the municipality. As we strolled through the market, my friend Fadil often said "everything has collapsed" (*sve je propalo*) and gestured toward the large abandoned crumbling sawmill, situated in the vicinity of the market. The sawmill was the main employer in the municipality during the socialist period.

In the postwar years, the sawmill was closed, privatized and closed again, while the workers were left without salaries and expensive machines were stolen. This is a common story throughout BiH, other Yugoslav successor states, and postsocialist contexts generally. It mirrors the disastrous privatization of state assets in the postsocialist, postwar years. "Imagine," Fadil continued, "everyone was working and earning money before the war, so there was no time to do what we are doing now. We are just walking pointlessly but we can't afford to buy anything."

Fadil is viewed by his fellow villagers as truly pious (*pravi vjernik*). It was not unusual to hear Fadil critically recounting how religious expression in socialist Yugoslavia was restricted, or how villagers' attempts to build a mosque were rejected by the state authorities. He often recalled how in the late 1970s his son was publicly humiliated by the teachers on numerous occasions for attending Friday sermons in the mosque. Yet for all his memories of restricted religious freedom during Yugoslav socialism, Fadil often viewed the socialist past positively. He was not alone in this.

Every Friday, Fadil met with his friends for a weekly catch-up in one of the local cafés before going to the mosque. Many of these men were his former coworkers at the sawmill. In addition to gossiping and exchanging news about their families, they would regularly discuss the current despair and political deadlock. They would also share memories of the time when they worked in the sawmill. Debating and remembering the socialist past is not confined to public cafés, however. When I started recording life histories of Fadil and the other villagers, one of the first things they wanted to share with me was, again, their working past. Family albums were filled with important personal documents hidden from public display: folders brimming with newspaper articles on fading yellow paper and old black-and-white photographs of villagers proudly posing as the vanguard of Yugoslav socialism in front of a skip, a tractor or a pile of timber. These fading fragments of villagers' socialist workplaces, now resting in the cupboards of their houses, were not kept simply for nostalgic reasons but as reminders of the "dignity and respect the workers enjoyed under socialism" (Petrović 2017: 19).

I begin with the story of Fadil not because it is exceptional. Tales of collapse live on and are felt viscerally among the villagers. But Fadil's story also tells us something rather common about how villagers blend religious experience and practice with statements about socialist and postsocialist political economy in their everyday historical work. Fadil's comment that "everyone was working and earning money before the war" poignantly illustrates how not *only* memories of the Bosnian war but also those of socialism constitute two interrelated temporal orientations toward the present: the postwar and the postsocialist. Although these temporal orientations have been critically scrutinized in recent years (Jansen 2015; Jansen, Brković, Čelebičić 2016), I employ them throughout the book with caution. My decision is driven ethnographically, since both orient much of the everyday historical work villagers do. Let me unpack them in turn.

POSTWAR

The Bosnian war (1992–95) was a violent departure from Yugoslav socialism.[2] The disintegration of the Socialist Federal Republic of Yugoslavia, of which BiH was part (1945–92), was marked by a series of armed conflicts over the territories of the crumbling federation. Being sandwiched between neighboring Croatia, Serbia, and Montenegro, the territory of BiH became a bone of contention between antagonistic state-making projects. On the one hand were centrifugal anti-Bosnian projects, with heavy involvement from the neighboring countries intent upon grabbing territory; on the other, centripetal pro-Bosnian projects that fought against these attempts (Jansen, Brković, and Čelebičić 2016: 5). At the same time, the increasingly heavy presence of the international, military and humanitarian communities, representing particular political and geopolitical interests, made itself felt in BiH (Gilbert 2016, McMahon 2017). The Bosnian war, during which more than half of the Bosnian population was displaced (approximately 1.2 million people), cost more than a hundred thousand lives, including the genocide of over eight thousand male Bosnian Muslims killed in Srebrenica by Serbian forces in 1995 (Duijzings 2007, Wagner 2008).

The war in BiH was officially brought to an end by the Dayton Peace Agreement, mediated by the US-led international community. The Dayton-brokered peace deal set out a complex consociational power-sharing mechanism between the three "constituent peoples": Bosniaks (Muslims), Serbs, and Croats. Furthermore, it established a new architecture for the now postsocialist, postwar state. The result has been an extremely fractured regime of state sovereignty and citizenship (Hayden 2013, Hromadžić 2015, Jansen 2015, Mujanović 2018). The effect of this international intervention is that administrative and governmental structures are haphazardly distributed across multiple institutions with overlapping and unclear responsibilities, making it difficult for Bosnian citizens to decipher and move through them, as we discover over the course of this book.

The Dayton consociational model has become notorious for its opacity. Postwar BiH consists of two entities—the Republika Srpska and the Federation of Bosnia and Herzegovina—as well as a smaller, neutral Brčko District centered on the eponymous town. The federation is further subdivided into ten cantons.[3] Despite the complexity of this postwar politico-bureaucratic arrangement, in their day-to-day dealings with this machinery, villagers simply referred to it as "the state" (*država*). Villagers held the state responsible for the collapse of the sawmill, due to shady privatization, and for the ongoing marginalization of their lives.

POSTSOCIALIST

Fadil's claim that "everyone was working and earning money before the war" reminds us that "the hard-to-name period after the postwar" cannot be separated from the temporal afterness of Yugoslav socialism, that is, from the postsocialist transformations (Gilbert 2006). The postsocialist condition emerged from a global historical juncture marking the end of the Cold War and the global rise of economic and political neoliberalism (Chari and Verdery 2009, Harvey 2004, Kurtović and Sargsyan 2019, Ortner 2016). The neoliberal transformations of the political economy across the former Yugoslavia paralleled similar devastating trends in other formerly socialist countries (Dunn 2004, Kideckel 2008, Makovicky 2014) as well as in countries that fell victim to predatory neoliberal reforms (e.g., Han 2012, Muehlebach 2012).

The Bosnian war and the postwar political economy of the Bosnian state, as Larisa Kurtović (2015) suggests, led to the plundering of public resources, a process well documented across the world (Harvey 2004). This process resulted in the politicization and privatization of social redistribution, now controlled by local ethnonational elites and their clientelistic networks (see also Jansen 2006). As a result, the Dayton postwar model of the Bosnian state—designed and implemented by the international community—was not only politically and economically unsustainable (ibid., 5). It also enabled, as Kurtović argues, "new forms of structural violence and created new (transethnic) surplus populations, that cannot be accommodated within the existing (and largely clientelistic) regimes of redistribution" (3; see also Gilbert and Mujanović 2015). There is now an unprecedented degree of precarity in BiH, and one of the highest unemployment rates in Europe, particularly among young people.[4]

To date, existing scholarship has focused primarily on the devastating effects these transformations have had on entire sectors of production in the industrial and mining towns that formed the economic backbone of prewar BiH. Indeed, postindustrial decline and dispossession are patterns that have unfolded across the postsocialist ecumene (e.g., Alexander 2004, Kideckel 2008), and beyond (Bear 2015, Sanchez 2015). What is missing from these accounts, however, is close attention to the damage done to the small municipalities and rural areas situated in the margins of the state (see also Bergholz 2016: 9–10).[5] In rural areas, the effects were devastating. Villagers' responses to pervasive precarity and marginalization have oscillated between outmigration to the cities, casual labor opportunities, informal economic activities, and subsistence farming and foraging. This is the context in which this book is situated. The postsocialist, postwar years have been dramatic and harsh. Making sense of this period is an intellectual project I share with Bosnians. As a result, my analysis has become thoroughly intertwined with villagers' attempts to live Muslim lives at this particular historical juncture.

Contextualizing Islam

Those interested in the study of Islam and Muslims in Southeast Europe, and in BiH in particular, will sooner or later notice how deeply this subject is entangled with debates on nationalism and identity politics (e.g., Bougarel 2018, Clayer and Popović 1997).[6] Nothing epitomizes this observation better than Ernest Gellner's classic *Nations and Nationalisms* (1983). In this book Gellner boldly and unforgettably wrote about Islam in BiH: "nowadays, to be a Bosnian Muslim you need not believe that there is no God but God and that Mohamed is his Prophet, but you do need to have lost that faith" (1983: 72). It is safe to say that Ernest Gellner was wrong, at least as far as the religious experiences of Muslims in the Zvijezda highlands are concerned. If we followed Gellner's argument, how could we explain, for example, the Ramadan memories of villagers like Fadil from the early 1950s: "there was no mosque where we could gather; the Communists wouldn't let us build one here, so we prayed in cramped houses." Or we might ask Professor Gellner how we should attend to the photos and shared memories of those who went year after year, decade after decade, century after century, on a three-day "little hajj" (*mali hadž*) to the Karići holy site (see chapter 6).[7]

These examples illustrate anything but "lost faith." Nonetheless, Gellner's argument lucidly captures something very important about the political and scholarly stance toward Islam and religion in Southeast Europe and, more broadly, in the context of the modern secular nation-state. This problem with the methodological nationalism dominates the study of religious experiences, conduct, and lives, portraying them as locked in a conventional geographical ordering of the nation-state, its borders, and secular political sensibilities.[8] This epistemological position reduces a vast array of experiences with the divine into discourses on the politics of identity and/or difference, and silences and de-historicizes other ideas and practices that play an important role in villagers' as well as urbanites' articulations of what it means to be Muslim and live a Muslim life.

In BiH, over the course of the twentieth century the category of "Muslim" came to signify an ethnonational identity and was eventually recognized as one of the constitutive national groups (*nacije*). This was further strengthened during the 1980s, when rekindled nationalist movements across the Yugoslav Federation (Perica 2002) drew heavily on religious symbolism and discourses—Catholic, Muslim, and Orthodox alike. The Yugoslav wars in the 1990s further exacerbated ethnonational discourses. Moreover, this ethnonational logic was reproduced in the Dayton agreement itself (see Hayden 2013: 289–374). It is beyond the scope of the book to fully recount the deep genealogies of how religious differences became translated into political differences and how this shift has influenced scholarly concepts and analysis.[9] The historical genealogy of institutional organization of Islam in BiH reflects how nation building and religious institutionalization have been entwined (see the sidebar in this introduction). For the questions I pursue in this book, however, I consider such a framework limiting.

The ethnonational identitarian framework turns any analysis, consciously or unconsciously, into a study of how religious discourses of difference operate as boundary makers, distinguishing Muslims from non-Muslims, and how the relations between Muslims and non-Muslims are configured (Barth 1969, Bougarel 2003, Bringa 1995). I do not wish to deny the important role such conceptualizations play in the political life of BiH, or of any other religiously plural nation-state in the world today. Yet one could easily flip this argument in order to move beyond the identity politics of fixed boundaries and difference. Instead, we could ask about the practical etiquettes that enable boundary crossing, and participation in the lives of others, including commensality and hospitality, conviviality, or the moral idioms of neighborliness.[10] Such practices of boundary crossing "rarely find their way into the records, as opposed to the 'events' that construct archives and define historical study" (Bryant 2016: 5).

The events that have defined the study of Muslim lives in BiH are those of ethnonational identity, identitarian conflict, and violence. In particular, the 1992–95 war is often taken as *the* point of departure and as an encompassing interpretive prism for understanding past and present. But as I document throughout this book, we need to open our research to other moral sensibilities and meaning-making practices that transcend the historiographies of the imagined community of the secular nation-state.

Beyond Muslim Identity

Writing about religion in the context of sectarianism and societies that are divided along identitarian lines, Ussama Makdisi aptly suggests that we need "to move away from the certainties and the chauvinism of religious, nationalist, and civilizational talk" because these certainties silence other modes of belonging and de-historicize other ways of arranging social and political life (Baer, Makdisi, and Shryock 2009: 940). In his critical intervention into accounts of the genesis of Bosnian nationalist imaginations, Edin Hajdarpasic argues that "the most discussed facet of this land, the one constantly revisited by politicians and scholars alike, was its 'national' or 'ethnic' composition. Such phrases seem self-evident, evoking confident projections of clear-cut population counts, but the numbers themselves necessarily conflate *a vast array of social relations* into deceptively solid 'ethnic' categories" (2015: 6, emphasis added; also Jansen 2005a).[11] It is this vast array of social relations and imaginings, including rural-urban dynamics, generational divides, or contestations over religious authority between the ulema and lay Muslims, and among lay Muslims themselves, that is flattened (almost to the point of disappearance) in writings on everyday religious experiences in BiH in the past and the present.

By shifting the focus toward *other kinds of relations* as these unfold in day-to-day situations, I do not wish to imply that villagers in the Zvijezda highlands, like anywhere else, would not discursively identify themselves with ethnonational categories in specific situations. Nonetheless, these categorical identifications obscure the ways in which villagers develop their relations with the divine; they do not constitute the language of the everyday, where engagement in politics, history or the lives of others unfolds *within* and *as* the realm of religious experience. It is more productive, as Douglas Rogers suggests, "to ask about *the practices* of fashioning individuals and collectives than to begin from (and usually end with) abstract categories of individualism or collectivism" (Rogers 2009: 51, original emphasis). Rather than starting my argument with the abstract category of "Muslim identity," in this book I ask how "people come to understand themselves and one another as human subjects and aspire to participate in moral communities" (51), be they families, neighborhoods, villages, political parties, mosque congregations, or the global Umma.

The focus on *other kinds of relations* is helpful in elucidating what it means to be Muslim in the flow of everyday life. Attending to these alternatives, as recent debates among the anthropologists of Islam have suggested, requires "a new and different understanding of the relationship between Islam, everyday religious experience and interpersonal relationships" (Marsden 2005: 22–23; see also Ahmad 2017; Marsden and Retsikas 2013; Osella and Soares 2010). How villagers relate to Islam as a historically constituted body of knowledge and practice, and how they articulate their ways of being Muslim, has been shaped by the shifting forms of secular modernity aligned to state socialist power, by commitment to nationalism, by experiences of violence and political instability in the wake of the collapse of socialist Yugoslavia, and by BiH's geopolitical and georeligious entanglements with the wider Muslim world. This book attends to Islam and Muslim lives in the Zvijezda highlands as a nexus of everyday religious practice and experience with the divine, coupled with villagers' self-conceptions of what being Muslim means. I track how this nexus unfolds in the flow of social life and is entangled in the histories of political and socioeconomic transformations and inequalities as they are configured in the postsocialist, postwar present. Ultimately, what interests me is the opportunity afforded by ethnographic research for tracing villagers' forms and practices of meaning making in terms of Islam (Ahmed 2016: 527). These practices span generations and are used to do a complex array of everyday historical work.

Not only does this approach move beyond ethnonational arguments about "Muslim identity," it also nuances the now-conventional approaches to the study of Islam rooted in the work of Talal Asad, which treat Islam as a coherent discursive tradition (Asad 1986). In the context of multilayered sociopolitical ruptures, such approaches are not very helpful. In rural Bosnia, the forms and practices of mediating Islamic religious tradition are often situated *in* villagers' material worlds—in their houses, fields, and neighborhoods—and these are understood *through* everyday historical work rather than in devotional or doctrinal positions that arise solely from the scriptural discourses that predominate in revived Islamic piety movements that have emerged "after socialism."[12]

Vital Exchange

July in the Zvijezda highlands is the time for making hay. In mid-July in 2009, the hay-making season was eagerly anticipated. Villagers commonly shared their concerns that much was at stake during haymaking due to the unpredictability of the weather. One unexpectedly heavy rain shower could easily damage the entire harvest. Everyone in the neighborhoods endeavored to be available to work during this period. Those villagers living in urban areas were returning in high numbers as well. Any free pair of hands was much needed, and neighbors regularly helped each other. Through their actions they were acknowledging the value of care, reciprocity, and good deeds—"today I will help you, tomorrow you will help me."

One hot afternoon, I found myself helping my next-door neighbor Fadil and his family. Worried about the gloomy clouds clustering on the horizon, we worked hurriedly and tirelessly for several hours, making a haystack that would preserve high-quality hay for the winter months. After everyone had finished, we all sat down and rested against the haystack we had just made.

A few minutes later, Fadil pulled a few dried stalks of grass from the haystack and silently held them for a while. Then he turned to his grandson while still holding the stalks in his hands and said "this is milk, thanks to Allah" (*ovo je mljeko, elhamdullilah*). Fadil's expression was subtle, evocative, and pregnant with meaning. It entwined the cosmological and the material: with God's blessing—secured through prayers for rain performed before the haymaking season (see chapter 4)—throughout the year hay is fed to livestock, which in turn provide milk, meat, and manure to regenerate the soil. All are vital substances that sustain the members of the household. Their abundance is manifestation of God's grace in the course of everyday life. But milk and meat can also be turned into much-needed cash by selling dairy products and thus improving household budgets in situations of economic marginalization (see chapter 2).

The expression "this is milk, thanks to Allah" entwines material resources and social reproduction with Muslims' religious sensibilities. By telling, showing, and instructing his grandson in front of other family members, Fadil embraced in a single sentence the intergenerational relationship of care between the house as a compound of people, the land, animals, and social practices of *re*production of life as an unfolding exchange with the divine. "This is milk, thanks to Allah" was an expressive trope, articulating how the house becomes a site of exchange with God underpinned by everyday historical work: through caring for the land, Fadil and his family secure the house's enduring strength and divine blessing (*bereket*), which sustain the household over time.

The story of Fadil captures the central argument I make in this book as it shows *the other kinds of relations* at work in expressing what it means to be Muslim in the flow of everyday life. In what follows, I argue that living a Muslim life in rural BiH is ordered by deep relations of obligation and care among the living, the dead, and the divine that are generations deep. These relations are governed by notions of exchange and reciprocity. Villagers' conceptions of what it means to be Muslim and live a Muslim life are ultimately oriented toward the quest for salvation in the afterlife (*ahiret*), a pursuit that influences their actions in the world here and now (*dunjaluk*). This moral horizon is defined by the fundamental question of *how to live*, rather than the identitarian question of *who I am*. Pathways oriented toward the afterlife are multiple and uncertain, but they are all generated by human activities, which ultimately determine villagers' relationship with the divine over time. The expressions permeating everyday village life, such as "only Allah knows," "if God permits," and "God is merciful" are inseparable from daily acts of help and care; they are woven into the vast web of interpersonal relations. Everyday historical work is consistent with villagers' apprehension that human activities have consequences for one's life trajectory and the afterlife. Everyday life, in other words, is where values are generated and religious experience is articulated. This historically unfolding, interactional relationship with the divine, as mediated through human actions and the cultivation of interpersonal relations and exchanges with fellow villagers, and by caring for the souls of the dead, is deeply ethical (Lambek 2015a). For villagers, human activities and commitments in the world here and now are literally *vital* for whatever pathway to salvation one may forge. To grasp the generative and creative force of human activities, across a vast array of relationships, all domains of social life, and through time, this book explores how villagers construe what it means to be Muslim and live a Muslim life as a *flow of vital exchange* with God.

Vital exchange refers to a moral horizon of action, and to the means by which villagers bring a perpetual flow of divine grace, abundance, and prosperity in their everyday lives.[13] Viewed from this perspective, living a Muslim life consists not so much of claiming a specific ethnonational identity but of taking part in day-to-day exchanges of blessing (*bereket*), prosperity (*nafaka*) and fortune (*hajr*), in good deeds and merits (*sevap*), and in prayers (*dova*) between the living, the dead, and the divine. Such notions as blessing, fortune, luck, destiny, and salvation, Samuli Schielke writes, don't always figure in the analytical toolbox of social scientists, yet their analytical purchase in an uncertain world is far-reaching (2015: 220; see also Gaibazzi 2015). Since divine grace is "a gratuitous gift, bestowed inexplicably, not as a reward for exemplary acts of piety" (Barraud et al. 1994: 20), this book traces the manifold *instances* and *sites* of vital exchange with God in everyday life, which are irreducible to the realms of Islamic orthodoxy and scriptural reasoning, just as they escape ethnonational categorization.

Fieldwork and Methodological Considerations

The region of the Zvijezda highlands in central Bosnia lies about thirty miles north of the Bosnian capital, Sarajevo. It is a place of stunning beauty. From spring to autumn it is verdant, with rich forests, countless streams, and pastures and colorful fields spread across the hills and down to the cool valleys, where one usually hides from the burning sun during the summer. In winter, life becomes more difficult. The tiny lanes connecting the villages to the main roads are blocked by snow, streams and water pipes freeze, and villages are often cut off from municipal services for days or weeks at a time. To reach any of the villages in the highlands, one has to drive between five and ten miles from the main highways on tiny, semi-asphalted roads. The roads leading to villages, built during the early Yugoslav modernization of the countryside in the 1960s, are sandwiched between steep hills and dark forests, and they often come to a dead end near the village. One then has to follow unpaved roads and paths that are muddy or icy in winter and dusty in summer.

The Zvijezda highlands are proudly depicted in local narratives as a place of natural beauty and remoteness. The star-shaped hills—giving the highland range its name—are seen as a shield that has protected the villages over centuries. Yet the very same villages are often mocked by urbanites as places of backwardness and peasant manners. In recent years, new characterizations have emerged among villagers that reflect the withdrawal of the state from their lives. Villagers nowadays articulate a sense of abandonment, hardship, and despair. These feelings are exacerbated by the everyday experience of coping with deteriorating roads and crumbling infrastructure that makes travel to and from the villages, and access to services, even more difficult.

In describing the Zvijezda highlands, I draw on language and metaphors that matter to villagers. Although they often invoke a sense of marginality and remoteness, this does not mean they are isolated from critical events. Nor are villagers isolated from globalized discourses on Islamic orthodoxy and Muslim politics, or from global transformations in the political economy. The location of this study in highland villages does not make it a priori less relevant to a general understanding of the large-scale transformative processes that have unfolded elsewhere in BiH and beyond. Rather, its location offers an analytically productive vantage point from which to explore how actually existing forms of everyday religious and historical experience are reconfiguring in postsocialist, postwar BiH.

This book is based on long-term fieldwork stretching over a decade, with multiple return visits. My original research plan was to study the Muslim ritual practices and sacred landscapes for which the Zvijezda highlands are well-known. By a twist of fate, while traveling around the region I happened upon the historically Muslim-only village of about 250 inhabitants that, for the purposes of this book, I refer to as Brdo (a pseudonym). I decided to base myself in the village, but I traveled extensively to other villages across the highlands. My original research plans disintegrated very soon after my arrival, as I came to understand the seriousness of rural marginalization and its effects on everyday life. The period of Yugoslav socialism (1945–92) had brought sufficient economic prosperity and independence to every household in the region. In the postsocialist, postwar years, however, in every village I visited, an average of six out of ten men were unemployed or worked in extremely precarious positions, without any regular contract, health insurance, or pension savings.[14]

Everyone tried to get by as best they could. This included the outmigration of the younger generations, which further reinforced the sense of marginalization and abandonment among those who stayed put. As in many other postsocialist rural areas across Eastern and Southeastern Europe (Creed 2011, Duijzings 2013, Humphrey 2002, Kaneff 2004), the decline in living standards was generally sharp compared with the socialist, prewar years. My initial research plans soon became enmeshed in new themes that related more directly to these socioeconomic conditions.

In Brdo and elsewhere in the Zvijezda highlands I observed and documented "the effects of long-term and extralocal processes as they are manifested and refracted in a multiplicity of small-scale processes, local practices and individual actions" (Berdahl 1999: 13; Green 2005). This had two important consequences for how my research speaks to wider trends in Southeast Europe, and in the former Yugoslavia in particular. First, I was able to assess the effects of postsocialist and postwar socioeconomic transformations and the ensuing rise of inequalities in rural areas that have seldom been studied. Furthermore, the fact that I lived in an area that stretched across the borders of the Sarajevo canton and Zenica-Doboj canton in the Federation of BiH enabled me to scrutinize how implementation of the Dayton Peace Agreement, which changed the inner territorial borders of the country, was affecting villagers' access to services and other forms of resource redistribution (Bringa 2016, Brković 2017). Finally, my focus on religious experiences and practices helped me ascertain the degree to which more "assertive" conceptions of Islamic discourses had gained traction in the countryside in the post-Yugoslav years and to explore where and how village Muslims locate, negotiate, and/or resist religious and spiritual authority (Ghodsee 2010). These three intertwined trajectories helped me destabilize the apparent fixity and coherence of collective identities that treat "Muslims" as one monolithic ethnonational category. In fact, I discovered that Bosnian Muslims are a community beset by multiple tensions, with ample cynicism and even mockery directed at their own political and religious establishment (Hromadžić 2015: 17).

Second, since my fieldwork spanned over a decade, I have been able to document the individual trajectories of numerous villagers from a longer-term perspective, rather than capturing a one-off snapshot of village life. This viewpoint also made me aware of the general absence of "the rural" not only from major debates on post-Yugoslav states, but from many studies of Muslim communities in the wider region of Southeast Europe, the Mediterranean, and the Middle East (Gilsenan 1982, Hart 2013, Marsden 2005). This is striking despite Stef

Jansen's insightful observation, made more than a decade ago, that the rural-urban perspective "constitutes the most widely shared non-nationalist framework for understanding events in the region" (Jansen 2005b: 154). Similarly, Jessica Greenberg points out that "there is perhaps no more contested social terrain than that of urban versus rural belonging" (2011: 96). These claims are made even more intriguing by the fact that more than half of the overall population in BiH continues to live in rural or semirural areas.

The bias against conducting fieldwork in rural areas is in my view largely influenced by two specters. First, the image of the traditional peasant community and its values has long been idealized and promoted by nationalist elites across Southeast Europe (Duijzings 2013, Hajdarpasic 2015, Kaneff 2004, Kurtović 2013). Secondly, the community-study paradigm has dominated the anthropology of Europe for decades (Halpern and Kideckel 1983). This paradigm treats villages as isolated moral communities that are effectively cut off from world affairs and state bureaucratic and religious institutions (Berdahl 1999; Herzfeld 1987: 8).

Rural life, however, is anything but parochial. It unfolds in a "complex web of relations between local, national, and international politics and economics" (Herzfeld 1987: 12), each with its own temporalities and imaginaries. Cities and villages are entwined in ambiguous, "messy entanglements" (Woods 2011: 293; cited in Duijzings 2013: 17). In turn, the study of these systems, which extend across multiple scales and processes, must be ethnographically grounded. As Daphnee Berdahl reminds us, it is "'in the actions of individuals living in time and place' that these forces are embodied, interpreted, contested, and negotiated" (Berdahl 1999: 3). Given the complexity at hand, what does "rural" mean to Bosnian villagers, if anything at all? How are postsocialist, postwar transformations unfolding in rural areas of BiH?

By asking these questions, I do not want to imply that there are two separate worlds in BiH, one urban, the other rural. The two categories are not empirically clear-cut and separate entities; rather, they are located within shifting horizons of experience, imbued with affective meanings and emotional idioms of belonging, and subject to "state effects" of different types and intensities (Mitchell 1991). The "rural" in this book operates as a scaling device whereby I track how villagers make and remake relationships with one another, with the municipal, cantonal, and federal realms of religion and politics, and with the world at large. These relationships are always contextualized. They are always negotiated within a localized and experience-near horizon—that of village life. In other words, by tracking the connections villagers make, I follow Berdahl's methodological recipe for doing village-based ethnographic research "beyond" the community-studies paradigm: exploring the effects of extralocal processes over long periods of time and looking at how these processes become part of (and sometimes subvert) local experiences and practices (1999: 3). This book is therefore an attempt to draw the "rural" back into anthropological research on post-Yugoslav societies.

A Roadmap

The book moves through diverse ethnographic encounters and sites of vital exchange. It is divided into two parts. The first, "Making and Unmaking Village Lives," delves into the question of how the postsocialist, postwar fabric of village life is understood and how it is infused with Islam in villagers' everyday historical work. In chapter 1, I introduce the house as the ground of one's life, family, and care, and as a particular transgenerational ambient of historical and religious experience. What it means to share a social space with others vis-à-vis newly emergent hierarchies and inequalities is addressed in chapter 2, which focuses on ideas of neighborliness (*komšiluk*) and proximity, giving special attention to their ethical textures, and their fragility. In the face of changing village sociality and neighborhood spaces, chapter 3 explores the moral economy of care and generosity toward others, tracking the forms of moral reasoning and practice that underlie multiple spheres of exchange in village life.

The second part, "Vital Exchange," offers a reversed perspective, exploring how Islam and religious experience are understood and how each is infused with the postsocialist, postwar predicaments as well as opportunities. Chapter 4 explores how Islamic time can offer improvised techniques for making meaning and organizing material and social life. It shows how temporal reasoning, articulated through daily prayer, fasting, and worship, is enmeshed with the new temporalities that have emerged from postsocialist, postwar junctures. Chapter 5 examines the role of prayer in Muslim life. How does the act of prayer, as a temporal experience, orient villagers toward the past, present, and future? What does the social life of prayer entail in the village context? Chapter 6 explores the spaces of veneration and prayer (*dovište*) in the highlands. These sacred sites offer a window into the historical, political, and religious transformations that have taken place over the last hundred years. I argue in this chapter that events unfolding around holy sites in the region are indicative of ambiguities and areas of contest that characterize religious authority, authenticity, and historical consciousness in postsocialist, postwar Bosnian Muslim politics at large.

Organization of Islam in Bosnia and Herzegovina

Islam and Muslim lives are chiefly organized through the Islamic Community of Bosnia and Herzegovina (IC-BiH; Islamska Zajednica u Bosni i Hercegovini). This form of official organization of Islam has been developing for over a century. Here I focus primarily on how its organizational structure presides over matters of religious authority, conduct and practice.

Between 1463 and 1878, the territory of Bosnia was part of the Ottoman Empire. Administration of Islam was institutionalized as part of the Ottoman state. It encompassed all aspects of Muslim lives, ranging from questions of faith and ritual, marriage, divorce, and inheritance, to education and jurisprudence. The highest functionary in this structure, the *shaykh al-Islam*, was seated in Istanbul. The shaykh al-Islam also appointed local Muslims to the ranks of provincial *muftis*, authorizing them with powers to run local Islamic affairs. This was also the case for Bosnia.

In 1878, Bosnia changed hands from Ottoman to Habsburg rule. Bosnia was under the administration of the Habsburg empire until the beginning of World War I in 1914, when the entire imperial structure of the ancien régime crumbled. The period between 1878 and 1914 was crucial for developing the organizational and administrative structures for managing religious life in the country outside of the parameters of a Muslim-ruled empire. The legacies of these structures have also continued to organize Muslim lives until the present, as it was a moment when Muslims became a religious minority in a non-Muslim setting. In the Hapsburg empire, religious life was organized around the state-recognized religious communities that had state-guaranteed religious freedoms. After becoming a religious minority, Muslims had to carve an autonomous space for themselves in the new political arrangements, not only as a religious community but increasingly also on ethnoreligious terms as a national group struggling for recognition. These attempts were met with an approval from the Habsburg colonial authorities, who wanted to cut the ties between their new Muslim imperial subjects and the old Ottoman Islamic authority in Istanbul.

To resolve the issue of religious and institutional authority, a new position of *Reisu-l-ulema* of BiH was negotiated with the new rulers and created in 1882, along with the council of religious scholars—Meclis-i Ulema (Amzi-Erdogdular 2013: 132–33). After two decades of struggles over the organization of Islamic affairs (education, jurisprudence, and endowments) as well as political recognition, a new institutional arrangement was approved by the Habsburg administration in 1909. The arrangement created a council of Islamic clerics and scholars (*ulema*) headed by the *Reisu-l-ulema* (grand mufti), and it further introduced "autonomy and elections into the administration of endowments and religious schools" (F. Karčić 2015: 130).

Following the successes of the Muslim autonomy movement in the early twentieth century, the postimperial period saw steadily increasing state control, particularly after moments of crisis. After World War I, BiH became part of the Kingdom of Yugoslavia. In 1930, all Muslim religious communities within the kingdom were lumped together into one unified Islamic religious community of Yugoslavia, and their autonomy was severely restricted by the state. After World War II, the new socialist regime took over Yugoslavia. The impact on all religious communities was severe. The secular socialist state kept control over religious communities. In 1946, Sharia courts and Islamic jurisprudence were completely abolished. Religious properties and endowments were nationalized in two waves (1945, 1958). The training of future imams was severely restricted. With the only exception of the madrasa in Sarajevo, all other schools were closed. Sufi (dervish) orders were banned in 1952 (Algar 1971). This changed with liberalization in the 1960s, also thanks to the constitutional changes in the Yugoslav Federation (1969 and 1974). The Faculty of Islamic Studies and the section for girls in the Sarajevo madrasa opened in the late 1970s. Moreover, the leading role of socialist Yugoslavia in the Non-Aligned Movement during the Cold War, created in this period numerous opportunities for the IC-BiH to foster transnational connections with Muslim-majority countries who were members of the Movement, and thus to realign the IC-BiH with a wider Muslim world (*umma*) (Fichter 2017, Rexhepi 2017).

Further major reorganizations and liberalization of the IC-BiH occurred in 1990, reflecting the wider wind of change brought about by the end of the communist rule across the now postsocialist world, returning more autonomy to religious communities. This liberalized structure continued to be in place during the disintegration of the Yugoslav Federation, from which a newly independent Republic of Bosnia and Herzegovina emerged (Barišić 2008, Walton and Rexhepi 2019). Soon after, the Bosnian war broke out, and the organization of Islamic affairs ran according to interim regulations and arrangements. The Bosnian war further strengthened the position of the IC-BiH as the guarantor of the Muslim religious community in BiH as well as an important political voice representing Bosnian Muslims as an ethnoreligious group (*nacija*).

In 1997, the IC-BiH approved a new constitution that also forms the basis for administration and organization of Islamic affairs in the present. It defines the IC-BiH as the chief authority for Bosnian Muslims in the country and in its diasporas abroad. Its Islamic authority and historical continuity are derived in the constitution from the Ottoman heritage, and grounded in the Hanafi school of jurisprudence (article 2). Here, it is important to note that the Islamic authority of the IC-BiH has been challenged in the past three decades by what the IC-BiH euphemistically calls the "new interpretations of Islam" (Duranović and Ljevaković-Subašić 2018). This euphemism lumps together various and rather diverse actors (Li 2019), foreign and increasingly local, who represent and proselytize different interpretations of Islam and organization of Muslim lives and who do not recognize the IC-BiH as their religious authority.

Muslim lives, governed by the IC-BiH, are nowadays organized along the following structure: The local unit (*džemat*)—village or borough—has its own permanent imam (*hodža*) or a deputy imam in places where no permanent imam has been assigned. Thus, at the level of everyday life, Muslim lives are organized and unfold in one's džemat—from one's birth to death. An association of džemats at the level of a district or a municipality (*medžilis*) is led by the chief imam (*glavni imam*). At the regional level, the local districts are organized within regional offices (*muftiluk*) led by the regional leaders (*muftija*). These regions are Banja Luka, Bihać, Goražde, Mostar, Sarajevo, Travnik, Tuzla, and Zenica, with an additional muftija for the army. There are also IC-BiH organizations abroad (*mešihat*) in Australia, North America, Croatia, Europe, Serbia, Slovenia.

At the top of the hierarchical structure is the Rijaset office, led by the *Reisu-l-ulema* (grand mufti), overseen by the council of the IC-BiH and its constitutional court. The IC-BiH is at present in charge of training and appointing imams. It also certifies religious teachers, approves religious curricula, and runs Islamic schools. The IC-BiH currently runs six madrasas (high schools) in BiH (Cazin, Mostar, Sarajevo, Travnik, Tuzla, Visoko), and two abroad (Novi Pazar, Serbia; and Zagreb, Croatia); and three university programs in BiH (Bihać, Sarajevo, Zenica), and one abroad (Novi

Pazar, Serbia). Furthermore, the IC-BiH is in charge of several research and heritage institutions, and of collecting and distributing alms (*zakat*) and charitable donations (*sadekatul-fitr*). The IC-BiH also provides an official umbrella for numerous dervish orders, which are associated within the Tarikatski Centar in accordance with the general theological orientation and jurisprudence of the IC-BiH, while respecting the specificities of the teaching and practice of these orders. Finally, the relationship between the IC-BiH and the state is nowadays regulated by the law about religious communities that guarantees religious freedom and protection while maintaining that BiH is a secular state. This organizational arrangement thus presents an attempt at carving an autonomous space for Islam in the context of a secular state in Europe.

PART ONE

Making and Unmaking Village Lives

1

Houses in Flames

It is the summer of 2014 and I am squeezed along with four other people inside an aging Volkswagen II. Tarik, his children, his wife Remzija, and I are leaving Sarajevo. We are heading toward the village of Brdo in a car belonging to a village neighbor. The last two weeks had been very hot and dry. Tarik was concerned about the old fruit trees in the garden of his half-century-old and now visibly crumbling house. But even more so, he was worried about the newly planted trees around his still-unfinished new house. After many years of being unable to find stable employment, Tarik and Remzija concluded that they would need to relocate closer to the capital, Sarajevo. Yet the move did not mean cutting off all the attachments that the family maintained and cared about *in* and *with* the village. The family dreamed about saving enough money to be able to finish their new house and return to the village. "The house"—old and new—thus became a central focus of the family's daily conversations about care, responsibility, and belonging to a place, but also a horizon of aspiration.

Back in the car on the way to the village. Tarik is listing all the trees, their position in the garden, their age, who planted them and when, and the years of the best yields. The apple tree in the corner next to the shed is forty years old. The plum tree next to the house, under whose shade we would regularly sit, is thirty-two years old, and its best yield was during the last year of the war in 1995. The former was planted by Tarik's grandfather, the latter by his father. The biographies of trees, houses, and their inhabitants are intimately intertwined.

The language of aspiration, family life, care, and belonging can take on many forms. It was through concern about the houses and the trees planted by his parents, grandparents, and himself that Tarik was able to articulate the story of his family, and thus of his own life. By regularly bringing his children back with him to the village and watering the trees together, Tarik and Remzija hoped to reproduce their sense of belonging and the duty of care in their children. Being in the car on the way back to the village, however, was also a reminder that the story unfolds within historically inflected social and political contexts: living on the margins of the uncaring state, long-term unemployment and heavy indebtedness. A conjuncture of these forces, unleashed in the postsocialist, postwar years, has driven many families away from the trees, the land, and the house, and hampered their dreams of settling in a new home in the village.

The trees, the gardens, and the houses don't only index people's property. They are also containers of histories, trails of past lives, materialization of care across generations, materials of religious experience, and bundles of relations and exchanges that are enacted *with* and *through* them. These elements of intimate relations and belonging, as Rebecca Bryant poignantly writes, "interweave in a tapestry that becomes the ground of one's life" (2010: 31). Yet this ground is nowadays profoundly shifting for many villagers. The suburbs of Sarajevo and other Bosnian cities are full of similar stories bearing witness to the scale and pervasiveness of the push factors and to the corrosive effects of the economic restructuring on rural communities.[1] In this chapter I take the house as a prism to shed light on the transformation of the intimate topographies of belonging and care, and the material world in rural BiH resulting from the postsocialist, postwar junctures.

Endurance

The conversation with Tarik in the car, as well as with other villagers over the years, has opened up the key dimension of the house as the ground of one's life: *endurance*. The house is a material manifestation of intergenerational kinship ties and a vehicle of historical continuity. In rural BiH, the notion of the house entails an inalienable compound encompassing the house itself, as well as the land—consisting of fields, meadows, trees, or pastures—animals, kin relations, and naming (i.e., patrilineal filiation and belonging) that endure over time.[2] But Tarik's life story also opens a series of questions: How have these conceptions of the house endured in the face of dramatic ruptures and transformations? What materials and practices of endurance are villagers endowed with in the present to reproduce the house at a time of rapid and violent changes?

Endurance can take on different forms. When dealing with the aftermaths of transformative events, Jane Guyer observes, endurance can become therapeutic and recuperative mode of agency. Guyer contends that endurance intertwines "many spaces of agency, imagination, and effort" (2017: 90) that are invested in an attempt to preserve specific components of life and thought "across thresholds of major change" (81). Building on Guyer's proposition, in this chapter I am interested in the key enduring strengths of the house that are gleaned from nurturing the house's living members and the land whereby the house as the ground of one's life is sustained. This is done so by fostering and cultivating a sense of guardianship, care for the land, and sharing the labor and its fruits. *Guardianship*, I argue, is a mode of relatedness, to one's family, to history, and ultimately to God that spans generations. In turn, I contextualize how these forms of guardianship have been entangled in ongoing transformations in rural BiH.

The Ethics of Guardianship: A History

The value of the house compound is realized by means of its historical continuity. The house compound constitutes a form of inalienable possession that must be removed from circulation in order to achieve such continuity. As Annette Weiner (1992) reminds us, for any form of possession to become conceived of as inalienable, it requires tremendous labor and care. The notion of guardianship articulates such historically constituted sensibilities and repertoires of people's engagement with property, inheritance, and obligations of care. In rural Bosnia, guardianship is first and foremost a form of ethical practice of care oriented toward "a skillful achievement" of continuity and endurance of the house (Weiner 1992: 7). This is a result of three historically interrelated logics of practice: local kinship (patrilineal ideology), marriage (village exogamy), and inheritance practices (partible inheritance).

Until the mid-twentieth century, village economy was formed by and large by subsistence farming. The relatively limited access to any new land due to a hilly and forested terrain in the highlands, combined with the ideology of *partible inheritance* patterns, resulted in the locally specific marriage and inheritance practices as counterbalancing mechanisms controlling land distribution and minimizing its partition. Namely, female household members married outside their kin groups and left the village. Women were compensated, usually with a dowry, in exchange for renouncing their rights over the inheritable land and the house. This cemented local conceptions of inheritable property as inalienable, including the houses. To illustrate my point further, let me turn to the village of Brdo.

Over the years of my fieldwork in Brdo I analyzed 250 marriages, spanning the past four generations and taking place over a period of around a hundred years. Only five marriages out of the total number took place between members of the village, and in all these cases they were also outside of one's patrilineal group. With rare exceptions, in which the imperative of partible inheritance was applied to the land and the house, women in the vast majority of cases were given a dowry. In chapter 3 we return to this point to further discuss what happens when a claim to a share of the inheritance is staked after it had been renounced.

The presence of the three logics of practice demonstrates a strong degree of historical continuity despite the political, social, and economic ruptures and transformations throughout the second half of the twentieth century and the first quarter of the twenty-first century. What we can observe here is a peculiarity of postsocialist transformation in rural BiH. Other former state socialist countries experienced dramatic ruptures in property relations and inheritance practices due to the state-led endeavors to abolish private property. Indeed, one of the cornerstones of the anthropology of postsocialism was its focus on the restoration of property relations after the collapse of the state socialist governmentalities, and more broadly the idea of property relations as such (Hann 1998; Hann 2003; Verdery 2003; Verdery and Humphrey 2004; for a critique of such an approach, see Thelen 2011). Unlike rural areas in other formerly state-socialist Eastern European countries, where the property relations have been restored in various degrees to its former owners in the post-1989 period, the socialist Yugoslav state did not collectivize the land and private property entirely. Although immediately after the Second World War there was an attempt to expropriate private land that exceeded 25–30 hectares and introduce agrarian reform, such attempts were eventually abandoned. In 1953, following another reform, the maximum size of private ownership was reduced to 10 hectares (Bringa 1995: 51; Davis 1977: 64; Leutloff-Grandits 2006: 77). In rural Bosnia, the majority of the population never owned such a huge amount of land anyway, hence these changes had very little effect on villagers' property relations and as a result little effect on inheritance practices.

Gendered Guardianship

The three logics translate into the gendered dynamics of guardianship as an ethical practice of care whereby continuity of the house is achieved. The practice of guardianship in the Zvijezda highlands goes beyond merely taking care of material inheritance (land, trees, houses), dominated by the preference for male siblings to inherit the house compound. This would effectively exclude women from taking any active participation in social practices of *re*production of the house compound, and from participation in vital exchange with the divine that brings prosperity, well-being, and blessing to the house enacted through guardianship. For both men and women, any act of guardianship is burdened by the deep sense of responsibility and haunted by the possibility of failing in one's obligation to maintain the chain of continuity of the house. Failing to do so would inevitably lead to betrayal of one's ancestors. Furthermore, it would cut people off from the sources of accumulated blessing (*bereket*) through a long-term cycle of vital exchange between the members of the house and the divine over generations (Brenner 1998: 179–80).[3]

Maintaining the household compound is a collective achievement. At the day-to-day level, the acts of care and guardianship are gendered in regard to *attentiveness* to particular domains of social life rather than forming a clear-cut distinction between the (male) outside and (female) inside domains of moral conduct and organization of social life (Bourdieu 1977, Hirschon 1978).[4] The discourses and acts of care revolve around two *overlapping* modes of guardianship, that of caring for the bequest, and caring for the living.

The Land (Not) for Sale

Fadil's father was considered by villagers to be a well-off landowner. Until his death in the early 1970s, he lived solely from his land. His two sons, both born in the late 1940s, Fadil and Bekir, and their families, continued to practice subsistence farming while also working in the timber and construction industries, respectively. They all lived together in one house until their father's death. Then they followed the trend common across rural Bosnia since the late 1960s of living separately in their newly built houses, as we see later in this chapter. This trend of household fission and dissolving intergenerational interdependence emerged from the incorporation of village households into the wage economy of the Yugoslav state, which brought increasing economic independence to individuals and nuclear families. Numerous villagers across the highlands also took the opportunity at the time to work as *gastarbaiters* in the Federal Republic of Germany, and later as construction workers in the Middle East in the late 1970s and 1980s. Nowadays, less than a third of families across the Zvijezda highlands live jointly under one roof. Despite the fission of the household, Fadil's and Bekir's families continue to share the bequeathed land and jointly coordinate the work on that land. The families conceptualize and relate to the property with a deep sense of obligation and care: they must manage it well so that it can be passed on to their children and grandchildren. It is now their families' responsibility to guard and cultivate the bequest that continues to give life.

Guardianship is binding. The house compound is given by one's father in order to be kept. This is a common moral discourse as much as an everyday ethical practice.[5] As a result, it was nearly impossible for me to track down any instances of land or property being sold in the villages. This was in sharp contrast with municipal and urban suburbs, where "For sale" signs were omnipresent. Today, as much as during the Yugoslav era, those families who do not use some of their meadows or pastures usually let other villagers use the land and take a portion of hay, money, or sacrificed ram (*kurban*) in return as a form of accorded (*halal*) exchange (see ch. 3). Similarly, the families who migrate to the cities, or who live in the diaspora abroad, do not sell their land or any other property. So far, there has always been a relative or a neighbor in the village who is asked to take care over the guardianship. And, as in the case of Tarik, who was rushing to water his fruit trees in the village, his guardianship continues even after he has migrated from the village. Abandoned land is morally sanctioned as problematic and sinful, as would be someone's attempt to sell the land.

In order to further consider the persuasiveness of this moral discourse, let us look more closely at two examples from the village Brdo. Nestled in a hilly landscape, the houses are clustered patrilineally. Two decades ago, in the late 1990s, one such neighborhood located in the slopes, collectively decided to build a septic system. It was a cooperative exercise: the neighbors collected money and organized themselves. After many weeks of discussions, the villagers concluded that the best location for building a septic tank would be in a small valley below the hillside where the houses were situated. Began, who also lives in the neighborhood, owned the land in the valley where the neighbors wanted to build the tank. Without much hesitation or persuasion, he agreed to the use of this tiny valley for the communal purpose, knowing that his house will benefit from the septic system as well, yet without renouncing his ownership over the land. In return, Began's household did not pay any construction costs, with the neighbors paying on his behalf as a way to compensate him. Moreover, Began's household can still use the valley as a pasture for his sheep.

This resolution did not occur in the second neighborhood. There, the only valley where a drainage system could be established is owned by old Hasan, who comes from the third neighborhood. Hasan is considered to be a descendant of a well-off family, and he owns an extensive portion of the land. Since he does not use much of the land, Hasan lets other villagers use it if they provide him with compensation in return—usually hay. Whenever Hasan passed Faruk's house, while herding a flock of sheep, Faruk loudly shouted "Hasan, yoo-hoo Hasan,

The land not for sale in the village.

let's make a bargain." Hasan usually waved his hand and followed the flock. Faruk is also a descendant of a well-off family and also owns a large portion of the land. Some of his fields share a border with Hasan's but are unsuitable as a site for the septic tank. Faruk tried to offer Hasan various fields of almost incommensurable quality and size on behalf of his neighborhood. Later, Faruk even tried to let Hasan choose whichever piece of his land he desired. If Hasan accepted this deal, he would definitely be better off. Yet Hasan remained unshakable.

Whenever I tried to get any hint of explanation as to why Hasan did not want to exchange the land despite the fact that he would be better off, there was often a prolonged silence, and then the neighbors simply said "it's his land." In the first case, we can see that although Began provided his land, he did not detach himself from the land. His family still uses it. Moreover, Began's house benefits from the septic system as well. If Hasan employed only calculative reasoning in making a decision and exchanged the land with Faruk, then he would be better off. Indeed, he could have chosen any piece of land that Faruk owned. But to Hasan the value of the land operates in the register of inalienable possession and is hardly commensurable. In order to exchange, as the second scenario indicates, Hasan would have to withdraw and alienate himself from the inherited land that ought to be kept and not exchanged. Even for Faruk, the decision to exchange the land was difficult and was discussed within the household, and with the neighbors, on whose behalf he tried to negotiate as well, for months. Faruk's decision and the desire to exchange were considered carefully and framed in the hierarchy of values with respect to the long-term benefits to, and well-being of, the household and even the neighborhood. Hence, such a decision was understood as the only one appropriate to the given circumstances, and as an act that did not sever Fadil's guardianship of the inherited house compound.

Eating Together

The second mode of guardianship revolves around the ethics of caring for the living. It is the domain in which women in particular assume the burden as well as achieve the continuity and endurance of the house over time.

So far we have learned from Tarik and other male villagers that the notion of the house is embodied in the trees, fields, and buildings that he was tirelessly caring for with the help of his wife and children, even despite their physical distance from the village. Listening to his wife, Remzija, and other women in the village, I received a slightly different perspective on what taking care of the house entails. Giving life and raising children were always mentioned as contributing to the maintenance of the bequeathed house compound over time. But as our conversations progressed, it became clear that for women the meaning of the house was folded into the everyday acts of commensality expressed in the idioms "living together" and "eating together."

The ideational framework of living together as a matter of eating together is a pervasive moral trope with regard to relatedness and family care in the Zvijezda highlands. The notion of "living together" requires a further analytical distinction here between the house and the neighborhood. Although the house and the neighborhood have historically constituted a prime socio-spatial nexus where village life has been and continues to be lived, the two are not alike (Bringa 1995: 41–58). As I discuss in chapter 2, neighborhood (*komšiluk*) is a nexus of sociality within physical proximity, articulating the values of hospitality and mutuality, as well as a site where neighbors can engage with each other's lives. The house, as the ground of one's life and intimate belonging, is a composite of kinship and property relations, and a local model for organizing material life, whereby the very conditions of life are sustained and reproduced with a deep sense of care that spans generations. This is expressed in the idioms of "eating" and "living together."

From the earliest moments of my fieldwork, I regularly encountered similar depictions across the highlands. For example, I had been living in Brdo for only a few weeks when, in late August 2009, everyone started to worry about preparing their houses for the upcoming winter. One day, during the obligatory large pot of morning coffee with his family, my landlord decided to go to the forest to collect some firewood reserves for the winter. On the way to the forest we crossed the field of our neighbor Nijas, who was working with someone I could not recognize from a distance. "Look, there is Nijas and . . ." I said. "Oh yes, that's Nijas and his *amidža*" commented my landlord's wife. "Amidža?" I asked, because I was not yet used to the local kinship terminologies. "You know amidža . . . well, Nijas's father's brother, they are all together," she explained. "What do you mean by 'together'?" I asked, as I remembered that Nijas's uncle lived alone in a separate house close to ours, and hence I was confused. My landlord's wife continued, "together, you know, they all eat together, like Mujo and Fadil, or like Menso and Raif, and like you do with us, we also live together." In her explanation that "they are all together" and "they all eat together," she articulated the key ideas through which villagers understand, experience, and enact the local meanings of the house, care, and relatedness in the processes of everyday life.

The idiom of "eating together" is more than just an act of consuming food together. Commensality is an important idiom of relatedness, family life and memory, materialized through the house that unfolds through time. The food needs to be prepared the way the members of the house like it and must suit their taste. Preparation and taste embody accumulated memories and skills that transcend generations (Sutton and Hernandez 2007). Entering Remzija's, Izeta's, and many other kitchen corners in village houses, I was introduced to the hidden world of all these invisible utensils with specific purpose, qualities, and stories that women attached to them. Not every baking tray (*tepsija*) is as good for baking bread or pita as "the blue one on the shelf that I inherited from my mother-in-law," Remzija repeatedly told me about the biographies of these objects (Kopytoff 1986). Women in the villages offered me the analogical biographies of these utensils stored in the cupboards of their houses, and their inalienable property qualities, in a way that was analogical to Tarik's descriptions of the biographies of the trees in his family gardens, connecting the families across time.

"Eating together" also points to the hearth as the physical and social center of the house. Old and new houses in the villages organize the space inside the house in a similar fashion around the hearth, where the family's daily life unfolds. But there is more to the hearth than just its interior architecture. When I visited Tarik and Remzija for the first time in their newly rented flat in a suburb of Sarajevo, Remzija immediately complained that she couldn't prepare food properly anymore. Her new electric oven did not work properly and was giving her a headache. The food she made was either burned or half-baked. Neither their utensils nor their cooking skills could be used to their greatest effect in the new environment. "How am I supposed to feed my family if I can't even give them a slice of bread?" Remzija exclaimed, expressing her frustration and desperation at not being able to make bread at home any more, while trying to make sense to the shifting intimate topographies of belonging and care. Tarik and Remzija weren't the only ones facing difficulties in their new suburban neighborhood. Following a series of consultations with their ex-village neighbors, who had moved to the suburb earlier, Tarik and Remzija decided to bring their wood burning stove—the hearth of the house—from the old village house and install it in the garden attached to their newly rented flat.

Intimate Topographies

If trees, houses, and the land embody genealogical memories, the food and the biographies of personal objects such as utensils index peoples' intimate topographies associated with the house (Bachelard 1969). Indeed, "eating together" refers to a particular ambience of familiarity, populated with intimate objects of everyday life and care that create a sense of homeliness and evoke what it means and feels like to be at home. Making food, and eating together takes place around a tablecloth (*sofra*) laid over the table or on the floor in the hearth of the house. The floor, the literal ground of one's life in the house, is covered by a rug (*ćilim*) that itself is often imbued with biographies connected with one's dowry, or a wedding gift. This is the place where children learn their first words, take their first steps, meet their relatives and neighbors, where family gets together, and where secrets are whispered to the attentive ears of parents and siblings.

The walls of the house are heterotopic sites in their own right, mixing the personal, the divine, and the secular. They are decorated with framed or wood-carved Islamic calligraphies, posters of Mecca, calendars with praying times and images of Bosnian mosques, family photographs, sometimes hanging right next to the fading black-and-white photos of Josip Broz Tito, the leader of socialist Yugoslavia. The surrounding furniture, windows, and walls are all decorated with embroidery and fine cloths that have their own biographies. While the embroidery covering the top shelf where the wrapped Qur'an is kept, Izeta explained to me, is one of the very few objects her prematurely deceased mother bequeathed to her when she was fourteen, the embroideries decorating the sofa were made over the years with other women from the neighborhood during their regular coffee get-togethers.

When I visited Tarik and Remzija, and also the other villagers who had moved away from the highlands to the suburbs, it was striking how similar the hearths of their rented flats looked to their village houses. And it was these items of personal property, the intimate objects of everyday life—an ashtray, a red coffeepot (*džezva*), a water jug, baking trays, a string of praying beads hanging over the door handle, and the decorative fabrics on the furniture—all imbued with the biographies of the past lives and family's togetherness, that transformed the four white concrete walls of a rented flat into an intimate topography of home. Time and again women commented that "I made sure I took everything with me," or "I carefully packed everything and took it with us. I did the same during the war when we were living in a stranger's house." In such everyday narrative reflections women were making historical analogies with the wartimes, when the families were forced to flee their homes and live in the houses of strangers, and the women's role was to maintain the continuity of the house despite challenging circumstances, whether resulting from the war or the effects of economic dispossession in the postsocialist, postwar years.[6] In fact, the biographies of many objects carry the stains of past wars as much as of socialism, reminding villagers what was damaged or lost, and conversely what remained. Their biographical qualities cannot be reduced to being mere vehicles of traumatic or nostalgic memories. What is important is the enduring capacity of these objects, cared for by women, to transform spaces into the intimate topographies where the members of the house can get together, live together, and eat together over time.

Intimate topographies can also stretch across distance. Intimate objects move, villagers migrate, and the life-giving and nourishing substances produced by women in the house circulate from villages to towns, and sustain the household members across distances. When Tarik finished watering the trees and spent another day working around the houses—old and new—it was time to go back to Sarajevo. The evening before our departure, a neighbor knocked on the door. Her son had moved to the same suburb as Tarik four years earlier. The neighbor asked Tarik whether we could bring a few dairy items for her son—cheese, milk, and sour cream. This was not an unusual request. Villagers who travel to cities for work are regularly asked to carry dairy items for others who left the village. A friendly request for this kind of help is seldom declined, since no one can be sure whether they will need to take part in a similar supply network in the near future. Home-produced food is one of the enduring strengths of life that "gives vitality to humans, animals, and other living things" of the house across generations (Gudeman

2016: 28). Whenever I joined someone from the villages who migrated to the suburbs of Sarajevo for a meal, sooner or later I was told whether the ingredients were "ours"—our cheese, our meat, our milk. The "ours" referred to the family house in the village. Eating "ours" was a metonymical extension of "eating together," while eating "homemade" (*domaći*) referred to products purchased from other villagers, or neighbors with their own rural-urban channels of supply. Anthropologists describe how, in the situations of scarcity and economic deprivation, rural-urban food-provisioning networks flourished in the socialist and postsocialist contexts (Ries 2009). But there is more at stake here. The food-provisioning networks maintain the house and the family relations through the acts of "eating together" across distances.

Houses in Flames

It was a lazy, hot summer afternoon, and we were sitting in the shade of the dogwood tree in the corner of Mustafa's garden, waiting for the temperature to drop a bit. It was too hot to do anything but talk and ponder. Is it better to live in a brick house? Mustafa asked his neighbor Edin, who had joined us for a cup of coffee. Or, is it better to live in a wooden house? He continued in his contemplation. Mustafa preferred brick houses. Old timber houses signified to him and to the majority of villagers ruralism, and epitomized peasant and class backwardness.[7] This was also why the architectural style of the newly built houses in villages, in the municipalities, or on the outskirts of big cities, were indistinguishable from the socialist era to the present. Edin liked timber houses. He disagreed with Mustafa as far as the aesthetics and insulation qualities were concerned. Nonetheless, he took the conversation and the argument in favor of brick houses in a different direction. "In Bosnia," he suggested, "our houses are in flames every fifty years; it's practical to use bricks so you don't need to start from scratch again and again."

This was an intriguing comment but not an isolated one. Different variations of this narrative circulate throughout the highlands. Bego, now ninety years old, remembers how a Chetnik soldier during World War II was shouting toward the forest where Bego was hiding at the time: "Burn the latrines so they won't have any chance to even shit here again." His vivid memories of that war when Chetnik troops attacked the villages are nowadays narrated as stories of villagers' endurance, vitality, and the strength to move on in their lives, rather than simply referring to suffering or hatred of the Other. Time and again villagers have rebuilt their homes, piecing their lives together from the rubbles and ashes of violence.

In the previous section, we saw how villagers mediate their relations with the living, the dead, and ultimately with the divine *in* and *through* the house. "The houses in flames" narratives, however, bring into sharp relief the house as a vehicle for villagers' everyday historical work. Indeed, the house is profoundly intertwined with critical events, ruptures, and transformations, which extend beyond the Zvijezda highlands.

"Our houses are in flames every fifty years" and "burn the latrines" are the expressive forms of the living remainders of the past in the present, and material and narrative analogies for engaging with one's history as a series of plunders, violence and ruinations that were brought upon villagers during the twentieth century. In other words, if the house evokes the ground of one's life, it also evokes its fragility. How do societies, with historical experiences of facing violence and devastation, reproduce the past for the future in and through fragility and loss of the ground of their lives in the present? Annette Weiner asks a similar question. In her response to this question, Weiner pointed to the capacity of an inalienable possession, such as the house, to act "as a stabilizing force against change because its presence authenticates cosmological origins, kinship, and political histories" (1992: 9). But what if that same stabilizing force, the house in our case, is undergoing metamorphoses itself?

Topographies of Abandonment

The transformation of the political economy of Bosnia and Herzegovina has had severe consequences for rural areas. In the areas that were destroyed during the war, the return of refugees and displaced villagers has not fulfilled the expectations of the international community (Jansen 2011). Although politics is often mentioned as a reason, the political economy of postsocialist, postwar BiH, characterized by a chronic lack of job opportunities and poor infrastructure in rural areas, needs to be included in the equation as well (Donais 2005).

In the Zvijezda highlands, the changing political economy of BiH has resulted in outmigration, abandonment of houses, and withdrawal from the land.[8] Nowadays, empty houses, torsos of looted buildings or unfinished red-and-grey brick-and-block villas, and abandoned, untended fields are scattered across the rural landscape and serve as enduring mementos of the hard work, hopes, and aspirations that the generations of villagers invested in their houses, and which have never fully materialized. Unlike in other parts of the country that witnessed mass atrocities, destruction of properties, forced displacement during the Bosnian war, and the non-return of displaced families, in the Zvijezda highlands the empty buildings and neglected land are crude symptoms of declining economic opportunities, poor living standards, and failed privatization in the postsocialist, postwar years.

Historical vicissitudes, embodied in the expressive tropes "our houses are in flames every fifty years" and "burn the latrines," have profoundly shaped the conceptions and practices of the house as a model of livelihood and rendered its fragility omnipresent. Bricks or timber? Village or town? The inherited house or a rented flat in a Sarajevo suburb? Such questions loom in the background of everyday conversations in the villages today. However, similar questions have been repeated time and again over the course of the last century. The house therefore needs to be attended to as a shifting "operational cultural ideal" in regard to how material life is organized, and how houses have been formed in a given historical moment and circumstances (Fernandez and Fernandez 1988). Its ideals and values are constantly in the making, emerging as a series of negotiated, often incompatible, understandings and practices inside and outside of the house, between relatives and neighbors, and between the villagers and the wider translocal political and economic forces.

The shifts and undergoing metamorphoses of the house can be traced through another trope, that of "the land gives life." We have encountered this trope already, as told by Fadil to his grandson. Its meaning has transformed over time. For the land to give life, one has to engage with it and take care of it. But is this possible anymore?

Across rural Bosnia, a common model of sustaining and organizing material life in the villages until the 1960s was the autarky of extended multigenerational house. "The land gives life" was an expression of a traditional peasant way of life that also became an ideal typical model for studying rural life in Yugoslavia, and southeast Europe more broadly.[9] The large-scale state modernization of the Yugoslav countryside connected the villages in the Zvijezda highlands by means of newly built roads with urban centers, and increased the mobility of the workforce.[10] This had two consequences for "the land that gives life" and the house.

First, as we saw in the case of Fadil and his brother in the previous section, male villagers turned their plowed fields into hay meadows and fully took part in the socialist wage economy, working outside of the villages, while women continued to maintain the vegetable gardens around the houses, as well as keeping a small number of livestock.[11] Although part of the locally produced diet was subsequently substituted by products purchased in the newly opened village shops, or brought from the urban centers, the value of autarky had never gone fully away.

Second, an increasing number of opportunities to participate in the wage labor market, in which male villagers predominantly took part, accelerated the processes of household fission. This affected the bequeathed "land that gives life" as well. Due to easier access to wage labor opportunities and spousal economic independence, young couples in particular attempted to earn their own living, save money and build their own houses (Bringa 1995: 42–47). Hand in hand with these changes emerged new meanings associated with individual and family property.

Since the 1960s, when multigenerational houses started to split, the land has been partitioned. As a result, fences have been erected between brothers and neighbors, and communal pastures have disappeared from the village landscape.[12] Since the mid-1970s, when all villages in the highlands became fully connected via the road links with urban centers, these processes intensified further. The materiality, architecture, and aesthetics of the house also changed in this period, in particular under the influence of those villagers who started working as *gastarbeiters* in the Federal Republic of Germany, and who became important agents of changing taste back in the villages (Bernard 2012).

The houses that have been built since the late 1970s are made from bricks rather than timber, which became an ideal image of the house. The craze for building one's own house, common across Yugoslavia at the time (Archer 2017), also became an expression of the rising inequalities between families who not only succeeded in saving enough money, but who also had enough bequeathed land in villages to allow such a partition of family property for the purpose of building new houses in the first place. Until the late 1960s, the stable number of multigenerational houses in the villages of the Zvijezda highlands ranged between ten and twenty, and no single-family houses. In the last three decades the number of single-family houses has tripled on average, and in Brdo it reached seventy houses, though nowadays many are empty.

When the debt crisis hit Yugoslavia in the 1980s, villagers turned back to their fields. "The land that gives life" regained the meaning of self-sustenance again. It was further exacerbated in the postsocialist, postwar period. Facing the retraction of state provision and access to labor opportunities, subsistence farming and kinship networks became the primary safety net for the marginalized and now largely unemployed villagers.[13] "Retreat to the household" (Pine 2002, also Humphrey 2002), a trend that is also common in rural areas across the postsocialist countryside more broadly, reinvigorated the house economy and care for the life-giving land. Ultimately, as Frances Pine suggests, such a retreat does not mean reverting to the old-style peasantry, but rather turning to a new way of managing self-sustenance in a context of economic dispossession and precarity. This shift, as Pine further argues, is "accompanied by a simultaneous drive towards new or more elaborate forms of consumption, urban values and exchanges, highly individualistic entrepreneurial activities, movement and mobility" (Pine 2002: 99).

In the Zvijezda highlands, the villagers' retreat to "the land that gives life" has been an ongoing process of reconfiguring how to organize one's material life vis-á-vis the wider reconfigurations in Bosnian political economy. For those villagers who stayed in the highlands, the house economy of self-sustenance bifurcated. First, subsistence agriculture for household consumption continues to be practiced by all households. The yields constitute a significant part of the household diet, with occasional sales of surplus to traders, at the local markets, or to villagers who migrated to the cities. Second, new cash crop seasonal activities have emerged in recent years. Cash crop production was encouraged by international aid projects, as well as by ad hoc cantonal projects in the early postwar years, but it has increasingly become part of villagers' entrepreneurial experimentations. These include greenhouse farming, meat production, beekeeping, and harvesting wild fruits, mushrooms, and herbs.

The products and cash circulate within the networks connecting villagers and village expats in the cities, and among their old and new urban acquaintances. The taste and demand of urbanites, especially their increasing revaluation of "homemade" and "organic" products, is now shaping villagers' own economic activities and experimentations with new forms of farming and production. Among the most frequent activities are dairy production, beekeeping, and the production of related honey and wax products, growing raspberries on their fields, or making specialized meat products (e.g., smoked turkey and lamb).

If "the land that gives life" continues to be a pervasive idiom of village life for those who retreated to the land, we need to consider what happens when the land lost its life-giving capacity due to people's withdrawal from it.

Empty Houses

How should we attend to land that could give life but no longer does? And what about the unfinished, empty houses that stand abandoned in the landscape across rural BiH? The mushrooming numbers of empty houses and untended fields in the village landscape embody traces of lives, sweat, labor, debts, neighborhood help and solidarity, and personal hopes, headaches, and aspirations that did not unfold as anticipated.

The postsocialist, postwar years brought about prolonged economic marginalization of the countryside. At the same time, this period engendered another wave of debt crisis—easily accessible microloans (*kredit*) that led to a spiral of indebtedness for many villagers.[14] This debt epidemic coincided with shrinking labor opportunities, and finding anyone without debt among the villagers was like finding a needle in a haystack. Faced with the impossibility of saving enough money to build a house, since the early 2000s loans have become a popular way for villagers to pursue the aspiration of building the ground of their life—a house.

This was the case for many villagers in the Zvijezda highlands, including Tarik, his wife Remzija, and their three children. I followed the family closely over the years of my fieldwork. The family used to live squeezed inside an old wooden house, built in the 1950s, that they inherited from Tarik's parents. Tarik was a well-respected guardian who cared tremendously for the bequeathed property. Still, there was no way he could bring running water or a bathroom into the old house. The family of five found living in the old house constraining and uncomfortable. Building a more spacious, brick house became a source of aspiration and hope, a dream of a better life. Access to *kredit*, combined with help from neighbors, enabled Tarik to build a basic roofed structure on the family land on the outskirts of the village by 2004. Since then, as Tarik was unemployed long-term, the family has struggled to pay off the debt and any further construction work on the house has been put on hold indefinitely. While still living in the old house, Tarik went to the new "house" at least twice a week, taking care of it as much as he took care of the old house. In the summer months, his children went regularly to water the apple trees that Tarik had planted in the garden back in 2004. The family had never given up the aspiration that one day they would all move in.

When I returned to BiH in 2014, it was therefore a bit of a surprise to find myself sitting in the living room of a spacious flat in a Sarajevo suburb. It felt spacious because there was very little furniture in the flat. Tarik was sitting next to me on the sofa. A few of the other objects in the room were familiar: a TV set, a couple of framed family photographs, green praying beads (*tespih*) hanging next to the door frame, and Remzija's handmade knitted decorative cloths carefully arranged on the few pieces of furniture and providing the sense of homely warmth that I remembered so well from their old house in the highlands. Five years after our first encounter, Remzija and Tarik had joined other villagers on the run from desperate circumstances to find a job and reside on the outskirts of Sarajevo, in Vogošća. "We're like refugees again," was Remzija's first sentence when she appeared in the living room with an ashtray and a cold homemade raspberry cordial, recalling her experiences of displacement. "What can I do?" sighed Tarik, and looked at me, while trying to roll a cigarette. Like many others, he couldn't afford to buy cigarettes anymore, so he started rolling his own using tobacco of variable quality obtained through friends or on local markets and which caused respiratory problems he hadn't had before. When he had finally rolled three cigarettes, he sat more comfortably. We had not seen each other for two years—a period that had profoundly changed the ground of Tarik's family life.

The years of failed attempts to secure a job in the Zvijezda highlands had led Tarik to try to seek a better fortune abroad, hoping that this would allow him to provide for his family but also to care for the bequest. This was a decision that was made with much hesitation, but also in the anticipation of finally having a chance to save enough money to move to the new house. So Tarik went to Kazakhstan as a construction worker. There, no one from the Bosnian building brigade received a salary. The agent from Bosnia who got Tarik the job went completely silent. All the Bosnians who arrived with Tarik were stuck in Astana without any means of leaving. Tarik and the others had to ask their families to buy them tickets and bring them home. "Most of us," he bitterly commented, "had to take another loan although the reason we went to Kazakhstan was to earn enough money to pay our existing loans back." When Tarik returned, his struggle to find a job continued and all the family's savings had gone into getting him back. In the end, it just became too much to bear. "Let me show you something," Tarik said, pulling out from under the coffee table a plastic box full of various pills that he had started taking in the last few years. The diagnosis he had received as a result of accumulated stress, while still in his mid-forties, was far too common a story in BiH: high cholesterol, high blood pressure, and diabetes. Moreover, Tarik still suffered from the aftereffects of the war injuries he sustained by being hit by shrapnel.

A few months before our reunion in 2014, Tarik's brother had found a job for him in a Sarajevo factory. Although the job was uncertain and irregular, and the contracts available in the factory ranged from a month to three months, it was Tarik's first regular income in many years. Now living in the village became an obstacle, as commuting was too expensive, and it turned out to be cheaper if the family moved to the suburbs of Sarajevo. No one seemed to mind the move. The children were excited, and there was a good prospect for Remzija to find a job as well. "It feels like our village here," they both said, and Tarik continued "my brother lives only a five-minute walk from here. And Najm from our komšiluk lives on the top of the hill, where Mevludin [another next-door neighbor] built a house, and he plans to use it for his kids once they go to the university."

So, had he left the village, the plans to finish his house, and ultimately the duty of guardianship, for good, I wondered? Having known him for many years, I knew how strongly attached he felt to the village, as well as to the property bequeathed to him. I also knew how much his family dreamed about moving to their new, bigger, and more comfortable house. What will happen to the house now, I asked? "We go back regularly, to do some work around the new house," both Tarik and Remzija replied, "cutting the grass, watering the apple trees, sweeping the floor." Then he added, "inshallah, I will build a bench and a table underneath an apple tree so we can sit in the shade and drink coffee next summer." Both were convinced, in their hopes and in their humble actions of care—watering the apple trees, cutting the grass, sweeping—that one day, the family would return to where the ground of their life and intimate topographies of belonging were located. After this conversation, Tarik took his mobile phone to call one of the village neighbors who regularly drove to Sarajevo for work, asking him whether he had a few free seats in his car. This is how we ended up squeezed into an aging Volkswagen II, heading toward the village to water the apple trees.

One June morning in 2016, I received the message that Tarik had passed away in Sarajevo. At the age of forty-nine he had a heart attack. His heart exploded from the pressure, as his daughter told me. Then she added, "here, in Bosnia, debts kill people—it was too much for him." The family did not return. The unfinished house, the apple trees, and the land were abandoned, joining an increasing number of houses without guardians, which no longer give life.

2

Locked Doors

"First search for a neighbor, then build a house" is a popular proverb in the Zvijezda highlands. Sifet introduced me to this saying in the early days of my fieldwork. When I visited him one autumn day in 2009 with another neighbor, Zahid, he seemed distressed. We were planning to attend a funeral (*dženaza*) that was scheduled to take place after the afternoon prayer in the mosque. Zahid and I sat down on the sofa. Sifet seemed unable to get ready. After a while, Zahid pulled out a packet of cigarettes from the pocket of his jacket while we were waiting. After finishing his first cigarette, Zahid's impatience rose, as there was still no sign that Sifet was ready to leave. It was time for another cigarette. I was aware that Zahid had an infamous reputation for approaching people in a direct manner, so when I saw that he was fidgeting and reaching for his third cigarette while mumbling to himself, I decided to break the silent tension in the room and asked Sifet what the matter was. Sifet welcomed the opportunity to direct his stress into a short pedagogical exercise:

> When someone dies in our village quarter, then the whole neighborhood (*komšiluk*) tries to help you and look after your family; people come to your house and ask you what needs to be done, they give you support; there isn't anything like that in the other village quarter. It is our custom that the body of the dead person stays in the house the night before the funeral and living persons sit next to the body through the night. I can tell you exactly who came to the house when

> my mother died: everyone from my neighborhood. Yesterday, the family from the other quarter couldn't find anybody who would stay with the deceased body through the night. Can you imagine what the people from that quarter are like? Yesterday, there was nobody who would look after the deceased body.

Participation in mourning for the soul of the dead is an expression of care for the dead as well as for the community of the living. Sifet found the absence of the neighbors from the house of the deceased impossible to understand. His inability to prepare for the funeral because of his anger and desperation was a result of what he saw as the increasing lack of neighbors' care that marked the previous night.

Let's consider another event that happened a few years later. It was the summer of 2012, and I had just returned to the Zvijezda highlands. In the first few hours of my stay in Brdo, I learned about a family tragedy that had occurred in one of the neighborhoods just a few months before my arrival. The story goes like this: One early April morning, the entire village was awakened by a terrible scream coming from the garden of Sakib, a villager. It was not Sakib but his wife, Mediha, who was screaming and weeping. When Mediha awoke around 5 a.m. and could not find her husband in the house, she went outside, only to discover that Sakib had hanged himself from a tree in the garden. The ensuing police investigation quickly concluded that Sakib had committed suicide. This took everyone by surprise, and the news spread quickly across the municipality, where it was widely debated in cafés even months after the tragedy. The obvious question that everyone asked was "why?" as Sakib was seen by his fellow neighbors as one of the more fortunate villagers. As his friends and neighbors emphasized, Sakib was the first villager to get a permanent job after the war ended in 1995. Unlike many in the village, Sakib had a regular and decent income. He also had a new spacious house, a nice wife, three young children, and he was highly valued among his neighbors for his good reputation of always helping others: he was lauded as a good neighbor. So why did he commit suicide? Rumors later spread that Sakib had accumulated debts and was not capable of dealing with them anymore. These rumors did not make it easier for his neighbors, family, and friends to understand his suicide. Sakib's suicide provoked further questions and vigorous debates. The "why" was discussed along with other questions: Why did nobody from the neighborhood know about Sakib's problems? Why did he not tell anyone about his debts? Why did people not care about one another anymore? Some of his neighbors even asked why people like Sakib had to live in a state where loans and life in debt were the only means of surviving and getting by, and suicide the only way of escaping them.

Fragility

How should we think about these two events? As personal tragedies? Certainly. But something else was at stake in the urgency with which villagers were debating these events. We can think of them as moments exposing how fragile the certitudes of everyday life can be. In turn we need to ask: How are such moments folded into the broader effects of the postsocialist, postwar transformations? How do villagers make sense to these transformations in their everyday historical work through the idiom of komšiluk?

In this chapter I explore the entanglements between such singular moments of everyday life and the ongoing effects of critical events. I am concerned with how these entanglements shape and punctuate village sociality, that is, the ongoing relationships villagers make with one another within neighborhood spaces, where everyday life unfolds. In her reflection on neighborliness, Veena Das aptly observes that "there is a fragility to the give and take in everyday life born out of an ethics of proximity" (2013: 219). In this chapter I examine the idea of komšiluk in terms of such a fragile ethics of proximity.

Komšiluk is a fragile concept. It is fragile in two ways: as an analytical category and as an idiom of lived experience. On the one hand, the Bosnian war triggered numerous scholarly debates that have attempted to ascertain "the

Dženaza (funeral) as an expression of respect, piety, and neighborliness.

roots" of civility and/or antagonism in multireligious and multiethnic Bosnian society. "Neighborliness," "neighbors," and "neighborhood" became frequent metaphors, analogies, as well as analytical tools that were cast over the dynamics of civility in Bosnian society, past and present. Indeed, the depictions of Bosnia and Herzegovina as a place where various communities met and lived together side by side, and the Bosnian war as a war between neighbors, have mushroomed since the conflict erupted, and they continue to populate the pages of academic and popular writing.[1] The question of whether or not komšiluk is inherently antagonistic, engendering intercommunal violence, or not, represents a conceptual deadlock and evokes the incompatibility of these respective analytical positions. This renders komšiluk vulnerable as an ethnographic object of analysis to these externally imposed conceptual frames.

On the other hand, as Sifet's laments suggest, the local conceptions of komšiluk are agonistic rather than antagonistic, and social rather than a priori political. Indeed, "one may not love one's neighbors," as Rebecca Bryant poignantly writes, "but one normally needs to get along with them" (2016: 14). In this chapter, I take Bryant's observation as a point of departure to argue that komšiluk refers to a form of sociality within proximity, whether in situations where the texture of social fabric has been a multiethnic setting, or not, as is the case of the villages in the Zvijezda highlands. Put differently, komšiluk is a social form and an ethical practice of a moral community emerging from living in proximity.

Unlike the house being a medium of deeply affective forms of relatedness and deep obligations of care, as we saw in chapter 1, the idioms of neighborliness are primarily born out of the pragmatics of sociality in proximity. And that is what makes komšiluk fragile in the sense of being subject to constant negotiation and working out how to move along with one's life while being enmeshed in the lives of others with whom one shares proximity. The questions about Sakib's suicide and the doubts as to whether his neighbors could have done anything to prevent the tragedy are a haunting reminder of how quickly *all* social ties born out of living in proximity can be cut off, and how the moral community is constantly on the verge of possible fragmentation and collapse.

Komšiluk, like other cultural conceptions of neighborhood, is "the site in which the life of the other is engaged" (Das 2010: 376). Its values and obligations are realized through the ethical practice of being a good neighbor, and "[as] a moral striving in its uncertainty and its attention to the concrete specificity of the other" (377), in which sociality becomes for villagers a moral project embedded in everyday life . This moral dimension of everyday life is recognized in "the apparatuses of everyday life—habits, excuses, pretences, concealment, as well as endurance, acknowledgement" (Das 2012: 145). This is why neighborhood sociality is potentially also an important dimension of religious experience. Pursuing and cultivating such an ethics of proximity—by taking part in mourning for the soul of a deceased neighbor or by caring for one's neighbors as the acts of good deeds (*sevap*) as I discuss in the following chapter—can become a mode of enacting and articulating vital exchange with the divine, and infuse komšiluk with otherworldly qualities.[2]

Yet villagers' reasoning about Sakib's suicide reminds us that komšiluk needs to be situated within the spatiotemporal configuration of large-scale postsocialist and postwar transformations of Bosnian society that deeply shattered villagers' lifeworlds. These unfolding transformations have reconfigured how villagers engage or disengage in the life of others and how the spaces of proximity become the spaces of distance.

Ethics of Proximity

Born out of everyday proximity, komšiluk in the Zvijezda highlands consists of tapestried networks of ties made up of giving and taking. These ties are oiled by small gestures of care and participation in the lives of others, ranging from borrowing tools, utensils, coffee, sugar, oil or flour, and regular visits; to helping with everyday chores around the house and in the fields; or participating in mourning for deceased neighbors. Yet the very same networks afford a constant stream of gossip that gives rise to disputes, turning friends into foes and old enemies into friends as villagers move along in their lives. Komšiluk, as an ethics of proximity, is constantly in the making. It unfolds in villagers' actions as well as in their reflections on these actions, whereby villagers strive to forge and maintain good interpersonal relations with neighbors in the flow of social life.

As the stories of Sakib and Sifet bring into sharp relief, komšiluk as sociality within proximity is perceived by the villagers as having altered dramatically. The rupture is considered to have taken place during the war in the 1990s, followed by the events and developments in the postsocialist and postwar years that Elissa Helms describes as "a time of major fluctuation in values, institutions, possibilities, and hierarchies of privilege" (2013: 5). The changing character of interpersonal relations in village neighborhoods commonly expressed through komšiluk-related idioms mirrors larger socioeconomic reconfigurations of Bosnia and Herzegovina, and in particular rising economic inequalities between the villagers that are felt and debated as newly emerged hierarchies between the "winners" and the "losers" of the postwar years.

Such newly constituted hierarchies deeply affect interpersonal relations, accentuate the fragility of sociality in proximity, and transform villages and village neighborhoods into sites of disengagement in the life of others. The discourses, and attempts to live up to the idioms of komšiluk as sociality in proximity show how people in situations of dramatic societal ruptures and upheavals often refuse to give up certain values they are not willing to part with, including the ways in which these are produced and realized (Robbins 2013). But what is it that villagers do not wish to part with? A quick excursion into the past might help us to better understand.

In their classic prewar ethnographies of Bosnian rural communities, William Lockwood (1975) and Tone Bringa (1995) clearly distinguish between kinship and komšiluk as the key principles of village social organization, and demonstrating that neighborhood mattered most in day-to-day interactions, in the processes of exchanging work and mutual help, and in visiting patterns. Both studies show that the core organizing principle of neighborhood networks was *residence* (Lockwood 1975: 65), and that komšiluk was "defined from the point of view of the individual household as those houses which immediately surrounded it, and with which it had relationships of mutual obligations, exchange, and support, reflected in the visiting patterns between them" (Bringa 1995: 55). Why is it that nowadays so many villagers who experienced forced displacement during the war, and those who left their neighborhoods in search of jobs and a better life in Sarajevo or abroad in the postwar years, are still considered as neighbors while others who continue to live next door are not worthy of a greeting? The extent to which can we take these prewar findings for rural areas across Bosnia, which experienced numerous ruptures and critical events into their lives, as an accurate description of the postwar years requires further research.

In the postsocialist, postwar years, komšiluk has become for villagers in the Zvijezda highlands an aspect of their daily aspirations to live good lives despite the radical changes affecting the very social morphology of village communities. So, to return to Sifet, on several occasions after the funeral he told me, "I just took for granted that komšiluk will always last," referring to reciprocal bonds and deep sense of obligation to care and engagement in the life of one's neighbor. The critical ruptures had turned these certainties upside down. He was not alone in feeling this way; and such expressions of doubt and uncertainty rendered the fragility of komšiluk painfully present.

Engaging the Lives of Others

"This komšiluk is so bad," Emina often used to shout from the window when she or her siblings had an argument with someone from their immediate next-door circles. In recent years, the open window and loud shouting had been further amplified by posts and comments on social media, and especially on Facebook. This time, however, she discovered that one of the next-door neighbors was gossiping about her, portraying her as flirting with men in the municipality where she went to high school. "It hurts when people lie about such things," continued Emina tearfully. She was in love with Asim, who had just left to work as a construction worker in Azerbaijan for six months to earn enough money to finish building a flat in his parents' house and then marry her. Every day Emina was impatiently counting the days to Asim's return. Watching the news on TV, something she did not care about before, became part of her everyday routine as she wanted to stay up-to-date in case there was any mention of Azerbaijan. She checked her mobile phone at five-minute intervals, awaiting a message from Asim. In the evenings, before Emina went to bed, she read all the messages they had recently exchanged. Nearly every night she prayed a prayer of good luck (*hajr-dova*)—and hoped to dream about Asim, and their happy future together. "But you know what," she told me after she had calmed down, "once Asim is back, I won't wait a second and I will move to his village immediately. We will have our own flat in his family house. People in his komšiluk are nice, and the village has all modern amenities that we will never have here. Our village, and komšiluk in particular, is not good. I am sure I will like it there, his neighbors are more cultured (*kulturni*) than here. If my parents don't let me go, I will elope."

Eventually Emina and Asim married, and she moved as planned. But Emina still cares about the komšiluk where she grew up. Since her move, whenever she calls her parents or younger siblings, Emina always asks about the news in the neighborhood, which she misses a lot. She also keeps track of and participates in neighborhood matters via social media. Visiting all the neighbors is one of the first things she does whenever she returns to the village. For Emina as well as for other villagers, caring about one's next-door neighbors in the give and take of everyday life is what komšiluk is about, despite all the ups and downs that living in proximity might entail. With the benefits of social media, Emina left the village but did not abandon her komšiluk.

Care and Good Deeds

Komšiluk as a site for engaging the life of others is articulated in particular in the actions and idioms of care (*briga*) that take multiple mundane forms (Hromadžić 2016). In villages, the first conversation I heard every morning in the neighborhoods where I was staying was "How did you sleep?" "Very well, and you?" or sometimes "Not at all" if someone in the house was ill or away. From as early as sunrise, villagers occasionally stopped for a short chat around a shared neighborhood water pump to exchange news, while the village was still half-asleep. The importance of such a mundane gesture of engagement in the life of other neighbors as asking a neighbor "how did you sleep?" is most painfully felt when it is absent, for example when two neighbors stop by the pump or pass each other on the tiny village paths and do not greet each other, negating an acknowledgment of sociality in proximity. Such silences can be just temporary, resulting from a quarrel, or may last for years, in particular if family property is at stake.

An equally significant form of care is articulated in idioms and acts of mutual help and generalized reciprocity. Women in komšiluk might stop by and help to wash a carpet or look after each other's children. Men may join in by chopping firewood or unloading a trailer with hay or trunks. "Real komšiluk," I was told by Zejna while she was helping to unload a truck of hay for her neighbor Nijas, is when "during the hay making season people regularly help each other." This description, however romanticized it might sound, needs to be taken seriously. As we saw in the previous chapter, caring for the land and subsistence farming has intensified in the postwar years due to economic hardship and marginalization of rural areas. The topography of the landscape surrounding the villages in the Zvijezda highlands is generally steep, making a number of meadows inaccessible to mechanized forms of grass cutting or transportation. Hay making thus continues to be a labor-demanding task that relies on highly orchestrated cooperative human labor—known as *moba* (Bringa 1995, Lockwood 1975)—in order to finish the task in a timely manner, as the threat of rain is constantly present. Yet, even such situations and enactments of neighborhood sociality, and exchange of small daily favors and good deeds are considered as manifestations of vital exchange and thus constitute an important dimension of religious experience.

Indeed, on a hot summer's afternoon, Nermin and Zakir, two next-door neighbors, got together in Zakir's backyard, and started carefully sharpening their scythes. Both did it simultaneously, sharing the same tools, working slowly and precisely and checking each other's scythes. When they had finished sharpening, Zakir asked me what the time was. It was 5 p.m., I replied. He nodded, gesturing with his head that it was time to go. Without even giving me the chance to ask where we were going, he said that Nusret, another neighbor, had severe back pain and was incapable of working on his meadows now, when the hay-making period was underway. When Zakir, Nermin, and I reached the path leading to Nusret's meadow, several other male neighbors were already waiting with their scythes. After reaching Nusret's meadow and taking part in the obligatory conversation and cigarettes, the men started cutting the grass. Their movement was coordinated and they worked fast, with a short break

Komšiluk in the making.

every half an hour to smoke a cigarette. The break itself was a continuation of neighborhood exchange as the packets of cigarettes and bottles of water were shared among the neighbors throughout the *moba*. After two and half hours, the meadow was cut.

Nusret, who was observing his neighbors at work, invited the men for coffee. When the neighbors gathered in the shadow of the veranda, Nusret's wife, Sabira, immediately brought coffee, while Nusret served water and cold non-alcoholic drinks. After a few cups of coffee, Nusret and Sabira served a festive-like four-course meal, and at the end sweet baklava. While they were eating and chatting, and then again when the neighbors were leaving, Nusret repeatedly thanked his neighbors for their help, emphasizing that what his neighbors did today was *sevap*—an act of good deed that earns good merits in the flow of vital exchange with the divine. The *moba* needs be attended to as a series of exchanges within the context of village moral economy that also includes the divine, rather than simply attended to through its transactional parts.

Rhythms of Neighborliness

Commensality plays an important part in social life in the komšiluk. During the holy month of Ramadan, neighbors regularly organize *iftar* (an evening break from fasting during Ramadan). Evening after evening, villagers provide food for one another. "Real iftar," I was told—and experienced on many occasions—"that's when people get together, they eat a lot, drink a lot of coffee, it's a joy, that's real komšiluk." So here we have yet another fragment of what living in proximity entails. The ethics and sociality in proximity unfolds here as an affective labor of emotions—feeding and feasting creates the feeling of togetherness, and "it's a joy" being together—entwined with specific temporal rhythms, namely the annual Ramadan cycle. Other actions and layers of sociality are carried out every day, such as the morning encounters by the water pump. Both the affective labor of emotions and temporal rhythms energize, intensify, and punctuate social exchanges, and cultivate interpersonal relations in neighborhoods.

"Unemployment has made everyone twice as busy" some villagers half-jokingly commented very often during the hot summer evenings on the cooling verandas. Indeed, for employed as well as unemployed villagers alike, the summer months are marked in the Zvijezda highlands by hard work on the fields (growing potatoes, beans, corn, onions, and seasonal vegetables), making hay, and preparing firewood for the harsh winter months. Hence, the mobilization of neighborhood networks and the orchestration of work have a profound impact on the character of social relations within the komšiluk. Leisure activities significantly decrease over the summer period. As villagers usually put it, "there is too much to do and the weather is so unpredictable." This shared perception of the unpredictability of the weather has increased in recent years, and villagers blame climate change. Furthermore, for the majority of villagers, this period is critical to surviving the winter months, when there is literally no opportunity to make any cash unless a household owns a cow and is thus able to sell surplus dairy products.[3] As Mirza, who is unemployed long-term and a father of two small children, kept repeating during the summer months, "Our house needs at least four stacks of hay and a truckload of potatoes to survive the winter, if God permits."

The different seasons of the year, workloads, and activities cultivate and orchestrate different forms of engagement in the lives of other neighbors. Yet sociality in proximity is also a matter of joy and pleasure, and male neighbors always find time to smoke a cigarette together; likewise, next-door neighbors and families find an opportunity to sit and drink coffee together, echoing the words of my village friend Mustafa that "even giving a smile to others is *sadaka*" (voluntary gifts also earning good deeds), rendering the everyday forms of sociality entwined with the otherworldly realms.[4] These small gestures of attention and expressions of care toward other neighbors, such as offering a cigarette or a piece of freshly made cake, are precisely those acts that "allow life to be knitted together pair by pair" (Das 2012: 139).

Making ends meet—barter exchange (*trampa*) of dairy surplus.

During my conversations about komšiluk, I was often told that "winter has always been made for komšiluk." Indeed, the winter period is marked by countless coffee visits in the neighborhoods. However, these are anything but random as they form a pattern of exchanging visits known as *sijelo*, which display a high degree of regularity (see also Bringa 1995: 92). Neighbors think carefully about who they will visit and when. Every *sijelo* visit is expected to be returned in order to keep the books balanced between the neighbors. Not paying visits back is offensive and hurtful. There is, however, another reason for the frequent visitations during the winter months in the villages: winter is boring if one doesn't have a job, and *sijelo* is a way to kill time. During the harsh winter months when the villages are snowed in, unemployed villagers become prisoners of their komšiluk, restrained to the physical space of the neighborhood as they have nowhere to go, and nothing to do but wait for better weather.

Finally, the ritual calendar adds another temporal layer to neighborhood life. In particular, the Islamic annual feast of sacrifice (*kurban bajram*), often understood as a feast of the neighborhood (Sorabji 2008: 103), regenerates neighborhood relations. During the feast, villagers ritually slaughter rams and exchange the meat between the households within the immediate neighborhood (komšiluk) as well as the extended neighborhood or quarter (*mahala*), as I discuss at length in chapter 3. An exchange of the sacrificed meat during this feast in the Zvijezda highlands reenacts the symbolic boundaries of moral communities of the neighborhood. The sacrificed meat (*kurban*) that circulates on this occasion year after year embodies the moral community of komšiluk and what the fragile ethics of proximity entails: to engage in the life of other neighbors is itself an act of self-sacrifice that earns good deeds and merits. To suggest this, however, does not remove komšiluk from the warp and weft of postsocialist, postwar configurations that altered and accentuated the fragility of komšiluk in new ways.

"Knocking on My Neighbor's Door"

Sakib's suicide, and Sifet's concerns about neighbors who refused to share sorrow and mourning, highlight the fragility of life in village neighborhoods. The sense of fragility is acutely felt in the flow of ongoing relationships that neighbors make with one another. The possibility of these relationships being cut off at any point is constantly present. If these two critical moments were sudden and unexpected interventions into neighborhood life, the outmigration and abandoning of the neighborhoods and villages has become an ongoing process and a permanent feature of village life in the Zvijezda highlands. From the very outset of my fieldwork in the highlands, I frequently encountered "locked doors" (*zaključana vrata*) not only as a trope in local conversations but also quite literally.

"Locked doors" became a cause of serious concerns and anxieties. One November morning in 2009, a message spread in Brdo that in a neighboring village a dead male body had been found in a stream. The body was decayed, suggesting that the man had died a few weeks before. The reactions of the villagers were straightforward and characteristically similar to the following statement: "Why had nobody been looking for him? Where was his komšiluk? Why did nobody help him? That village is not good, there are too many locked doors." Whenever this event was mentioned in the following weeks, either in Brdo or in the municipality, it always brought bitterness, embarrassment, fear, and a reminder of the fragility of komšiluk. With the increasing outmigration from the villages in the highlands, this could have easily happen elsewhere as well.

I visited the village where the body was found on a number of occasions. During my visits to the village, I always stopped for a chat with Zilka, a widow in her early sixties who knew me through her relatives in Brdo. One day, without any prompting, she started one of our conversations by lamenting about the vanishing village and neighborhood sociality, and a lack of care for others. When asked what she meant exactly by komšiluk in the context of her laments, she replied by pointing to the houses surrounding her own: "If something happened I couldn't knock on my neighbor's doors because there are no neighbors anymore. Everyone is gone." Her observation was not inaccurate. The surrounding houses were indeed deserted. The doors were locked and many fields and gardens untended. Moreover, as I learned from the village imam (*hodža*), the Saturday Qur'anic class (*mekteb*) was becoming more empty year by year. After one of the classes the imam showed me the attendance book, and turned the pages to go back in time, pointing to the names of children and with a sad voice he told me: "Aziz—Vogošća, Nizama—Sarajevo, Aiša—she was an outstanding student, now she is in Munich," referring to those children who moved with their parents away from the village, and where they went. Whereas in 2009 he struggled to get more than a dozen children to the *mekteb*, ten years earlier he had struggled to accommodate and keep the attention of more than thirty children in an overcrowded classroom. When I returned in 2014, there weren't enough children in the village anymore, so the Saturday classes had been canceled. As far as he was concerned, no further proof was needed: there were too many locked doors in the village.

These critical moments—a neighbor's suicide, a decaying corpse in a stream, an empty classroom, and abandoned houses with locked doors—created a discursive space and a vocabulary for situating and reflecting on the changing character of social relations and idioms of care within the komšiluk, and for living village life in the context of the sociopolitical reconfigurations of the past two decades.[5]

In chats, during coffee visits, or at the Friday sermons (*džuma*) in the municipal mosque, the motifs of disengagement in the lives of others reappeared again and again, and the specter of the "locked door" haunted most of the conversations. These examples of lamenting villagers, however, are anything but the laments of elderly generations regarding the deterioration of life in the present compared to the past. On the contrary, the omnipresence of the "locked doors" trope is shared across a wide range of villagers who, rather than merely lamenting, are trying to come to terms with the unfolding postsocialist and postwar changes.

The increasing number of locked doors is the result of economic marginalization that impacts rural areas across the politically designed lines of division of Bosnia and Herzegovina.[6] The loss of job prospects, limited access to medical services, limited decent education for one's children, and deteriorating road infrastructure are the key push factors that drive villagers from the Zvijezda highlands out to the suburbs of large Bosnian cities, Sarajevo in particular. There, villagers like Tarik and Remzija often pursue precarious lives in the grey zones of job and housing markets, hoping to be able to remake their lives and homes once more.

Fragility of Proximity

The idiom of "locked doors" captures the increasing outmigration from the villages, but it also expresses the ways in which interpersonal relations have metamorphosed for those villagers who have stayed, or have been left behind in the countryside. How do these changes affect komšiluk as a moral project and the site of the everyday in village life? There are two overlapping forces reconfiguring the ethics of proximity. First, the newly emerged "hierarchies of suffering." Second, rising socioeconomic inequalities that turned villagers into the "winners" and the "losers" of the postsocialist, postwar reconfigurations.

BITTER COFFEE

"Shall we go and visit Bakir?" I suggested to a friend one winter afternoon. It was snowing heavily, and we were bored. "Nah," he mumbled, adding, "Bakir's coffee is always bitter." My experience of Bakir and his wife, Emina, was that they were rather generous hosts. "What's wrong with their coffee?" I naively asked, only to receive the simple answer "nothing"—but with underlying ironic undertone. Only later did I learn that there was indeed nothing wrong with their coffee as such. The expression of bitter coffee referred to memories of the war that continue to shape the ongoing relationships in the neighborhood, between the two neighbors. In the eyes of my friend, Bakir was a traitor for allegedly trading with humanitarian aid during the war.

The rural-urban divide is one of the major nonnationalist frameworks for understanding deep cleavages and large-scale changes unfolding in the post-Yugoslav states (Jansen 2005b). Yet the reconfiguration of social redistribution and the emergence of new "hierarchies of privilege" (Helms 2013: 5) have had significant effects on the ongoing interpersonal relations across the rural-urban divide. Among such new cleavages, the hierarchies of suffering play a prominent role in reconfiguring village sociality. In her perceptive ethnography of the process of identifying the missing victims of the massacre in Srebrenica, and the internal dynamics among the survivors and returnees to Srebrenica, Sarah Wagner explored the newly constituted "hierarchies of suffering" that emerged in the aftermath of the Srebrenica tragedy.[7] Wagner's work is important as it shifts the focus from the Bosnian war and its afterlives as a matter of ethnonational tensions, in this case between Bosnian Muslims and Bosnian Serbs. It looks instead at how the newly emerged "hierarchies of suffering" draw new lines of tension and reconfigure interpersonal relations within communities, enclaves or villages as well as wider scales of Bosnian society (Wagner 2008, Jansen 2007). The notion of "hierarchies of suffering" has wider implications for the unfolding dynamics of social redistribution in postsocialist, postwar Bosnia. It refers to the creation of moral hierarchies of value whereby the claims for humanitarian aid and other benefits during the war as well as in the postwar years have been justified and legitimized by ordering, categorizing, and bureaucratizing individual misery and hardship (Bougarel 2007, Johanneau 2016, Klepal 2018).[8] In the Zvijezda highlands, neighborhood relations have been hampered by the cowardliness of fellow villagers during the Bosnian war, who often succeeded in the postwar years by climbing over the shoulders of others. The sense of injustice among neighbors keeps many of these wounds fresh.

A coffee visit is an important aspect of neighborhood sociality. This is the moment when local, as much as regional or global politics are discussed, along with village and neighborhood matters. Meeting over coffee also gives villagers an opportunity to articulate, negotiate, and grasp particular war memories, unrewarded personal sacrifices, and changing interpersonal relations in komšiluk and village life. This is all the result of the very conflict that the villagers endured (Helms 2010). The war and immediate postwar memories that the villagers share with one another disclose various layouts of intra-village tensions and animosities and reveal sources of long-lasting bitterness and injustice among villagers and close neighbors (Sorabji 2006). The enduring "bad memories" that overshadow interpersonal relations among villagers in the present offer a complementary perspective on the question of reconciliation that in the Bosnian context is framed chiefly as a matter of relations between ethnonationally divided communities (Jansen 2011). Yet the 1990s war was deeply revealing of neighbors' characters and personal qualities irrespective of individual ethnonational belonging, as for some villagers it became more important during the war to save their own property rather than that of their neighbors.

As Zahid put it to me one day in an outburst of anger after being refused help from a neighbor, "and do you know what the worst thing is about the war? [Silence.] That human life is not even worth a pot of potatoes. I'll tell you what, if another war broke out now, I would kill half of the village. This man [the neighbor who refused to help] was given petrol to get my ill father from the village but he moved his livestock instead [referring to the time when the village was under shelling]."

Indeed, it did not take too long during my fieldwork to learn about those neighbors who took advantage during the war and acted cowardly, selling humanitarian aid rather than sharing it, or not helping others. As I learned on another occasion about the father of a family of six who fled after their village was completely burnt down, "He left the poor family with us, and disappeared to trade on the war's black market. I took care of them while he was getting rich. In the end, when he returned to pick up his family, he gave me a packet of cigarettes and kept his money."

Anyone who did not stay during the war in BiH and fled abroad instead was judged to be equally problematic, if not cowardly (see also Jansen 2007). By contrast, evening after evening, the loss of children, brothers and sisters, fathers and mothers was remembered, and the hardship of those villagers who had often not received any respectable compensation or recognition of their suffering was discussed. Twenty years after signing the Dayton Peace Agreement that ended the 1992–95 war, the moral hierarchies of suffering thus continue to keep many wounds and injustices alive.

As often happens, time has healed many bodily wounds, personal breakdowns, and tragedies. Time also brings former foes back to the same table to drink sweet rather than bitter coffee together again, to allow "life to be knitted together pair by pair," as Veena Das puts it. Yet, as these stories also attest, it is important to recognize that in communities that strive to come to terms with societal ruptures, political violence, and suffering, the cowardliness of specific neighbors during the war and its aftermaths are not washed off easily from the shores of memory, and the taste of bitterness prevails (Thiranagama and Kelly 2012). In the Zvijezda highlands, these prolonged tensions have become enmeshed in villagers' perceptions of the "winners" and "losers" of the postsocialist, postwar socioeconomic transformations.

OF WINNERS AND LOSERS

The long-term aftermaths of violent conflicts generate, as Heonik Kwon argues, "an array of interpretative controversies at community level" (Kwon 2008: 13). Such controversies erupt about the conflict itself, the hierarchies of suffering, and also about the ensuing clashing perceptions of the "winners" and "losers" within the communities. Interpretative controversies and discontent are common across the villages in the Zvijezda highlands. In particular, such controversies erupt with regard to the hierarchies of suffering and how these are entwined with widening socioeconomic inequalities. The rising inequalities are commonly perceived by villagers as a result of uneven access to the provisions of the war and postwar humanitarian aid in order to gain more livestock or machines, often by those villagers who acted in a cowardly way during the war. The very same individuals often managed to capitalize on their cowardly gains and now pursue individual benefits at all costs without regard for their fellow neighbors. This generates multiple tensions due to the fear of breaking apart the neighborhoods. In turn, the new winners of the postsocialist and postwar transformations sully interpersonal relations in the villages, and turn village neighborhoods into sites of disengagement.[9]

In 2012, during the three-day feast celebrating the end of Ramadan (*ramazanski bajram*), I was having coffee in the house of Zakir. While his wife was preparing coffee and cakes, I asked Zakir about his komšiluk, specifically how many of his neighbors he visited and how many visited his house. The question "who has come to your house?" is commonly asked during such festive occasions because reciprocal visits to all households in one's neighborhood are an important part of the feast etiquette. As it was the late afternoon of the third day of the feast, Zakir did not expect any more visitors. Most of the neighborhood visits take place during the first day. He therefore started listing the names. After finishing the list, Ragib's household was missing, yet Zakir, for whom komšiluk was everything, visited him on the first day of the feast. In previous years I had learned that Ragib's household is considered to be part of the neighborhood although the house is no longer in physical proximity. Ragib's family used to live in the komšiluk, but since Ragib became a successful owner of a sawmill, he moved his premises to the outskirts of the village, where he built a huge and spectacular house. In the symbolic village geography, the household continued to be considered part of the neighborhood, and hence was included in all festive activities.

After Zakir finished listing all the names, I asked him if anyone from Ragib's family had come. My question was received like a twist of the knife in a fresh wound. Zakir started complaining about Ragib. But he wasn't the only one complaining about him. The widely shared feeling about Ragib among neighbors was that since he had become a successful entrepreneur, he did not care about neighborhood relations anymore. He did not chat with people and did not even "give others a smile." He simply did not care anymore. Yet he exploited everyone whenever he could, especially the unemployed male villagers who were desperate to get even a badly paid, uninsured job in his sawmill. Such a list of criticisms may be easily interpreted as the complaints of a jealous neighbor. But for Zakir it wasn't jealousy that made him so bitter. It was the breakdown of the ethics of proximity and not caring anymore that mattered so much to him and to other neighbors. In fact, it was painful for Zakir not to be able to have a cup of coffee in his own house with Ragib, as the two of them used to be very close neighbors and friends before the war. The bond between them was further strengthened during the war when they spent a lot of time together on the frontline protecting the village. Now, Zakir was convinced that the laissez-faire spirit of the postsocialist, postwar years had created a widening gap between the villagers, and turned villages into sites of disengagement where people did not care about each other anymore. He continued:

> In 1996, the situation in the village was terrible. No one had a job, and we relied only on humanitarian donations and our fields. I told Ragib, who seemed to have an entrepreneurial spirit, to open a sawmill in the village. I helped him, and gave him 500 KM [Bosnia and Herzegovina convertible marks, approx. €250] in 1996 so he could open the sawmill, make some money, and give jobs to people in the village. At the time, he had just opened a small grocery in his cellar, so I gave him the idea and the starting capital. He was paying it back only slowly, usually in coins now and then, no more than 50 KM [€25] at a time [gesturing with hands to show how he was carrying the coins], but I did not care as it was good for all of us here. It turned out to be a good idea; the business has gone well ever since as you can see, his family owns three houses in the village, has expensive cars, Jeeps, and tractors. Yet he has come to my house only once since, when I was really sick and paralyzed for six months. He came and gave me 50 KM, saying "I have never forgotten your help—here you are." I did not care about the money, but why did he not ask whether my family is OK, or needs any help as I could not move and had to shit in the bed. Even worse, when I eventually recovered, I could not find a job for years and he has never offered me any help when I had to feed my young daughters. When I eventually convinced his son rather than Ragib to give me a chance, a few months after I started working at his sawmill, I was the first one who was made redundant when the economic crisis hit the timber industry. That's what happens when people have money. They do not care.

Zakir's life story is full of twists and turns. Yet the way he portrays Ragib as someone who managed to climb over the shoulders of other neighbors is shared unanimously in the village. The story of one neighbor disengaging from the lives of other neighbors, however, is not exceptional but rather commonplace. From the first days of my fieldwork a decade ago I encountered cases of villagers pursuing their own interests at all costs and thus without taking care of others. These stories and the stories of hierarchies of suffering are intertwined. The postwar development produced a class of villagers who managed to obtain tractors or other farming mechanization equipment through somewhat opaque donation programs run by the international aid agencies and the cantonal and municipal offices during the postwar years.

The donation program was targeted at those individuals who owned more than 10 hectares of land and were able to farm, but most commonly at those who had personal "connections" (*veze*) with municipal politicians and political parties (Brković 2017). The result was another dividing line created between the households. Some households historically had more land in the villages than others, better social status, and connections, and those without these privileges. The level of infuriation was further fueled by the fact that one of the crucial requirements for obtaining a tractor or any other donated equipment was that the recipient would make them also available for the duration of at least four years after the donation to other villagers so the entire community could benefit from the donation. However, no mechanisms have ever been put in place to ensure that the recipients were actually helping others with the donated equipment. This was a story common across the highlands.

In the absence of any accountability, those villagers with the donated equipment were either not sharing at all, or charging other villagers money for the use. The standard fee for using a tractor was usually between 20 and 50 KM [€10–€25], an amount that is rather high by village standards, considering the high level of unemployment or living only from minimal income. "This tractor should be ours," was the reaction that I often heard from those less-fortunate villagers when they had to pay for the use, or when any of the owners passed us in a donated tractor in the forest or on the village paths. In the villagers' eyes, these donations have considerably sullied the ethics of proximity and the values of mutual help so strongly associated with the moral imagination of care and mutual help in the komšiluk. As a consequence, the great majority of the villagers without mechanization or access to donations often have nothing to reciprocate aside from paying or creating debts.[10]

The rise of new hierarchies did not stop with the decline of the postwar international donations and aid programs. In recent years, numerous municipalities have started a donation program that gives greenhouses to those who live in precarious conditions and yet are able to produce vegetables. The requirement for the recipients of the donation was that those who received the greenhouse would donate a part of the harvest to other poor villagers, or to the local soup kitchens that are feeding families living under the poverty line, for the duration of four to five years.[11] The actual mechanism for distributing the greenhouses is opaque. The donation of these greenhouses has often been used as a form of political bribery during local elections, and nobody checked whether any vegetables had actually been donated to those in need. Instead, a number of greenhouse owners have started selling rather than donating vegetables to their fellow villagers. Thus the "greenhouse effect" was that the donation enabled their recipients to start making money without participating in exchanges of mutual help or charitable donations. The tractors and the greenhouses have, in the villages, become materialized testimonies through which increasing economic inequalities and emerging social hierarchies created through money and personal connections have been reflected and articulated. On the one hand, they index a failure of the corrupted state that does not care. On the other hand, tractors and greenhouses are associated with those villagers who increasingly do not care either, and index the very reconfiguration of sociality within neighborhoods.

Locking the Doors

I began this chapter with a question: how are the moments of everyday life, such as a neighbor's suicide or refusing to participate in mourning for a deceased neighbor, folded into the larger effects of the critical events of the war and the postsocialist, postwar transformations? The entanglement of such moments and critical events renders komšiluk inherently fragile. For some villagers, the effects of such entanglements were more favorable than for others. Villagers like Zakir had to eventually lock the doors of their houses and move from the village to the city. Zakir left after he was made redundant by Ragib. He joined Tarik, Remzija, and other former village neighbors in the Sarajevo suburbs. When I met Zakir in Sarajevo, he kept assuring me, and thus himself, that his house wasn't locked up for good. We both knew this was wishful thinking. It was an expression of hope and aspiration to live a good life that Zakir associated with being in the village but that had become increasingly difficult to sustain. "Do you think you will return soon?" I asked him. There was a moment of silence, and then Zakir said "I was hoping that after the war things would go well, meanwhile everything has gone in a completely different direction, as there is more envy among neighbors, and everything is getting worse and worse. How could I survive there?" On that evening, Zakir felt like a failure, for whom the return to the village seemed like a fading dream. Zakir's experiences were in contradistinction to those of the winners, such as Ragib, who exploited the opportunities of the postsocialist laissez-faire environment, as well as those villagers who became successful recipients of donations after the end of the war, and who could thus remain and live a relatively comfortable village life without engaging in the lives of other neighbors. Unlike Ragib, Zakir thus followed the path of Tarik whose heart, like komšiluk and its ethics of proximity, was ultimately too fragile.

3

Halal Exchange

In the summer of 2013, I received a short Facebook message from a Bosnian friend, Edib: "This could only happen in Bosnia and Herzegovina," followed by a link. I clicked on the link and an article about the greengrocer Jusuf Solo appeared on my computer screen. The article was titled "Halal to You! Whoever Has No Money to Pay, Will Get It for Free." It described how the greengrocer Jusuf was giving away fruit and vegetables from his stall for free (*halal*). As he explained in the article, the greengrocer gave away produce for free to anyone "who can't earn, and who doesn't have any income." He added, "I was asked why I give food away for free [. . .] people come to my stall, staring, and can't believe it. But there is nothing miraculous in what I am doing: everyone who gives for free, will receive back a thousand times more from Allah. Only Allah knows best." When he was seventeen, Jusuf left for Russia, where he worked and earned good money. "Thanks to Allah, and the help of good people," he mused, "I made it, I earned enough, and I have a good life. It is now my turn to help."

The article was widely circulated among my friends at the time on social media, but the story it conveyed was not unusual or extraordinary—on the contrary. Stories about people giving away food for free, and giving small donations to people who need medical treatment, frequently circulate in the public sphere in BiH today, and are mediated by Facebook, TV and radio channels, newspapers, and amateur posters displayed in public spaces, or exchanged by word of mouth in the cafes, local weekly markets, or on the doorstep of a next-door neighbor (Brković 2016, Jašarević 2017).

Anthropologists have widely documented how moral impulses and sentiments of care travel across social and religious boundaries (Mair and Evans 2015). For example, a local soup kitchen in one of the municipal towns in the Zvijezda highlands was started in 1997 by a Franciscan humanitarian-charitable organization, and regularly feeds about 150 people from all walks of life. The kitchen relies on irregular contributions from the municipal and cantonal budgets, and on the regular generosity and mercy (*merhamet*) of kind people. The list of those who voluntary donate to the kitchen is long, and as diverse as the municipality's sociodemographic makeup. As one of the workers in the kitchen told me in 2014, there is "an entire Muslim village where people collect whatever they grow in their gardens and fields and bring it in their cars; things like potatoes, onions, plums, or homemade jam." This donation is considered by the villagers as *zakat* (obligatory annual alms) to the kitchen. A local Bosnian Croat entrepreneur who runs the bakery and a supermarket donates sixty-five loaves of bread every day. But the care and money also flows transnationally, as there are many other individuals living in diaspora in Austria who donate money every month.

The reach of the polite requests to give, help, and care for friends, neighbors, or complete strangers is wide-ranging, and so are the impulses to give: from donations to individual case-specific "humanitarian actions" (Brković 2015), collecting money for medical treatment to giving alms (*sadaka*). Villagers' encounters with such requests on the streets of the municipalities, or among those who wait patiently outside the local shops, mosques, and churches, mirror prolonged economic predicaments, and the withdrawal of the state from social redistribution vis-á-vis the grassroots solidarity. One significant aspect of this gift economy was a sentiment among my friends and interlocutors that Larisa Jašarević poignantly describes as being "insanely generous" (2017). Indeed, despite being heavily indebted, and long-term unemployed, villagers facing the urgent immediacy of a request for help always found some change in their pockets to give without hesitation, saying "forgiven" (*halal*). "People here have *merhamet* [mercy] in their souls," I was often told by someone who struggled to get by but who continued to give "insanely" whenever asked. Others simply said, "you know how difficult it is to ask for help, so it is even more difficult for those who can't give." The forms of giving and caring captured in the greengrocer's story, which my "insanely" generous friend Edib shared with me, need to be understood within this spatiotemporal configuration of postsocialist, postwar BiH.

These reconfigurations have brought about economic uncertainties and insecurities. Although the political economy arguments underlie many daily ways of getting by in BiH, it would be too reductionist if we render these reconfigurations solely within the realm of political economy. In this chapter I discuss the practice of giving "the halal way." In Islamic scriptural reasoning, the category of *halal* stands for allowed, permissible, lawful, and moral actions and forms of conduct, as opposed to the category of *haram*, that of unlawful, prohibited, and immoral conduct. However, as I illustrate throughout the chapter, these categories are lived and experienced rather hermeneutically as a matter of judgment, evaluation, and performative acts in specific historical situations (Lambek 2015a).

The act of "halal giving" to those who struggle to access even basic provisions is more than an expression of a critical social commentary on the current political situation and on economic deprivation. On the one hand, for the greengrocer Jusuf, as well as for other Bosnians who regularly care and give the halal way, the postsocialist, postwar Bosnian state, which does not care for its citizens, is perceived not only as corrupt and dysfunctional but also as being *haram*, that is, immoral and polluted. On the other hand, during my time in BiH I quickly became accustomed to the frequent attribution of "halal" in the sense of forgiveness, mercy, and grace to a myriad of acts, practices, events, and things, including acts of care for oneself and others. "Halal," I was commonly told, "is everything that satisfies Allah." Drawing on the recent debates in the anthropology of morality and ethics (Laidlaw 2014, Lambek 2015a), I argue that this framing of halal as a mode of moral action "that satisfies Allah" stems from the cultural conception of social actions whereby acting the halal way is an act of value creation that is commensurable with respect to the historically formed conceptions of what I describe as "halal metavalue." Here, I follow Michael Lambek's argument that across human history there has been a dialectic between "establishing absolute values," such as halal metavalue, "against which everything else is relative and to be measured—hence rendered commensurable to one another—and discovering things that render those absolutes relative in turn" (2015b: 227).

In this chapter I track how halal metavalue is established and rendered as a flow of vital exchange in different moments of everyday life. I analyze these processes as an *economic theology* of halal exchange. I borrow the concept of economic theology from Marcel Mauss's discussion of those forms of vital exchange whereby "the thing given produces its rewards in this life and in the next" (Mauss 2016: 162; Anderson 2018; Mittermaier 2013). Indeed, the greengrocer Jusuf was lucky, thanks to Allah's help, and the generous people in Russia who helped him, so now he can give back. Jusuf's story of success and generosity is one of personal luck and good fortune that he subsequently redistributes as divine abundance (*bereket*) to anyone "who can't earn, and who doesn't have any income," and which in turn earns good deeds (*sevap*) for Jusuf's personal path to the afterlife.

An economic theology of halal exchange embraces several fields of moral-cum-economic activity such as good deeds (*sevap*), prosperity and wealth (*nafaka*), and primarily divine abundance (*bereket*).[1] By looking at villagers' everyday economic predicaments of getting by through the lenses of the economic theology of halal exchange, this chapter shows how villagers make sense to these economic effects unfolding in postsocialist, postwar BiH today.

Ethics of Giving

Let me first distinguish between charitable almsgiving and halal exchange. Charitable giving lies at the very heart of Islam and what it means to be Muslim. It has constituted the backbone of Muslim societies over the centuries and became a means whereby Muslims addressed the fundamental questions of how people should relate to God and to one another in a just way in an unequal world (Singer 2008). Charitable giving also plays a key role in constructing Muslims' self-conceptions through everyday practices and actions. Indeed, one's piety is realized not only through obligatory prayers and submission to God but also through modes of interactions and exchanges with fellow human beings, and in particular through the well-intentioned acts of caring, giving, helping, and sharing (see Anderson 2011, Mittermaier 2019).

Islam distinguishes between obligatory alms (*zakat*), which constitute the third of the five pillars of Islam, and *sadaka*, an act of charitable giving or beneficence (Singer 2008: 20). Almsgiving is rooted in the conviction that one's wealth and fortune should be shared with anyone in need. All wealth and abundance are ultimately generated by and belong to God, and should be shared as evenly as possible rather than accumulated, in order to ensure that justice in the world here and now is achieved, and one's account settled in preparation for the afterlife. The act of almsgiving "purifies" one's wealth and makes the remaining portion pure and lawful—that is, *halal* (Benthall 1999: 29; Singer 2008: 36–37). The ways charitable giving and alms collection is organized today varies among individual Muslims and communities across the globe, and BiH is no exception.

As with other modern authorities of religious practice operating within the ambit of the secular state, the Islamic Community of Bosnia and Herzegovina (IC-BiH) is nowadays not only the officially recognized chief authority of Islamic orthodoxy but also the official authority for collecting alms. The annual collection of alms follows the general trend of the Hanafi school of the Sunni Islamic jurisprudence. Anyone whose wealth meets or exceeds a minimum threshold (*nisab*) should pay zakat.[2] The annual value of *nisab* is decided by the IC-BiH, and in 2019 its value was 6,640 KM ($3,860). But this centralized collection is a relatively recent phenomenon. Historically, almsgiving was redistributed locally by individuals directly to those who were in need (Duranović 2019). During the early years of socialist Yugoslavia (1945–58), the rich Ottoman-era founded endowments (*vakuf*) including the land, buildings, houses, and mosques that belonged to the IC-BiH were by and large confiscated by the socialist state along with the property of other churches.[3] When the impoverished IC-BiH attempted in the late 1960s and early 1970s to assemble resources to open the Islamic Theological Faculty in Sarajevo (opened in 1977) and the madrasa for women (opened in 1978), it issued a resolution in 1968, followed by a series of fatwas agitating for the centralized collection of zakat to be gathered through the network of its local branches. This decision was not always viewed favorably on the part of local imams, who were allegedly ambivalent or firmly against it. Some opposed the process of centralization, as it meant losing control over donated resources; others, described in the official documents as "half-educated theologians" and "conservative," interpreted the attempts to centralize zakat collection for building projects as being against the principles of sharia (IC-BiH 1973: 155–57). The leaders of the IC-BiH traveled extensively at the time, in particular around Ramadan, to explain the importance of the collection and appeal to the sensibilities of local imams and ordinary Muslims to give their alms to the IC-BiH to ensure that "every single dinar donated as *zakat* and *sadekatul-fitr* will reach the fund" (156).

Since the initiative to collect enough resources for the two educational institutions in the 1970s succeeded, the IC-BiH remained the main collector of alms donations and also their redistributor in BiH in the postsocialist, postwar years, when it further developed the infrastructures of Islamic charity.[4] The main areas of redistribution are nowadays oriented toward welfare, with students, educational institutions, and social and charitable work-related institutions the main beneficiaries. Given the socioeconomic predicaments of the country, the IC-BiH has been very active in mobilizing diasporic networks around the globe to increase alms donations. Some of the banks in Bosnia operating according to the principles of Islamic banking (the BBI Banka) have begun offering "zakat services" locally and internationally to the diaspora. The IC-BiH also runs a dedicated website, with clear step-by-step explanations about what zakat is and why it is important, including an online zakat calculator (*zekat kalkulator*), and where to pay.[5]

Collection point for sadaka alms, a poster explaining how to pay annual zakat during Ramadan in Sarajevo.

In the Zvijezda highlands, villagers participate in the centralized almsgiving only in a limited way. The mandatory zakat is out of question for the great majority of villagers, as they barely have enough resources to get by. However, during the holy month of Ramadan, when giving alms in the last ten days of the feast is considered to be particularly rewarding in the personal preparation for the afterlife, the word *vitre*—the Bosnian vernacular of *sadekatul-fitr* (an obligatory alms paid during Ramadan)—is on the lips of nearly every person, including those villagers who do not fast or pray during the holy month. Local imams often commented on the scale of villagers' beneficence: "villagers love vitre, everyone gives it, even those who drink [alcohol] and don't go to the mosque." The older generation of village imams similarly often told audiences, during Ramadan evening meals (*iftar*) or in the mosques, a popular story about a dispute that arose between Ahmed effendi Burek (1876–1948), a well-known old Sarajevo cleric, and a more modernist one who wanted to issue a fatwa against those who did not fast or pray during Ramadan, suggesting that their vitre should not be accepted. The old ulema, Ahmed effendi, allegedly responded: "Listen, this religion is broad, and everyone takes something from it. Some people take *namaz* [obligatory daily prayers], and others just vitre and nothing else. And you want to take this only bit of faith from them? Let it be, only Allah knows." The story is very popular and circulates widely in villages as a moral tale. Other imams described villagers' compulsion to give vitre as "having something 'foreign' in your wallet."[6] This figurative language of almsgiving as something that does not belong to one's wallet poetically expresses the obligation to give alms, whereby one's wealth is purified and made halal (moral and lawful).

Nonetheless, during my fieldwork I also encountered numerous villagers who adamantly refused to give anything to the IC-BiH. They argued that it would be stolen by the imams, and they gave it in their neighborhood instead. This was often the case in the villages that hosted a temporary imam during Ramadan because there was no regular imam. The temporary, appointed imams are paid through a money collection received from individual households in the village. These payments were often a source of bitter disputes and arguments, as every household was expected to contribute an equal share, including those who struggled financially. That at the end of Ramadan the imam would take up to 1500 KM (€765) from the village—an amount that many villagers could only dream about—was unacceptable to them, and also a reason for not paying vitre to the imam. Others who also refused to give alms to the IC-BiH argued that although they respected it in principle, the redistributive mechanisms were limited in their reach and effectiveness. So, for example, there was the above-mentioned Muslim village that donated the annual zakat on behalf of all households in food and vegetables to the local soup kitchen. Others refused on the theological grounds, referring to a verse in the Qur'an to give first to those in one's proximity, saying:

> There are people who don't work, have no salary, make their living just from the land, but it is unlikely that these individuals will appear on the list of the beneficiaries of the IC-BiH, and yet they are in desperate need. There are two types of people in need. The first have literally nothing. And the second, have a tiny bit, but will never have enough, even though they are working. So, for example, in our neighborhood we have someone like Mahir, who is not working. For some time, even his wife had no job and yet they have two kids, and no income. He was badly injured during the war and used to receive benefits, but the state just cut them off. How on earth will he manage to get on the list of beneficiaries to receive any help from the state? So we collect vitre and give it to him.

Voluntary gifts—sadaka—on the other hand, are one of the fundamental elements that glue together everyday sociality, and articulate social justice and care in the villages. Acts of sadaka are usually described as "a kind word" (*lijepa riječ*), or as an act of turning one's attention and care toward others. Sadaka is an act that earns good deeds (*sevap*). These acts of sadaka are intricately interwoven into the forms and practices of daily social exchange and shape the everyday ethics of proximity in village life.

Following the villagers' vocabularies of ethical practice, I maintain a conceptual distinction in this chapter between almsgiving (zakat, vitre, sadaka) and "halal exchanges." Villagers attribute the moral value of acting the "halal way" to a myriad of acts and valuations including almsgiving. Put differently, in the economic theology of halal giving, not every act of halal giving automatically means almsgiving, but every act of almsgiving is a halal act.

Sacrifice as Halal Exchange

If "halal is everything that satisfies Allah," how is the conception of halal as metavalue "against which everything else is relative and to be measured" (Lambek 2015b: 227) established? According to Michael Lambek (2015b: 237) blood sacrifice often lies at the root of value, and serves as an act of creating metavalue. In turn, the coexistence of regimes of value requires "the work of ritualization" (Keane 2001) and "cosmological authentication" (Weiner 1992) to establish hierarchies and maintain the boundaries between them. Ritualized blood sacrifice is rather common across many religious traditions (Bloch 1992). Here I am concerned with the Abrahamic religious traditions, in particular the Islamic tradition. Although there is considerable performative variability in Islamic ritual practice of the feast of sacrifice (Bowen 1992, Delaney 1991), the act of blood sacrifice brings divine abundance and grace and is followed by generous redistribution of the sacrificed meat. Participating in the ritual is an expression of one's piety and social standing as well as the ethics of proximity and care for others.

My first encounter with an act of halal exchange in the Zvijezda highlands was in the early days of my fieldwork during the Islamic feast of sacrifice, recognized locally as kurban bajram. It takes place two months and ten days after the end of Ramadan, and coincides with the hajj. In the villages, kurban bajram is a four-day feast during which a ram is sacrificed on the first day. The sacrificed meat (*kurban*) should then be divided into three parts. One third is given to the poor, who cannot afford to sacrifice an animal (this is often done by donating the meat to the local soup kitchen), one third is given to neighbors within one's neighborhood, and the final third is consumed by the household and one's kin. This redistributive logic ensures that divine abundance, bestowed in the sacrifice, circulates within these networks.

During my fieldwork, the feast was already on everyone's lips several weeks before it actually took place. Everyone I talked to wanted to participate in the feast. However, over coffee in the privacy of their houses, many of my friends and interlocutors often expressed doubts as to whether they would actually be able to afford to sacrifice a ram. Villagers contrasted these current anxieties and predicaments about the possibility or impossibility of performing sacrifice with the prewar times when everyone in the villages was able to and did perform the sacrifice. Indeed, in order to be able to sacrifice a suitable ram, the ram needs to be more than one year old. Moreover, a great deal of attention is paid to how big and heavy the ram is, its weight, color, and the presence or absence and shape of horns, and sometimes also a biography of the breeder, all of which establish the value of the ram as suitable for sacrifice. The most valuable rams, often put on public display, attract attention well before and after the feast, symbolizing the wealth and prosperity of their owners. To acquire a ram of desirable value thus requires considerable economic investment, including enough resources to feed the animal properly (ideally only with corn) to increase its size and weight in the months before the feast.

Deciding whom one ought to give sacrificed meat to is another step in the preparation for the act of sacrifice. Unlike in Muslim societies with hierarchical social fabric and strong vertical relationships where the feast takes the form of redistribution between socially unequal persons (Lyon 2004, Werbner 1990), in the Zvijezda highlands the kurban bajram is recognized as a feast of the neighborhood, and thus every household in one's neighborhood is visited and given the sacrifice. This means that the feast carries a persuasive moral narrative of mutuality and equality, and the circulation of the sacrificed meat weaves nonhierarchical horizontal relations between persons living in physical proximity. Yet as discussed in the previous chapter, despite the circulation of such discursive depictions of loyal and caring neighbors among the villagers, it has become less common for *all* households to participate in the sacrifice and its subsequent redistribution. The line between those households that can and those that cannot perform the sacrifice mirrors the new economic hierarchies that have emerged between individual households, that of the winners and the losers. Does this development mean that neighborhood solidarity and valuing nonhierarchical horizontal relations would completely vanish?

In Brdo, in the past decade, the number of households in the village who could afford to sacrifice a ram has decreased by around one third.[7] Whereas in prewar Yugoslav times animal sacrifice was practiced in all households, nowadays only well-off families, and those households who retreated to subsistence farming, can afford to perform the sacrifice.[8] The households in the village with the means to sacrifice continue to redistribute sacrificed meat, including giving to those who cannot afford it anymore. So whereas the prewar kurban bajram was deemed to be an "actually existing horizontality" of balanced reciprocal giving, postwar socioeconomic development and the massive indebtedness of many households have brought about a shift in circulation of the sacrifice toward "actually existing verticality" as the giving of blessed meat gained a redistributive character for those villagers who were still well-off. To address the question of how this transformation reconfigures neighborhood solidarity and the value of horizontal relations, we need return to halal metavalue. The widening socioeconomic gap between individual households, which manifests itself in the decreasing ability of villagers to take part in the sacrifice, is bridged in everyday practices by the work of ritualization, which maintains the value of horizontal social relations unsullied. It is the way the sacrifice is given—the halal way—that establishes halal metavalue against which any other exchanges between villagers can be measured and made commensurable.[9]

While writing about the feast of sacrifice, anthropologists of Islam have primarily paid attention to the very act of sacrifice, its public discourses, and how the scriptural orthodoxies and local practices of the feast intersect or differ (Bowen 1992, Brisebarre 1993). Largely unexplored, however, is the rhythm of the entire sacrificial complex, of which the act of sacrifice is but one part. Furthermore, what actually happens after the act of sacrifice, during the moments of giving sacrificed meat (*kurban*)? The way kurban is exchanged is the case in point here, as it is not only meat that circulates at that time. An act of giving during the feast is a performative act that also entails an exchange of words. Indeed, it is words, rather than the objects of exchange (sacrificed meat in this case), that specify, as Webb Keane suggests, "what kind of action is being performed, from whom the prestations come, to whom they are directed, and what kind of act they perform" (2001: 74). In turn, the performative act of giving the sacrifice is an act whereby halal metavalue is established, and against which any act of exchange is measured as halal exchange.

The act of giving the sacrifice has a highly elaborated etiquette of performative utterances (Lambek 2015c). Although I draw here on the case study from the village of Brdo, I have observed over the years the very same etiquette in other villages as well as in municipal towns in the Zvijezda highlands (also Sorabji 1989: 67). A person giving sacrificed meat always brings it to the doorstep of the recipient's house. The recipient says "kabulosum," in this context meaning "I agree to accept this," at the very moment of receiving. The giver then utters "halalosum," in this context meaning "you don't owe me anything." To ensure the performative act of halal giving is not sullied, the recipient, even if they have sacrificial meat to reciprocate, never gives back immediately. Giving kurban the halal way requires bringing the sacrifice to the house of the original giver. An overall choreography of giving sacrificed meat performatively and temporarily disables immediate reciprocity of direct equivalence (Dresch 1998: 125), thus establishing the incommensurability of halal metavalue.

Giving sacrificed meat is a performative act of halal giving, during which not only sacrificed meat but also words are exchanged. The word uttered while receiving the sacrifice, "kabulosum," derives from the Arabic "makbul," meaning "accepted from God." In turn, "halalosum" is a compound word, composed from "halal" and "olsun," meaning "forgiven to you," or literally "halal to you," conveying that the sacrifice is an instantiation of divine abundance, mediated by the giver. It is then the efficacy of the performative acts associated with the sacrificial complex that both establishes halal metavalue and maintains the circulation of sacrifice within the horizontal realms between villagers, whereby divine abundance is mediated by everyone involved in the exchange networks. What emerges here is an economic theology of halal exchange that may help us to understand why all households in the village Brdo, even those without any means of purchasing a ram for sacrifice, continue to be actively involved in the annual cycle of exchange of sacrifice and mediating divine abundance. Without their acceptance of the sacrifice, well-off households that can afford to give would not be able to access an ongoing flow of vital exchange (Mittermaier 2014: 524).[10] Let me now turn to the instances of how halal metavalue enables transvaluation and commensurability across divergent value domains.

Halal Money

One winter morning during my fieldwork, I helped Remza from the neighborhood where I was living to search for another neighbor, Resula. At the time, Remza's household had been receiving a two-liter bottle of milk every other day from Resula, whose family is well-off and owns a flock of sheep and three cows. The cow owned by Remza's family had just given birth to a calf, so all Remza's efforts at the time went toward feeding the calf as well as possible in order to sell it to earn much-needed cash, which would help sustain the family for at least four months. It is common practice in the villages that whenever someone's cow is pregnant or is suckling a newborn calf, neighbors supply the house with milk during the period. How should the extra supply of milk be reciprocated? This is a pertinent question, as many families rely on selling homemade dairy products to secure or supplement household income. This was also the case with Remza, who went to negotiate with old Resula over how an extra supply of milk ought to be paid back. When we finally found Resula, she just said, "you don't need to give us anything. If we need something, we will tell you; and if we don't, then it's halal." Remza's family had been struggling, like many families in the village, with unemployment and debts, and trading in surplus dairy production was their only regular source of income. Following this conversation, Resula never asked for anything, and the bottles of milk that she had given Remza's household became halal.

This example, like that of the greengrocer Jusuf, illustrates how halal metavalue operates across different value domains as instances of halal exchange. We need to pause here, however. As Lambek (2015b: 239) suggests, the act of sacrifice opens "moral vectors," introduces "specific commitments" and establishes the "seriousness of the ensuing values and acts that are at stake." In day-to-day situations, halal metavalue, which is established in the performative acts of the ritual sacrifice and exchange, is performed as virtue (i.e., being a good neighbor, spouse, Muslim). In other words, it is realized by means of virtuous acts and the exercise of judgment as to how and when an exchange will be acted on as a halal exchange (218). Hence Resula's decision not to ask for the milk to be paid back, instead considering it as being offered the halal way (free of charge); likewise, the greengrocer's decision to give any fruit or vegetables from his stall to anyone in need. Consequently, virtuous acts involving the performance of exchanges of goods and services the halal way are part and parcel of the economic theology of halal exchange as they mediate divine abundance and grace among fellow villagers.

If the socioeconomic restructuring in postwar years caused social redistribution in BiH to decline, the economic theology of halal exchange continues to offer villagers an ethical practice, whereby economic and divine resources (i.e., abundance) can be considered as commensurable in relation to halal metavalue. It is again the work of the performative acts of halalosum and kabulosum in the moment of exchange and the kind of virtue they perform. These performative acts maintain such exchanges within the realm of halal metavalue rather than within the realm of monetary value.

The situations in which Islamic economic theologies have been invoked to address and reanimate the realm of socioeconomic ruptures and transformations are multifaceted (e.g., Maurer 2005, Mittermaier 2013, Osella and Rudnyckyj 2017, Rudnyckyj 2014). In her work in rural Turkey, Kimberly Hart shows how village Muslims implement the moral conception of *hayir* (good deeds) to respond "to the social effects of economic change, as well as to address their personal quests for salvation" (2013: 74). These concerns are not dissimilar to those of my friends and interlocutors in the Zvijezda highlands. As Hart shows, village Muslims utilize and cultivate the virtuous acts of hayir to create "networks of charitable activity, [and] distributing goods" (76). The value domain and hayir acts unfold as a form of economic redistribution and social justice, as local instances of sadaka or almsgiving, and as an act of generosity. As Hart puts it, a good deed "is spread across small acts, the accumulation of which show attention to all needs, not only material inequities" (78).

Hart's observation poignantly illustrates two points. First, it shows how the realm of culturally specific metavalues unfolds in individual virtuous acts of "small gestures" of generosity and care. Even the simplest offering, such as giving cookies and surplus olive oil, or gestures of compassion between well-off and poor villagers, as Hart documents, are small acts of sacrifice that earn good deeds. As such, these acts are situated in the wider moral texture of vital exchange with the divine. Second, this argument ethnographically questions the often-overdetermined forces of market effects (Brenner 1998, Mittermaier 2013, Rudnyckyj 2010). Instead, it shows how the logic of the market intermingles and entwines with other logics and conceptions of value in the Zvijezda highlands.

A good deed is an instance of the economic theology of halal exchange rather than a metavalue in and of itself. Nonetheless, small gestures of generosity, care, and self-sacrifice if performed as virtuous acts of good deeds establish the "seriousness of the ensuing values and acts that are at stake," namely halal metavalue (Lambek 2015b: 239). By tracking the instances of such virtuous acts in daily situations in the village we can see how halal metavalue enables transvaluation and commensurability across divergent value domains and instances of exchange between villagers.

Mediating Abundance

Let me begin with the case of two brothers, Bilal and Nehrudin. Nehrudin left the village about fifteen years ago to settle in the capital, Sarajevo. However, he still owns some land around the village. Bilal, who owns a cow and a horse, has been taking care of several hay meadows belonging to Nehrudin. Bilal has never paid Nehrudin to use the land, even though he sells the hay produced from Nehrudin's meadows, using it to feed his cow and horse, which are also a source of extra cash from time to time. Nehrudin has never asked for any payment. Bilal, nevertheless, has been sending Nehrudin dairy products that he could otherwise sell in order to earn more cash. The current arrangement, however, as both brothers expressed on many occasions, is halal.[11]

Similarly, the villager Fadil from another neighborhood happened to have high honey and apple yields regularly. For pious Fadil, this is a sign of divine abundance, a gift from Allah. Therefore, every autumn Fadil redistributes a portion of the surplus in the neighborhood rather than accumulating or selling it, because it is halal to do so. Put differently, having access to hay, milk and dairy, and other yields is conceived of as a divine abundance (*bereket*) and as fortune and wealth (*nafaka*) that need to be mediated and shared, rather than accumulated at the expense of one's neighbors and of those who suffer (economically in this case). These acts of small-scale neighborhood redistribution and self-sacrifice are performed as virtuous acts of halal giving, during which the words "kabulosum" and "halalosum" are exchanged as well, rendering such exchanges within the realm of the halal metavalue.

Halal Exchange in an Unequal World

Even small gestures of generosity, care, and self-sacrifice are not void of monetization and calculative logic. The moral conundrum emerges from the tension between acting virtuously in regard to historically established metavalues vis-à-vis the difficult socioeconomic situation of the postwar Bosnian reality. These considerations come chiefly into play in situations in which money and payments are implied in helping one's neighbors. As discussed in chapter 2, the rising inequalities impact the ethics of proximity in the neighborhoods. Given these increasing economic inequalities, and the role that money plays in everyday acts of help and care, the question of the incommensurability of these exchanges becomes a case in point.[12]

Let me consider how the rising inequalities within the villages transform the conduct of mutual help and assistance within neighborhoods. During the years of my fieldwork, it has become common to pay a sum of money in return in those instances when the person who asked for assistance was not able to reciprocate. But helping a neighbor and being paid in return are two different exchange orders operating in different regimes of value. So, for example, having a tractor to carry firewood or hay from distant places, both of which are crucial for daily household functioning, or having a horse for plowing the hilly fields that surround the village, have become an asset. But we saw how these assets were sometimes unjustly gained. The villagers who owned them are the very same well-off villagers who also have resources to purchase rams for the sacrifice. In turn, whenever anyone else needs help with plowing or transportation, there is no possibility for them to reciprocate in kind. This is the moment when money comes in, as the villagers make reimbursements in cash to cover the costs of petrol, amortization, and time. As in the previous case, these transactions are commonly performed as virtuous and are accompanied with the exchange of words that qualify the act of help as an instance of halal exchange. The exchange of words takes place over coffee in the recipient's house, starting with the question "What do I owe you?" which is immediately followed by rhetorical denying of any debt, "Nothing." However, this denial takes place without uttering the word "halal." Only after the question is raised again does the recipient give an amount that she considers adequate, or according to her means. Only then is "halal" uttered without immediately checking how much money she was given. By performing the transactions within the realm of halal metavalue, any amount is acceptable and my village friends referred to such forms of cash as "halal money" (*halal pare*) instead. These instances, of course, should not be romanticized. During my fieldwork, I often overheard or was told by the owners of tractors or horses that they were not paid enough to even cover their expenses. They never raised this issue publicly, however. The reaction that usually followed was "but what can I do if they are struggling to get by?" referring to these disadvantaged villagers. In Brdo, there were two tractor owners who became notorious lamenters. Yet even they never asked for more money, and whatever they were paid was considered halal. As a result, the two men tried to keep themselves busy and made themselves occasionally unavailable so as to avoid any request for assistance, rather than asking for more money. If however they happened to be asked, especially in public under the moral gaze of the neighborhood, it was hard to decline.

In the Zvijezda highlands, small gestures of help and care performed the halal way manifest villagers' attempts to keep any potentially monetized transactions outside of the regime of direct equivalence (Dresch 1998: 125), and position them rather as virtuous acts in regard to halal metavalue. In other words, the invoking of halal metavalue acts in situations of increasing monetization of exchange, and rising economic inequalities among villagers as a virtuous act of "generalized moral abstraction of value across otherwise incommensurable domains" (Maurer 2005: 104). The economic theology of halal exchange unfolds in the villagers' ethical practices (virtue) as a process of transvaluation of economic value (cash) into halal metavalue (deeds).

Good Deeds and Kind Words

Villagers often described acts of sadaka as "a kind word" (*ljepa riječ*), or as an act of turning one's attention and care toward others. These acts are intricately interwoven into the forms and practices of daily social exchange and shape everyday ethics of proximity in village life. These range widely, from spontaneous acts of help and small gestures of care to sharing happiness with a neighbor, such as celebrating a newly purchased refrigerator. For Fadil, who invited me one day to a ride in his old tractor, the act of care for others was enacted in his spontaneous effort to repair one of the eroded paths that leads to the forest, fields, and hay meadows in the hills above the village. Fadil did not need to care about driving his tractor whenever and wherever he needed, as he could still drive over the holes in any weather conditions, unlike many of his neighbors, who had to wade through large swamps. Yet he decided to drive his tractor around the village for several hours and load it with stones, which he then used to repair the path so everyone could use it in any weather. When he and I finished the repair work, he expressed the hope that "it will help the neighbors, and will satisfy Allah." Indeed, "everything that satisfies Allah is halal."

Fadil's gesture of care opens another sphere of exchange, that of performing good deeds. When Fadil and I finished our work on the path, he said to me "today, you've done *sevap*." *Sevap*, or *dobro djelo*, refers to an act of good deed that earns merits in the flow of vital exchange and its benefit is realized by the community of fellow villagers. Sevap is another ethical act that satisfies Allah and oils the fragile sociality in proximity over time. Performing good deeds in the Zvijezda highlands, however, has also become a way of addressing the issues of access to scarce resources that enable people to live a "normal life" in postsocialist, postwar BiH—jobs, education, and social security. Accessing scarce resources has been widely described in the context of socialist and

Doing good deeds (sevap)—voluntary clearing of the village paths after a heavy snowfall.

postsocialist societies as a gray zone of illicit economic practices and moralities (Henig and Makovicky 2017). Anthropologists working across the socialist and postsocialist societies pervasively show that what international commentators and policy makers tend to describe as "illegal" or "corrupt" behavior does not fit into the local conceptions of such categories, and also into the hierarchies of moral values (Humphrey 2002).

In Bosnia and Herzegovina, the vernaculars people employ to navigate this ambiguous sphere of everyday life are *štela* and *veze* (Brković 2017). A *veze* is "a relation, a connection"; it is sometimes called *štela*, in situations when people talk about "a relation that needs to be fixed" (Brković 2015: 268). These two terms describe actions in the ambiguous sphere of illicit economic practices where mediation or leverage of access to resources are negotiated (Brković 2017, Koutkova 2016). Yet international policy makers operating in the country have been quick to describe such practices simply as "soft corruption" (UNDP Report 2009). In the great majority of debates among policy makers and social scientists alike, corruption and related illicit economic practices are conventionally understood within the cost-benefit or transactional framework as a way of securing advantage and access for oneself or one's own (Haller and Shore 2005, 2). This understanding of the term "corruption" is also commonly shared among villagers in the Zvijezda highlands.

This does not mean that villagers would not participate in an ambiguous sphere of various forms of informal brokerage, leverage and cultivating connections in accessing jobs, health care, permits or education. Although these activities and exchanges are not always understood as illegal, nonetheless they are conceived of as morally dubious, and therefore potentially haram-like (immoral). This often creates a moral dilemma for villagers between Muslim morality and the postsocialist, postwar predicaments of getting by. In addressing the moral dilemma of how to get things done in the halal way, villagers' actions in the grey zones have become informed by and performed according to the social etiquette of good deeds and merits, recognized and articulated as doing sevap.

Negotiating access to education is one of the spheres where doing good deeds takes place in the situations of moral conundrum. There are ongoing and vivid debates in rural as well as urban areas across the country about whether or not accessing education in BiH requires a degree of personal connections (*veze/ štela*). The perception during my fieldwork was that this includes elementary schools as much as high schools and universities. These perceptions weren't entirely unfounded. The latter in particular have gained attention in local media and international reports after numerous public scandals erupted around the more explicit, jarring forms of corruption in the institutions of higher education.

Over the years I often heard from many university students that getting a university degree has been for many students more than just a matter of having good personal connections (*veze/štela*). It also sometimes requires a considerable amount of money, depending on the subject studied, and one needs to calculate not only university fees but also additional money for "ensuring" success in exams. Numerous students I talked to over the years had to mobilize their *veze/štela* networks either to enroll into or to make it through the system. The lower stages of education are not an exception. Often, however, I learned that the cases of leverage or providing access were neither classified nor understood as *veze/štela* but rather were conceptualized and pursued as a good deed, that is, as sevap.

This was also the case for Mustafa, who is simultaneously a village imam, a high school teacher in the municipal town, and also a neighbor with extended kinship networks in the village. These three layers of his personhood straddle particular moral registers, duties, and obligations, that of Islamic moral authority, civil servant, and kin, respectively. In everyday situations, Mustafa has to negotiate often contradictory expectations emerging from these different strands while maintaining his moral accountability and self-worth in order to be a good Muslim. In his daily conduct, he emphasizes the notion of good deeds (*sevap*) as a form of everyday ethics that enable him to balance such diverse and often contradictory expectations and obligations, and yet to live the halal way as a good Muslim.

As a local imam and a high school teacher, Mustafa has networks of access with regard to influencing things that are dense and wide. It is no surprise that he is often approached after prayers in the mosque, as a moral authority, or over coffee, as kin, to "fix" various issues. We became close friends as we exchanged books and spent long hours discussing them. As he often confessed to me, people approach him with unrealistic expectations not only of what he can do, but also of what he is willing to do. He makes it very explicit that he does not want to do anything that would be considered *veze/štela*, as he was fed up with it and with the fact that nothing seemed to work without it in BiH. But this does not mean that Mustafa would refuse to help his fellow villagers that he meets in the mosque or to his village fellows he meets on village paths. This was the case on one autumn day when Mustafa was walking home through neighbors' gardens. Nurfet, who is his neighbor and a distant relative, nearly dragged him in for a coffee, as he wanted to ask him for help, but not in public. In Nurfet's living room, it took some time to dispense with the obligatory conversational niceties. Only then did Nurfet ask if Mustafa could help his daughter enroll for the prestigious subject of economic management at the municipal high school where Mustafa taught. During this conversation, Nurfet tacitly pointed out to Mustafa that the two of them were distant relatives and close neighbors. Moreover, Nurfet also carefully reminded Mustafa of his socioeconomic situation, that of being the only breadwinner in the house, yet with a small and irregular salary from the village sawmill, and having four kids and massive debts. There was no way for Nurfet to ensure that his daughter would get enrolled without any *veze/štela* connections and assistance.

Mustafa was reluctant to help Nurfet as a distant relative. This would imply to him exactly what *veze/štela* was. Participating in *veze/štela* matters would be for Mustafa acting in a haram way. At the same time, he well knew Nurfet's difficult situation and was thus concerned about the well-being of his family, which was in need. This matter of concern falls into the register of Mustafa's everyday ethical practice, that of acting the halal way and doing good deeds (sevap). Mustafa eventually decided to intervene in the selection process, and Nurfet's daughter was enrolled, although her grades were slightly below the required average. Mustafa had to explain to the selection committee that her poor grades were due to her difficult family situation, rather than being just an average student. Nurfet and his relatives reciprocated with sentiment by thanking Mustafa on many occasions, saying "may God bless you." Mustafa's response was always "halal to you," meaning in this context that his help was morally acceptable, and more importantly, it was a gratuitous act, free from obligation (halal), and that Nurfet's family did not owe him anything.

Although other villagers, as well as a number of teachers, knew about the enrollment process, none of them questioned what Mustafa did or invoked this case as an instance of using connections for personal gain, as they did in the case of some other students. On the contrary, the overall arrangement was evaluated and recognized as an act of good deed. This does not mean that villagers would not pursue access to increasingly scarce resources in other situations through *veze/štela*, as has been widely documented across BiH on the whole. Yet it is important to ethnographically appreciate that, in doing so, villagers recognize the moral conundrums that the pursuit of access might entail, and respond to the unfolding situations as best they can. In the Zvijezda highlands, the idioms of good deeds and vernacular conceptions of charitable giving instantiated in the form of kind words and taking care of others provide the villagers with powerful moral idioms through which the day-to-day struggle to get by and gain access to resources can be reimagined as halal acts and thus rendered as a matter of vital exchange.

Of Debt and Forgiveness

If there is one widely shared depiction of everyday life in BiH today, it would probably be living in debt (Jašarević 2017). Ranging from the high-interest microloans that have plagued the country, and the delayed or indefinitely postponed salaries, to the country's massive indebtedness, these are instances of how the experiences of life in debt increasingly reanimate people's reflections on life itself in postsocialist, postwar BiH. "I wish I had a regular income," "debts killed him," or an Islamic healer advertising himself in newspapers as a "fighter against sorcery, misfortune, unemployment and indebtedness" are just a few examples from my field notes. How does debt on such a massive scale entwine with the economic theology of halal exchange? We have already seen what ethical dilemmas monetary payments and personal interventions for help and services might create. This raises a question about debt and forgiveness in village life. If the economic theology of halal exchange unfolds in acts of transvaluation of economic value into halal metavalue, how does such economic theology attend to various forms of debts? What does the act of *halalit* (to forgive, to be merciful) entail?

In her splendid analysis, Larisa Jašarević (2012a, 2017) shows how notions of the good life and a decent death in postwar Bosnia and Herzegovina are undermined and underwritten by debt. Jašarević aptly illustrates how, due to their need for quick cash, many Bosnians in precarious economic situations are selling family graves, thus cutting off "persisting obligations and exchanges between the living and the dead" (2012a: 25). The ability to manage one's debts or the lack thereof, and more generally facing these troubles with a "lack of abundance," have become a pervasive part of everyday experience across Bosnian society at large (with the sole exception of ethnopolitical elites, Kurtović 2015). Is death the only escape from debt then?

I was first alerted to these questions in the early days of my fieldwork in the Zvijezda highlands, while attending a Muslim funeral (*dženaza*) in a nearby village. It was at the very end of the outdoor prayers, when the crowd gathered around the coffin (*tabut*), and the imam leading the ceremony asked the assembly to "forgive" (*halalit*) the soul of the deceased. In the context of the funeral, the utterance "halalit" is an act of forgiveness of any debts and sins the deceased person may have accumulated during their life in order to purify their soul. There are other profoundly life-transforming events, when the living ask for forgiveness—for example the hajj. When someone decides that they would like to undergo this pilgrimage, they sponsor a feast (*mevlud*) and a collective prayer (*ikrar dova*) in the mosque before their departure to Mecca. The crucial and highly emotional moment during the event is when the pilgrim-to-be stands up and asks the assembly in the mosque to forgive (halalit) all the person's debts and for all their sins to be canceled before leaving for Mecca, otherwise the pilgrimage would not be accepted by God.

Jašarević describes the act of halalit as a radical forgiveness in the context of postmortem exchange, and I would also include other events that transform the courses of people's lives, such as the hajj. The act of forgiveness can also be tracked in the instances of small everyday gestures of assistance and help, when halalit "dismisses an unreturned or excessive gift or favor" (Jašarević 2012a: 35). Put another way, the act of forgiving, if performed the halal way, transvalues debts as a matter of halal metavalue and divine abundance, as we saw in the case of Resula telling Remza how an extra supply of milk ought to be paid back. However, the possibility of forgiving inevitably implies a possibility of not forgiving, or *remembering* the debt, as Jašarević also points out.

The haunting possibility of not forgiving ("I won't halal you") is always present, and such situations do occur. An unforgivable debt also haunted Osman, who I knew for many years. Osman is a retired salesman known for his passion for bargaining, and he is well-known for being good at it. But he is also aware that his fame and reputation is not God-given but rather needs to be constantly cultivated. During one of my return visits to the village where Osman lives, I noticed that his house had recently been decorated. Pleased with my comment and without any further prompting, Osman described how the person who did the new tiling in the house bartered his work for a sack of Osman's hay and the agreement was finished in the halal way (no one owes anything). Because the builder's cows seemed to like Osman's hay, he called Osman again a week later and asked for more hay. This time, it was a bargained monetary transaction, and the agreed price was 110 KM (€55). The builder picked up the sacks of hay, and the following day sent 100 KM via Osman's next-door neighbor. Later during the week Osman met the builder at the market in the municipality, where the builder told Osman in public "here are the remaining 10 KM, but I will not halal it to you" (*neću halalit*). Osman, confused, offended, and publicly humiliated, asked whether there was anything wrong with the hay. The builder replied that this time the cows didn't like Osman's hay, and he had to throw it away. As the hay was not rotten, he could not claim the money back. Even though Osman got his money, this exchange did not leave him in peace and he has brought it up on various occasions afterward. What if, he sometimes asked himself in the company of other villagers, the builder thinks that I deliberately sold him worse hay? The neighbors kept reassuring Osman that he has nothing to worry about, as Allah knows his motives and is his witness that he did nothing wrong, yet this particular exchange haunts Osman. For Osman, as for other villagers, any well-intentioned act is halal, as it satisfies Allah who is the ultimate witness of their actions in the flow of social and vital exchanges. When somebody utters "neću halalit" (I won't halal it to you), it casts a specter of debt on these exchanges, and debts can spoil both individual preparation for the afterlife and interpersonal relations.

There are other instances of "not forgiving." They often ensue from an uneven accumulation of value through manipulating inheritance or property, and the land. During my fieldwork, tension arose between siblings over inherited property. Partible inheritance is a widely shared moral ideal (see ch. 1), but in reality it is also highly gendered. After I documented several dozen case studies of inheritance negotiations within households across the Zvijezda highlands, it was clear that women who marry outside of their villages rarely claim a share of the family land or any other family property, whereas brothers divide the inherited property equally or keep it intact. In turn, women receive compensation, for example in dowry expenses.[13] This practice has its roots in the legal notion of *miraz* (from Turkish/Arabic *mirat*, "to divide"), describing any property passing to a daughter (Hammel 1968: 18–19; Lockwood 1975: 64). However, as far as I could trace it, any *miraz* beyond dowry has been seldom demanded by women in the villages. I came across only two instances of women claiming a *miraz* on property, namely the land. This happened several years after the two women, Lejla and Amina, married into distant villages, and did not maintain any vital relations with the village apart from very occasional visits and phone calls. Both cases opened a number of emotionally charged debates, social commentaries, and a diagnosis of the disruptive postwar development in the country that has turned siblings into enemies.

In particular, in one of the cases it turned out that Lejla was generously compensated in her dowry in the late 1990s. Now, two decades later, Lejla wanted to sell her part of the inherited land to her own brothers. Lejla's family was struggling to deal with debts they had accumulated over the years due to mismanagement of high-interest microloans, and so attempted to claim the share in order to resell it. The land in her native village looked to Lejla and her family like a source of immediate cash revenue. However, as we saw in chapter 1, land in the Zvijezda highlands is considered a form of inalienable possession that is guarded over generations and that links individuals and families over time. Moreover, as Annette Weiner (1992: 4) suggests, "kinship is a decisive marker and maker of value" in the manner in which it expresses and legitimates the relationships between productive resources and social relations. In the highlands, this relationship is primarily conceived of as a realm of halal metavalue.

In turn, Lejla's attempt to claim the *miraz* back opened different "moral vectors" and commitments contrary to the existing values at stake (Lambek 2015b). It meant withdrawing not only from kinship obligations but also from halal exchange, instead imposing the calculative logic of economic value and profit that makes everything commensurable, including the land of the ancestors or kinship relations. It is perhaps hardly surprising, then, that the entire discussion among the villagers in both cases was centered on the fact that the two women did not want to renounce their respective *miraz*. Although these were rather unusual cases, the two "not-halal-events" have since become a haunting reminder of how easily an act of (halal) forgiveness can slip into the moral conundrum of debt relationships.

PART TWO

Vital Exchange

4

Cosmological Time

The Beads, the Calendar, the Clock

Every time I visited Osman in his house, he never failed to point to a wooden plaque with carved calligraphy and a clock with a picture of Kaaba in Mecca. The plaque was neatly placed on top of the television set in the living room. It was a present from his daughter; she gave it to him at the end of Ramadan several years ago. Osman has never fasted during Ramadan. He tried a few times but did not last more than a few days. Although he regularly attends Friday sermons (*džuma*) in the municipality, prays during the annual prayers for martyrs, travels to most of the annual collective prayers for rain in the summer months, and takes part in the Ramadan evening prayers (*teravija*) in the village mosque, he does not perform the obligatory five daily prayers (*namaz*). However, he likes the aesthetics of the Kaaba clock. It deserves to be displayed prominently in the house.

In the corner of the same room, there is a barely noticeable string of thirty-three faded green beads (*tespih*) that hang on the blue-painted door frame and that Osman's wife, Mediha, takes from the door frame and brings to the small back room five times a day to pray. A wall calendar hangs next to the beads, with color photographs of Bosnian mosques, old and new, and the days, weeks and months of the given year. It contains a schedule of praying times arranged according to the Islamic lunar calendar (*takvim*).[1] The very same calendar also contains the dates of significant Islamic feasts, including Ramadan, ramazanski bajram, and kurban bajram, and regionally specific annual events. Finally, there are also war-related commemorative events listed. The beads, the calendar, and the clock are materials of temporal reckoning in the house of Osman and Mediha, neatly interwoven into their daily rhythms, actions, and movements. The beads, calendar, and clock blend national, religious, and secular temporalities together.

The materials of temporal reckoning in village life are multifaceted and vary between individuals, households, and villages. Indeed, whereas Mediha follows the daily prayers with the *tespih* in her hand, scheduled in the calendar and punctuated by the clock, Osman does not. Osman follows many of the war-related commemorative days and often travels with other villagers to attend the ceremonies to pray for the souls of the martyrs across the country, unlike Mediha. As their different engagement with the beads, the calendar and the clock illustrates, the temporal materials are not prescriptive to one's action and conduct. Rather, the materials of temporal reckoning give orientation and tempo to social life (Munn 1992).

The calendar on the wall of the house is a remarkable tool of time measurement, with multiple modes of temporalization merged into one object. It combines the globally dominant time-reckoning device—the Gregorian calendar—with the Islamic lunisolar calendar and the Julian calendar that dominates Orthodox Christian practice, as the key materials of Islamic temporal cosmology in the villages. The imprints of the Julian calendar are echoed in the scheduling of the rituals of vitality and regeneration that punctuate the numerous ritual and farming activities (Bringa 1995; also Bloch and Parry 1982). The repertoires of time-reckoning derived from the Julian calendric traditions date back to Ottoman or even pre-Ottoman times (Hadžijahić 1978). These repertoires continued to shape the rhythms of social life in many villages during Yugoslav socialism. In the postsocialist, postwar years, the repertoires have also been revitalized and revalued in many other villages due to the resurgence of subsistence-farming production as well as that of public expression of religious life, as we see later.[2]

The juxtaposition of the beads, the calendar, and the clock opens up a series of questions explored in this chapter: What is the role of Islamic temporal cosmology in villagers' lives? How do the materials of temporal reckoning co-constitute villagers' religious experience? Addressing these questions, I contend, is crucial for understanding how critical events have been embraced and understood through the Islamic temporal cosmology and meaning-making practices in villagers' everyday historical work.

Cosmological Time

Radical breakdowns and ruptures—be they political, violent, or environmental—are intricately folded into the lifeworlds of individuals and communities. Critical events, as Veena Das (1996, 2007) reminds us, continue to shape temporal textures of everyday life and everyday historical work long after the events have passed. The ethnographic studies of the afterlives of forced displacement, political and sectarian violence, natural disasters, or humanitarian interventions have shown time and again how the aftermaths of critical events produce not only traumatic memories, but also expectations and anticipations in people's attempts to restore a degree of normalcy in their lives. Critical events thus give rise to the modes of temporal reasoning in the lifeworlds of affected individuals and communities which valorize not only past-oriented temporality in order to come to terms with the (traumatic) past but also future-oriented temporality (Bryant and Knight 2019, Kleist and Jansen 2016).

Anthropologists of post-Yugoslav societies have attended to the modes of future-oriented temporalization emerging from the postsocialist and postwar ruptures primarily through the study of particular imaginings, and anticipations, such as hope, and explored how these play out and unfold in individual and collective life-trajectories (Greenberg 2011; Jansen 2015; Jansen, Brković, and Čelebičić 2016). Yet, as the beads, the calendar, and the clock in Osman's house illustrate, the modes of temporal reasoning are more textured. There are other temporalities and modes of temporal reasoning at work that should not be ignored. How are these infused with, and articulated through everyday religious experience, meaning making, and practice? The value of secular forward-moving temporality favored in the existing scholarship needs to be paralleled with the modes of temporal reasoning and practice that are derived from Islamic temporal conceptions. Rather than treating them as separate, it is more productive to elucidate how these temporal orientations are entangled and generate configurations of temporal reasoning in a given historical-political nexus.

The modes of temporal reasoning and orientation unfold in everyday life as a matter of one's fate and destiny (*nafaka*) mediated by God's grace and blessing (*bereket*) in one's life. These are realized in the course of social life through the historically formed repertoires of vocabularies, practices, materials and sensibilities that shape and infuse both Muslim subjectivities and social relationships in the villages. As Douglas Rogers writes, "diffuse experiential categories such as ethical sensibilities, expectations, and modes of historical consciousness must somehow become material in order to be efficacious in the practical creation and reworking of ethical selves and relationships" (2009: 15). To ethnographically elucidate the textures of these "parallel repertoires" of temporal reasoning, I find it helpful to use Kimberly Hart's characterization of what she describes as the cosmological construction of Islamic time in village life. It relates, as Hart describes, "to the life course of the individual, as punctuated by rituals and the work of daily prayer, fasting, and worship" (2013: 45).

Yet the cosmological construction of Islamic time in the villages is entwined with other temporal wholes, namely secularism, capitalism, and nationalism, all of which rubbed shoulders over a long time in the Zvijezda highlands. By turning my attention to the textures of Islamic time in the villagers' lives, I do not wish to resort to a kind of "allochronic" argument (Fabian 1983). Rather, I turn my focus toward multiple sites where these temporal modalities are negotiated and articulated and, as Adeline Masquelier poignantly observes, how they become productive "techniques for making meaning and organizing social life" (2013: 474). In the following chapter we see further how these repertoires of Islamic temporal modalities are folded into and infused with the effects of the critical events of the war and the postsocialist, postwar reconfigurations. But for now, let me turn to the temporal repertoires punctuating daily prayer, fasting, and worship.

More Calendars

The central idiom of villagers' engagement with Islamic temporal cosmology is through the act of prayer (*dova*). Performing dova is an act of individual or collective piety. But dova is also a mode of action with consequences for oneself and others. Its performance is oriented toward accessing the good (*hajr*), prosperous destiny and wealth (*nafaka*), and divine abundance and blessing (*bereket*) not only for oneself, but also for the living here and now, and for the dead. Dova is interwoven into the material and temporal textures of everyday village life. Consider the following statements:

> "Every year we have had the hay under the roof before the dova for rain in Kolakovići [village] was due."

> "I have never sown beans before Jurjevdan [May 6] and never after the first *dova za kišu* [prayer for rain]."

> "Wait [with activity x] until dova [for rain]."

In the summer, statements and actions like these are part and parcel of day-to-day concerns. This is because the concept of dova figures centrally in the local ritual calendar of the prayers for rain. The ritual calendar, along with the weather forecast, is constantly followed on television, radio, and smartphones, and shapes labor activities in the fields, as well as affects villagers' considerations regarding when to take annual leave, or when to schedule a visit to relatives living in Sarajevo or in the diaspora abroad.

During the harsh and boring winter months, villagers switch back and forth between the broadcast weather forecasts, smartphone applications, and the Islamic religious calendar hanging on the walls in villagers' houses. Osman, Fadil, and other villagers find the calendar helpful in assessing the possibilities of severe snowstorms, or how many more freezing days they should expect. These ongoing weather concerns have never been taken lightly, due to their impact on scheduling work activities, and in the winter on organizing alternative transport arrangements for children to get to school from stranded villages that cannot be reached by the bus.

When the holy month of Ramadan arrives, the local IC-BiH branches distribute free wall-poster schedules of Ramadan prayer times (*ramazanska vaktija*) that find their way onto the walls of villagers' houses. Yet during the holy month it is a special Ramadan TV program and the digital clock, available on many channels, that punctuate the household rhythms of prayers, feasting and piety. This prayer time schedule mediated through television synchronizes the rhythms of the holy month across the individual households, villages, towns, and the country at large rather than local mosque loudspeakers (Armbrust 2006).

The poster-like Ramadan prayer schedules serve as more than a festive decoration on the walls of village houses, or as devices to punctuate prayers. In the past ten years, the shifting dates of Ramadan following the lunisolar calendar have coincided several times with the electoral calendars (2008, 2012, 2016). At the time, during public election rallies and in mosques, the representatives of the leading Bosniak (Muslim) political party SDA (Stranka Demokratske Akcije; Party of Democratic Action) distributed printed Ramadan prayer schedules with the party logos and photos of their candidates, blending national, religious, and secular temporalities together.

There are two chief calendric repertoires of Islamic temporal cosmology that punctuate prayer, fasting, and worship in village life. One is derived from the Julian calendric tradition, organizing outdoor worship as well as the organization of material life. The second is derived from a scriptural Islamic tradition, and from the practices and conceptions of individual piety in particular (Mahmood 2005).

Piety under the Open Sky

In the afternoon of May 5, 2009, Malika and Samira, two neighbors, were having coffee together in Malika's house while their husbands were away at a funeral. I had just returned from a long trip around several villages on the other side of the highlands and was invited to join them for a cup of coffee. "You haven't brought us *sihir* [sorcery], have you?" Samira half-jokingly welcomed me. Observing my perplexed face, she immediately added that the next day was Jurjevdan, May 6, and that the night before Jurjevdan people were susceptible to *sihir* attack more than during any other day of the year (also Bringa 1995: 225). That evening after 8 p.m., Malika, who prayed regularly only during the major religious feasts, had prayed the fourth daily prayer (*akšam namaz*) in the kitchen of her house. Subsequently, she wrapped the Qur'an in a cloth, uttered "bismillah" before she crossed the doorstep, and walked around the house three times while reciting the prayer for good luck (*hajr-dova*).[3] What Malika, Samira, and the other women in the village did on that night preceding Jurjevdan was an act of vital exchange whereby they sought to receive blessing and protection of the house and the living from Allah for performing hajr-dova. Moreover, the women's conduct manifested how calendars coalesce and temporal textures entwine in the Islamic temporal cosmology in the highlands.

The date of Jurjevdan, May 6, is derived from the Orthodox Christian tradition of celebrating St. George's Day according to the Julian calendar. This date marks the transition to the summer period.[4] Together with Alidjun, recognized by the Orthodox tradition as Ilinden, or St. Elias's Day, and celebrated on August 2, Jurjevdan constitutes a crucial calendric backbone in the cosmological construction of Islamic time, but also in social practice in the Zvijezda highlands.[5] Jurjevdan in particular structures the ritual calendar of the annual outdoor prayers for rain (*dove za kišu*), and to which village Muslims refer in everyday discourse as dova.

The places of gatherings and prayers, known as *dovišta* (pl.; sing. *dovište*), are most often outside the villages. Dovišta can be found around the old Ottoman Islamic tombs (sing. *mezar*), mausolea (sing. *turbe*), and the tombs of martyrs (*šehitluci*). Some of the dovišta are associated with the traces of the dervish brotherhoods, and recognized in the vernacular as such—the Sheikh's lodge (*Šejhova tekija*), and Sheikh's spring (*Šejhova voda*) for example. The dovište "Kurban stone" (*kurban kamen*), a white-painted flat stone in a meadow in the hills, is a site where according to vernacular histories the troops of the Sultan Mehmed II celebrated the feast of sacrifice—kurban bajram—during the conquest of the Bosnian lands in the fifteenth century (see Afterword). But the outdoor sites of regular veneration are also found around the tops of the hills, springs, caves, and lime trees, thus reflecting the fact that the practice itself has a long historical continuity across central Bosnia (Hadžijahić 1978, Muftić 2004, Mulahalilović 1989).[6] Dovišta and prayers for rain constitute a richly textured repertoire of temporal reckoning and are an important dimension of Muslim piety and religious experience in the highlands.

Each dovište has a fixed date for the prayer, reckoned by counting the Tuesdays or Sundays after Jurjevdan. Sunday was introduced to the ritual calendar during the era of socialist Yugoslavia as a way to make it easier for the local branches of the IC-BiH to seek approval for organizing the gatherings from the state authorities, though a small number of villages have maintained Tuesday as the day of the prayer for rain.[7] In the village of Dolina, studied by Tone Bringa in the late 1980s, there was an annual prayer for rain, which was organized around the local mausoleum and tombs. The prayers were held on the seventh Tuesday after Jurjevdan. In Bringa's case, the prayers were attended "exclusively by women and the prayers were led by local *bula*" (Bringa 1995: 172; also Baskar 2012). Furthermore, Bringa argues that "the prayers for rain, which are clearly a fertility ritual, should be the concern of women" (172). In the Zvijezda highlands, on the contrary, the organized collective prayers for rain are annual gatherings of primarily male Muslims to pray for rain in order for their fields to be fertile, and for prosperity and blessing of the house.[8]

Choreographies

Shrines and holy sites, large and small, spectacular or unnoticeable, are spread across the Eurasian landmass. As Bruce Grant (2011) suggests, they offer a window into the historical, political, religious, and social transformations and continuities that have taken place around them. Muslim sites for the prayers for rain in rural Bosnia are no exception in this unfolding story of frictions between this-worldly sovereignties and otherworldly realms. The state socialist secular intervention into the ritual calendar that moved many of the prayers for rain from Tuesdays to Sundays exemplifies how the two temporal logics and practices—secular and Islamic—have been entangled for a long time in the highlands and continue to be so. Yet it was the IC-BiH that implemented such interventions. This long-lasting entanglement can be best observed in the choreography of prayers for rain. Chapter 6 says more about the choreographies of Muslim holy sites, but here I am concerned with the question of choreography in relation to temporal entanglements.

The prayers for rain are mainly held under the open sky at dovišta. Until 1945 there were fifty or sixty dovišta throughout the northern areas of central Bosnia including in the Zvijezda highlands (Muftić 2004: 221). There prayers for rain continued in numerous locations during the socialist times despite the fact that the state monitored—if it did not suppress entirely—public manifestations of popular religious practices. The local explanation for holding prayers for rain is that during socialism, the farther you traveled from the municipalities (i.e., the more remote the dovište was), the less likely the prayers were to be (fully) suppressed. Although any collective gathering still had to be approved by the state authorities, for the sites and gatherings located on the margins of the state, such approval was usually granted.

Since Yugoslavia disintegrated and religious life was liberalized, numerous sites of prayers for rain have been renewed and some new sites have been created. Some of the dovišta have been embraced within nationalistic cosmologies and uplifted to the status of nationalized sites of commemoration (see chs. 5 and 6). In the Zvijezda highlands, the number of active outdoor dovišta does not exceed thirty-five today, as many of the prayers for rain have been relocated to the mosques (ch. 6).

The official organization of prayers for rain is under the responsibility and control of the local branch (*medžilis*) of the IC-BiH. The local branch is also responsible for preparing a schedule (*raspored dova*) for all places where the prayers take place in the region. The respective local branch also schedules imams to lead the prayers during these gatherings.

The schedules take the form of a pocket-sized printed spreadsheet-cum-calendar, which are distributed to the mosques during Friday sermons in April, although the majority of villagers know most of the dates by heart and can work out the date quickly by counting Tuesdays or Sundays in relation to Jurjevdan or Alidjun, respectively. In the house of Mediha and Osman, the schedule was attached to the calendar on the wall. In other houses, the schedule was kept with other visible calendars, or wrapped with the Qur'an on the shelf.

Between Rain and Storm

Although the orchestration of prayers for rain became an important site for exercising state control and intervention, there is yet more at stake. Let me return to the statements about the importance of prayers for rain in relation to the organization of material life and care, and in particular in scheduling and punctuating villagers' work in the fields as both constitute an important dimension of villagers' religious experience. As these statements illustrate, prayers for rain centered around the days of Jurjevdan and Alidjun are a means to temporalize material life and care in the Zvijezda highlands. Seeds are not sown before Jurjevdan. Hay needs to be safely stored under the roof of the stall by the end of July, when a dova is due. In villages, time, labor, and leisure are punctuated by constant references to "before" and "after" Jurjevdan, Alidjun and the respective prayers for rain.

Prayers following after Jurjevdan are described as Jurjev prayer (*Jurjevske dove*). The time after Jurjevdan is associated in the local discourses with fertile rain and water that regenerates the fields, gardens, and meadows and that freshens the air, and also with the processes of growing crops and hay and later with haymaking. The midsummer period is marked by Alidjun, and the prayers that follow are known as Alidjun prayers (*Alidjunske dove*). The midsummer period is characterized by hot and dry sun and occasional storms and fires. Thus, activities that follow Alidjun are associated with work on the fields and harvest as the land becomes drier. Alidjun is also the time in the highlands when potatoes need to be "woken up." On the date of Alidjun (August 2), villagers go to their fields to dig out a few potatoes in order to check their quality and thus anticipate the time of harvest, which is usually about a month later.

Although there is no sharp dividing line between the two dates in labor tasks around the houses and the fields, the Jurjev-Alidjun temporal axis of rains and storms shapes the cosmological construction of Islamic time in village life. It bundles agricultural activities and vegetative processes into the rubric of vital exchange through the idiom of dova, whereby divine grace is bestowed on the fields, meadows, and villagers' labor, mediated through the prayers for rain. In turn, to recall Fadil's words from the introduction ("this is milk, thanks to Allah"), the divine grace is materialized in the fields that give life and vitality to the house and to its members, who take care of them.

Rhythms of Piety

Collective ritual prayers for rain, their calendars, and the organization of material life and care are not the only textures of Islamic temporal cosmology. Other textures shape "the work of daily prayer, fasting, and worship" (Hart 2013: 45) in village life—the rhythms of piety. By piety and pious conduct, I refer to villagers' articulations of their relationship to God mediated by prayers.

The discourses surrounding Islamic piety among Bosnian Muslims, villagers and urbanites alike, focus on the practice of namaz (Ar. *salāt*)—five daily prayers and their performance.[9] Such conceptions of piety have also become a dominant focus in the literature on Islam and Muslim lives in Bosnia and Herzegovina. Ernest Gellner's hyperbolic statement "nowadays, to be a Bosnian Muslim you need not believe that there is no God but God and that Mohamad is his prophet, but you do need to have lost that faith" (1983: 72), or portraying Bosnian Muslims as those who do not regularly pray, became a common characterization (Bougarel 2018). However, such arguments tacitly erase the multifaceted conceptions of religious experience, and further cement the ethnonational perspective on what it means to be a Muslim in BiH. There have been several recent attempts to engage with the formation of Muslim pious subjectivity on non-ethnonational grounds, in particular among Muslim women in Sarajevo. Yet such accounts again tend to reduce the complexity of religious experience into issues of regular prayer and veiling, and thus into a particular Islamic discursive tradition (Mesarić 2017).

These two positions illustrate how problematic it is to frame the performance of piety as a clear-cut binary. As anthropologists have increasingly recognized, conceptions of Islam and living a Muslim life that lives up to the ideals of these conceptions are often contradictory, fragmented, ambiguous, and entwined with other aspirations (Marsden and Retsikas 2013, Schielke 2010). Such a narrowly focused conception of piety is unhelpful for the material discussed here.

Approaching Muslim piety as a clear-cut binary misses the nuances and intricacies of what constitutes religious experience. The notion of namaz encompasses an array of practices, emotions, and reasonings (Bowen 1989), but also temporalities and rhythms. Let me address the sites where the rhythms of piety are articulated and negotiated in village life.

Mindful Piety

Although the practice of namaz is recognized in the villages as one's duty (*farz*), the great majority of villagers do not perform namaz regularly. For villagers performing namaz is not an "either/or" rule but rather *one of the ways* the individual relates to the divine. Being a good Muslim does not mean that one either prays or does not. Malika, who wrapped the Qur'an into a cloth and walked three times around the house while praying hajr-dova on the night of May 5, also prayed all five prayers on that day as well as on the following day, the day of Jurjevdan. On other days, she prayed three times or not at all. Osman regularly goes to the mosque on Fridays, and follows all prayers during Ramadan, but he doesn't perform namaz otherwise. Thus the intensity and frequency of performing namaz differs not only between individuals. It also varies according to the day, week, season, as well as significantly during life cycles and according to life crises, and individual historical experiences, in particular with regard to the critical events of the war.

On the other hand, everyday rhythms of Muslim piety in the Zvijezda highlands cannot be reduced solely to the practice of namaz. Many villagers, young and old, often made jokes about those who pray regularly only because it was sanctioned by the Islamic discursive tradition as a duty. Such a form of abiding deference is often described by villagers as pointless. Although numerous individuals in every village were vocally adamant about the importance of namaz, many villagers associated the emphasis on namaz as the ultimate expression of one's piety with the moralizing discourse of imams and the religious establishment of the IC-BiH.

During my fieldwork, I often accompanied male villagers to džuma in the municipal mosques. There, week after week, the imams constantly reminded the assembly about the importance of namaz. During the major Islamic festive days, the appeal not to omit namaz was regularly repeated by the leading ulema in their public speeches, and amplified in newspaper articles, in interviews on the television, and on social media.[10]

Yet the discourse on the importance of namaz was regularly mocked by my interlocutors. "They are paid to pray, I am not—I have to feed my family," Osman, along with other villagers, often ironically commented as a response to the appeals, expressing the disconnect between the religious establishment and villagers. Osman's comment resonates with the observations of other anthropologists that living a Muslim life is a mindful and creative activity that requires an individual to exercise practical judgements in a range of situations as they emerge in the flow of social life (Lambek 2015a, Marsden 2005). Indeed, villagers debated these matters with one another daily over a cup of coffee. The widely shared view on the question of what it means to be a good Muslim was that any person ought to act first and foremost in a morally accountable way, rather than counting how often someone prays. Consider the following exchange between two neighbors, Ragib (aged sixty-three) and Zakir (forty-three), one afternoon:

RAGIB: Well, it's time to go to the mosque to pray.

ZAKIR: Why? You don't need to go there. It's pointless. No one will come. You can easily pray at home. You are like my brother! Whenever he does not work, he goes to pray at the mosque—that's weird, he could easily pray at home.

RAGIB: I tell you what, whenever you can, you ought to pray in the mosque.

[SHORT SILENCE]

RAGIB: I have read the Qur'an. Do you know what is written there? That Allah is merciful, but one thing is unforgivable, and this is [not doing] namaz.

> **ZAKIR:** Well, maybe I don't pray regularly, but this is not so important. It's more crucial to be a good Muslim—I don't cheat anyone, I don't steal, nothing of the kind. And God should know that, and I hope it will be so.

Similarly, Aiša, one of my neighbors, shared with me her reflections on a situation in which she was asked by an older female neighbor in a judgmental way why she had not attended a prayer at the mosque:

> And what does it mean to be a better Muslim? Is it someone who prays five times every day and does not even know why? Or is it she, who is veiled and does not know why? Or is it someone who carries her faith in her heart, feels it in her soul, yet does not harm anyone and on the contrary tries to help everyone in the way that it should be? And with the expectation that this is the way Allah wants it? Maybe I do not pray regularly, but it does not mean that I am a bad Muslim.

Conversations like these about daily namaz are common among the villagers. The attitudes of elderly Ragib toward Zakir, and the elderly women in the mosque toward Aiša, further nuance the point this chapter makes about the rhythms of piety. It is not only the religious calendar and the exercising of individual judgement but also the rhythms of the life course that impact the individual conduct of piety, and how such modes of action are evaluated by fellow villagers. Indeed, elderly villagers, I was often told, "have time" to structure their days to perform daily prayers and go to the mosque if they want to, and many do so. Yet there are other commensurable and efficacious forms of vital exchange whereby villagers can relate to God, such as doing good deeds for others, taking care of bequeathed property, or praying for the souls of the dead, that villagers pursue and that make one a good Muslim, as Zakir observed in his conversation with Ragib.

These manifold forms and articulations of piety situate the quest for being a good Muslim and living a Muslim life first and foremost as a form of moral striving with regard to how one relates to the divine. Yet such moral striving needs to be situated in the nexus of the singularity of the situation, individual judgment, Islamic discursive traditions, and the specificity of the given socio-political configuration.

Given the historical vicissitudes of the twentieth century, which have transformed Muslim lives in the villages significantly, the rhythms of piety need to be considered not only with regard to individual life cycles but also to different generations. In the Zvijezda highlands, different generations of villagers inevitably conceive ways of being Muslim and what living a Muslim life entails differently. These conceptions differ among those brought up in the pre-1950s socialist times, when religious life was not yet constrained by communist ideological policies, and those brought up during or after the disintegration of Yugoslavia. Furthermore, the increased religious ethnonationalism since the 1980s, exacerbated by the 1992–95 war, and the transformation of the post-Yugoslav political and religious landscape, have significantly reconfigured these debates between villagers as well.

In the exchange between Ragib and Zakir, we learned that the elderly Ragib is rather like Zakir's brother, who "whenever he is not working goes to pray at the mosque." Zakir's brother Nurfet hardly followed any of the daily prayers during Yugoslav socialism. Instead, he was enjoying the German marks that his father earned in the Federal Republic of Germany. In 1998 Nurfet moved to the outskirts of Sarajevo, where he started attending the local mosque regularly, initially only because he was bored in a new place, and looking for company. Subsequently he learned to recite the Qur'an in Arabic and became an assistant of the local imam.

Finally, the practice of namaz is codetermined by the effects of public piety, and its presence or absence respectively. In many villages across the Zvijezda highlands, the local mosques were built only in the 1980s or mushroomed in the late 1990s and early 2000s. Yet there is no imam permanently settled in many of those villages, and hence the village mosques are not used regularly. In such cases, the house is the main site of daily prayers, and the practice of piety is individualized and gendered in the private sphere of the house. There women continue to play the chief role as the guardians of spiritual life, piety, and transmission of Muslim values and practices, including conducting namaz (Bringa 1995, Sorabji 1989, Sorabji 1994).

In turn, the individualized rhythms of piety performed in the house change in intensity over the course of the year. The winter period provides more opportunities for daily prayers than the summer months when villagers are working on their fields and around the houses. Annual collective rituals that actually take place in the mosque, such as Ramadan, followed by the two major feasts (*ramazanski bajram* and kurban bajram), are also periods of heightened observance of namaz. So are the periods that immediately follow the death of someone close when prayers for the soul of the dead (*tevhid*) are performed on the day of the funeral, after seven days, forty days, six months, and one year. Yet, even those villagers who observe namaz all year long do not necessarily perform all five prayers every day.

The Rhythms of Ramadan

The annual rituals of Ramadan (*ramazan* in Bosnian spelling), ramazanski bajram (Ar. *Eid al-Fitr*) and kurban bajram (Ar. *Eid al-Adha*) are moments of intense piety and the most important feast of the Islamic calendar in villages across the highlands. Ramadan itself brings specific time-reckoning practices and rhythms. These are orchestrated along the axes *sehur-sabah* (beginning of the fasting in the morning followed by the morning prayer), and *iftar-akšam* (the break of fasting in the evening followed by the evening prayer). In villages without permanently serving imams and with the mosque loudspeakers switched off throughout the year, during the Ramadan period the village soundscape transforms and becomes punctuated by the *ezan* (call to prayer), which is played loudly from the mosque's amplifiers. Although the IC-BiH distributes the Ramadan calendar (ramazanska vaktija) with the exact times for fasting and prayers to all villagers in the mosques, the main technology of temporalization and time reckoning, as I suggested before, is the series of Ramadan programs on the televisions, along with the digital clock and smartphones, and less so the blaring amplifiers.

Ramadan changes the rhythms of piety. The duties regarding the five daily prayers and fasting during Ramadan are again regularly mentioned by the Islamic religious authority as important virtues with regard to good Muslim conduct. Although the number of villagers who would follow namaz regularly was low, the number of villagers who fasted and prayed during Ramadan was high. In fact, only a handful of villagers were not fasting. Among children, fasting was a popular game when it came to testing how many days of the holy month they could abstain from eating and drinking. In Brdo, drinking habits also changed in relation to alcohol consumption. The local grocery would refrain from selling alcohol at all during Ramadan. During a period of my fieldwork that coincided with Ramadan in 2009, one villager was seen drinking a bottle of beer in public near the mosque. He was criticized and mocked for months afterward, and the story is regularly recalled a decade later.

In his reflection on Ramadan in contemporary Egypt, Samuli Schielke (2009: 25) suggests that intensified pious conduct during Ramadan is for many Muslims a way to come to terms with less intense levels of worship and religious observance during the rest of the year. Schielke and other authors raise an important point about ambiguity, ambivalence, and fragmentation in the moral conceptions of what being a good Muslim entails in regard to scripturalist discourses on pious conduct. For ordinary Muslims, these conceptions are shaped not only by an Islamic discursive tradition but also by other "grand schemes" and ethical repertoires, as well as by the period of Ramadan and the rest of the year.

The modes of piety in the Zvijezda highlands remind us that these debates, led by villagers themselves, are not as clear-cut when it comes to the sharp division between "being good" during Ramadan, as Schielke puts it, and "not being so good" when it comes to piety during the rest of the year. For villagers, the notion of piety and pious conduct is more elastic and poetic, understood as an ethical practice that unfolds with different intensities and rhythms in the flow of life in relation to the individual pursuit of vital exchange. Many villagers who fasted and prayed during Ramadan conceived of the period between the end of Ramadan and kurban bajram, which lasts for about nine to ten weeks, as a continuity rather than discontinuity of intensified prayers. Pious conduct during the rest of the year does not rely solely on moral imperatives such as "being good at Ramadan" that are derived from an Islamic discursive tradition. On the contrary, piety as an ethical practice emerges from specific situations and responses to these situations such as having a dream vision or facing a prolonged life crisis, rather than from a dichotomous morality and practice of piety "during" Ramadan and non-pious conduct "after," as even the categories "during" and "after" can be inherently ambivalent and contested. To illustrate a range of possibilities on the continuum I conclude this chapter with a series of conceptions of pious conduct associated with Ramadan.

Moral Commitments

Some of the villagers living in the highlands were also following the mystical (Sufi) path of Islam. Their conduct articulated a more mystical Islamic teaching than the mainstream teaching of the religious establishment of the IC-BiH. These villagers emphasized the contemplative-cum-embodied facets of fasting during Ramadan that cultivate one's soul by taming one's body. Ramadan was an exemplary opportunity to cultivate the self through taming one's *nafs* (a set of one's desires and needs), in the quest for detachment from the mundane and material world here and now (*dunjaluk*).

The important lesson for those who fast is the realization that fasting is only a mimetic act that can be endured only temporarily. Ordinary human beings start looking forward to breaking the fast after just a few hours. Ramadan is an exercise that cultivates Muslims' awareness of who is the Lord and who is a mortal human. Hence, the time of Ramadan brings to the forefront the realization of what it means to be a human (*insan*) before God.

Although this highly reflexive and contemplative articulation of the meaning and purpose of Ramadan was shared only to some extent in the households and neighborhoods of these followers, it was not part of the common understanding and vocabulary shared among most of the villagers. Many villagers understood the meanings and purposes of Ramadan, and especially their observance of fasting, differently. A recurring argument in everyday debates before, during, and after Ramadan was that "it is worthwhile to fast" without providing a more elaborate narrative. Ramadan and the observance of fasting were conceived by some villagers as *adet* (customary tradition) that ought to be followed no matter what. Other villagers, however, approached the period of intensified piety and fasting during Ramadan as a matter of self-cultivation in their attempts to be good Muslims, and improving their relationship with God.

So here we have local conceptions of Ramadan showing different articulations of piety during the holy month. The former conception entwined the practice of piety during Ramadan with the ongoing practice of self-cultivation as a way to become closer to God. The latter proposition—"it is worthwhile to fast"—needs to be situated in a wider domain of villagers' social experience with the divine during the rest of the year. Indeed, during the four Ramadans I have spent in the highlands over the past decade, villagers paid tremendous attention to who visited the mosque regularly, who attended *teravija-namaz* (the night prayer during Ramadan), and who was fasting. Whereas during the rest of the year I barely heard or witnessed any negative comments on an individual's religious observance (the only exception being when someone got drunk in public), Ramadan was valued as a time of a rather different pious conduct and heightened moralizing of piety.

Soon after the beginning of Ramadan, villagers switched to a distinct evaluative moral grammar and started commenting on those who neither fasted nor attended the prayers in the mosque. In contrast to the conversations during the rest of the year, even my friends who were otherwise relaxed in their attitudes and personal conduct began to employ value judgments such as "bad behavior," or lack of respect for *adet* (custom). There were regular arguments and debates between neighbors on these matters during Ramadan. Disagreements and tensions were usually generated by two clashing conceptions of moral values, reasoning, and expectations that emerged during Ramadan, namely, between being a good and caring neighbor and being a good Muslim, which during the rest of the year would be considered as inextricably intertwined rather than divisive.

In chapter 2 I described everyday life in the neighborhood as a moral project where villagers engage in the lives of others. Villagers are expected to pay a visit to their neighbors on various important and joyful occasions. The Ramadan period is definitely not the right time for doing so, however, except to take part in the collective meal (*iftar*) that neighbors organize for one another in turn. Yet a few days before the beginning of Ramadan in a neighborhood in Brdo, Muradif and Hanifa's family succeeded in getting running water for their house after many years of carrying water from the communal well. This was a very important and celebratory moment for them, and hence the neighbors were expected to come and pay a visit to share their joy. Yet no one from Muradif and Hanifa's family fasted or attended the prayers in the mosque during Ramadan, unlike their neighbors, who were very involved in Ramadan. In the end, nobody came. This created a tension because the neighbors could not pay a visit as the evening prayers ended well after 10 p.m., and the following morning those who were fasting had to wake around 3 a.m. to prepare for another day of fasting. What happened was that after a week of waiting Muradif got very angry and told Hanifa that she should not talk to anyone in the neighborhood unless they came to visit and apologized. A few days later, Hanifa walked around a group of other neighbors who were sitting in the shade of the garden and waiting to break the fast; she quietly asked them how they were going, rejecting their invitation to join them, although she has otherwise usually done so. Then Hanifa said, still half-whispering, "we have been expecting you to come but you didn't come, and Muradif is really angry now because he thinks that this komšiluk is not worth anything at all." The women thanked Hanifa for the invitation, and replied politely that now it was Ramadan and Muradif should not have expected their fasting neighbors to visit them. Hanifa walked away without replying. The group of neighbors was disappointed and upset by the comment for a while, and then one of them, Rašida, reflecting on how the rhythms of piety can sometimes create conflicting moral expectations between being a good neighbor and a good Muslim that are difficult to live up to, said: "So what! No one can expect me that to walk around the village and hang around with someone for a coffee or whatever. It's Ramadan! It is worthwhile to fast! But they don't fast, so how could they understand? They ought to wait until the end of Ramadan, but I tell you what, they don't know what is worthy."

Similarly, Zehra, a widow in her late fifties, was attending an iftar organized by one of the houses in her komšiluk, her son phoned her to tell her to return urgently home because someone from the village had come to visit her for coffee. "Do they know that during Ramadan people should not walk around and hang around with others pointlessly or without any invitation?" lamented Zehra while leaving the dinner and rushing home in order to serve coffee to her guests, knowing that she would not be able to make it that night to the mosque for the Ramadan prayers. But she also knew that the visiting family was going through a very difficult period with massive indebtedness and one member undergoing cancer treatment. Hence she could not just deny them hospitality. Despite her laments, for Zehra, who was balancing contradictory commitments within the moral rubric of vital exchange, it was more important to engage in the lives of others on that night rather than go to the mosque.

These situations reveal that villagers are not vehicles solely enacting an Islamic discursive tradition and religious duty in their practices of piety. Rather, the ways villagers articulate their relations to the divine are entwined with other moral commitments and punctuated by multiple rhythms and repertoires of time reckoning in constituting villagers' religious experience in the course of social life.

* * *

I started this chapter by asking about the role of Islamic temporal cosmology in villagers' lives. Although the cosmological conceptions of Islamic time in village life provide villagers with a parallel temporal grammar of punctuating social activities, meaning-making practices, and individual relationships to the divine, they are intricately folded into the temporal textures of everyday life, which is not just about piety and Islam but rather about how these temporal textures are interwoven. And the ways in which an Islamic temporal cosmology and the modes of temporal reasoning emerging from the postsocialist, postwar ruptures overlap and intersect is the theme that is explored in the following chapter.

5

Praying and Witnessing

"I remember the time," Aiša told me, "when my husband was injured during the war. It was in 1994, and I prayed hajr-dove [for good luck] every day until he was cured. Elhamdulillah [thanks to Allah], God was merciful and made his life easier again." While talking to me in her house, Aiša was holding a pocket-size book of *Zbirka dova* (collection of prayers), which also contained the dova for good luck. Aiša's grandmother gave her the book when she was a teenager back in the 1980s. Aiša keeps the book along with the Qur'an wrapped in a cloth on a top shelf in her living room. She turns to the book and recites the prayers whenever she seeks divine intervention for her family or herself in moments of crisis. The vicissitudes of her life that have led her to search for an intervention have been multiple. They include personal illnesses or those of family members, debts and unemployment, stress and anxiety, school exams, prolonged family separation, or protection from the war. Time and again, I observed in the Zvijezda highlands the way that past experiences of hardship during the war, and economic predicaments and marginalization in the postwar years, are entwined with searching for divine intervention and assistance mediated by *dova* in a similar way to that described by Aiša on that afternoon in her house.

By a twist of fate, I became acquainted with Sadeta, a dream-healer living in the Sarajevo suburbs, early on in my fieldwork (see Edgar and Henig 2010). I found out about her services around the same time by sheer coincidence from friends in Sarajevo and the Zvijezda highlands who did not know one another.

My friends were all flocking to the kitchen table in her apartment in search of help. When I pointed out this serendipity to Sadeta, her calm reaction was that God wanted me to meet her.[1] Indeed, people and dreams come to Sadeta rather than her seeking them out. I have had opportunities to meet with Sadeta on numerous occasions since our first coffee in 2009. Without any prompting during our first conversation, Sadeta brought up the theme of the Bosnian war and the divine intervention mediated by the dova:

> Once during the war I attended a tevhid where I talked to a *hafiz* [a person who memorized the Qur'an by heart] about my dreams. Afterward he said, "now I'll give you a special dova against *sihir* [sorcery]." We had never seen each other before! He realized that I had a gift from God to help people. Then he wrote down the prayer, which needed to be repeated seventy-seven times, and also wrote down his telephone number and told me to return fifteen days later. During these two weeks I dreamed one night about an old woman and she told me, "pray . . . and don't be afraid of shells, bullets, or anything." You need to understand that it was during the war, my husband was old and ill, and I had to go out every day to fetch water and food. So I prayed as she told me every time I left the house. When I saw the hafiz after two weeks, I asked him about the dream because the woman in my dream didn't tell me how many times I should pray the dova. She only told me the words of the prayer. And the hafiz told me to repeat the prayer 1,479 times between *akšam* [evening prayer] and *jacija* [night prayer] whenever I wished, to go out for food for example, and God will help me. And now I repeat this prayer whenever someone needs God's help.

Sadeta and her late husband survived the Sarajevo siege. Aiša's husband recovered from his injury, and thanks to God's grace she did not lose anyone during the war. Divine interventions, whether mediated by prayers or dreams, are not reducible, as Diana Allan suggests, "to idle yearnings or escapism" (2014: 138). Rather, they introduce "possibility and intentionality in everyday relations, allowing desires and afflictions to be articulated and acted upon" (138). Indeed, Aiša's and Sadeta's narratives invite us to consider how, in the wake of critical events and their aftermaths, the idioms of dova and piety become productive techniques in reconfiguring villagers' social worlds, and for making sense of critical events and moments of rupture.

In moments of ruptures and radical societal changes, Joel Robbins suggested, "something does not just happen in time but rather happens to it" (2007: 12). Following this observation, we need to ask not only what ruptures do to time and temporal orientations, be it secular or Islamic, but also what ruptures do to one's sense of being in history. Listening to Aiša and Sadeta, I could not help but ask myself what everyday historical work does in the event of ruptures and critical events. What happens in the case of ruptures when all narratives break down and have to be pieced together again? And how does a person reinsert their voice back into her life history? The need to remake and recalibrate temporal orientations can often be observed in the context of conflicts and their aftermaths. Examining everyday historical work, as Rebecca Bryant argues, can help us "to understand how people remake everyday realities in the wake of war" (2014: 681).

On Prayer: Temporal Orientations

In chapter 4 we saw how the act of prayer figures as the central idiom of villagers' engagement with Islamic temporal cosmology. As I go through the transcripts, audio files, and field notes which I took while talking to Aiša, Sadeta, and others, I can see and hear time and again how performing dova becomes an efficacious and therapeutic act, as it enables one to address one's anxieties and uncertainties both immediately and prospectively.

Yet there is more at stake than seeking solace in moments of distress. The social life of critical events cannot be separated from the constructions of religious experience. The performance of dova, I argue in this chapter, produces a temporal orientation. It gives Aiša and Sadeta a vocabulary with which to engage with the critical events of the past, with the predicaments in the present, as well as with the yet-unknown future (Bryant and Knight 2019). The frequent references to acts of dova that quickly populated the pages of my field notes play an important role in situating and grasping critical events and moments of rupture, whether individual or collective, not as "traumatic memories" but as a vehicle of historical experience.

Anthropological studies of historical experience have examined "the variety of modes in which people learn about and represent the past" (Stewart 2012: 7; see also Palmié and Stewart 2016). These studies have documented how the past is culturally mediated through dreams, ritual iterations, and spirit possession in the present, and informs prospective social actions (Bandak 2019, Lambek 2002, Stewart 2012, Tambar 2011). The omnipresence of dova in everyday lives and vocabularies among villagers hints at analogous forms of cultural mediation of the past in the present. An act of prayer can also produce a sense of immersion in the past, can connect various temporal layers, times, and epochs in one's historical consciousness here and now, and can become a mode of historical experience (Stewart 2016, Tambar 2011). Dreams, the effects of prayers, miracles, or visions, as Amira Mittermaier contends, are hard to contain in secular regimes of historicity and temporalities. They belong, to follow Mittermaier's lead, "neither simply to religious traditions nor to secular imaginations; they are both immaterial and inherently political; they are as much about the present and past as they are about the future" (2015a: 119). And as Diana Allan adds, dreams can become "an intellectual and imaginative resource people can draw on in moments of adversity, allowing them to project themselves into the unknown and make it more tractable" (2014: 138).

What does this mean for acts of dova? In his *On Prayer*, Marcel Mauss writes that prayer is a mode of action that "is often as rich in ideas and images as a religious narrative" (2003: 22). Furthermore, Mauss suggests that prayer needs to be understood as a social phenomenon, that is, taking place "in a social landscape populated with fellow beings" (Bandak 2017: 4; also Anderson 2011). Mauss' argument, in the light of Aiša's and Sadeta's stories, I suggest, needs to be amplified as follows: an act of prayer is as rich in ideas and images as a historical narrative that can reveal, as Andreas Bandak poignantly argues, "quite a bit about what is negotiated in the social worlds we study," including peoples' hopes, anxieties, and desires (2017: 1–2). Here, I suggest that we should attend to acts of prayer as a mode of historical-cum-religious experience.

In this chapter I interrogate what kind of historical work the act of dova entails. I ask what repertoires and techniques of religious experience villagers employ to remake and recalibrate their temporal orientations toward the past, present, and the future. I trace how dova works in villagers' lives in addressing the ruptures and predicaments that have emerged from the disintegration of socialist Yugoslavia, the war, and their aftermaths, including economic hardship and marginalization. The argument progresses from the present temporal orientation, to the present-future, and finally to the present-past orientations.

Postwar Anxieties

There was a sigh followed by silence when Malika put her mobile phone back on the coffee table. Her daughters immediately recognized that Zakir, their father and Malika's husband, had not texted them yet that day. Sighs and silence had punctuated the household's routines for many months. "I wonder how he is doing there," she asked herself many times every day, before repeating how she couldn't sleep since her husband had left. Together with other male villagers from the Zvijezda highlands, Zakir had left for six months for construction work in Azerbaijan. The decision to go abroad was difficult for the families to make, and everyone kept postponing it for weeks and months as the last solution to their problems. None of the villagers who left for the former Soviet republic had

"Killing debts"—a farewell to long-term unemployed villagers who are going to work abroad.

been able to find a job in the highlands for several years. In the case of Zakir, it was as long as a decade. The families were getting by as well as they could: engaging in subsistence farming, selling dairy surplus, and collecting whatever they could sell during the summer periods, including mushrooms, wild strawberries, blueberries, raspberries, rose hips, and also timber all year round. The income generated from such activities, however, was unstable and hardly sufficient to cover the most immediate costs, including children's transport to school and other expenses associated with their education, electricity bills, and food, and, inevitably, repayment of microloans. The pressure of accumulated debts and microloans had become unbearable both economically and also in terms of how they affected the health and well-being of Zakir and others.

The link between health and debts is deeply intertwined in postsocialist, postwar Bosnia. In her work, Larisa Jašarević (2017) tracks how indebtedness has become a commonly shared experience and articulation of life in BiH today, and more broadly how the workings of the economy and the market have become part of peoples' experiences of their bodies, health, and social relationships. This was also the case for the four male villagers who left their families hoping to earn money in a venture abroad. In the months before he made up his mind to go to Azerbaijan, Zakir suffered from severe headaches, nausea, and insomnia. "The debts," he kept repeating, "are killing me." At the time, I often saw from the window of my room at night his silhouette projected onto the walls of the living room, with the TV on and smoking one cigarette after another until the early morning hours when, exhausted, he finally fell asleep. The stress and anxieties that he suffered from resulted in his being diagnosed with high blood pressure and receiving prescriptions of pills from the municipal medical center.

Since her husband left, Malika was now suffering from anxiety and insomnia. She spent her sleepless nights performing dova and reading the Qur'an. She often shared her feelings with close neighbors over a cup of coffee. "Whenever I pray," she told me, I ask Allah PBUH to protect my husband, and I ask dear God to give Zakir hajr and *nafaka* [wealth]. Since he left I have not been able to sleep properly. Fortunately, there are dove I can recite and pray in the evening that calm me down, and this is better than any pills."

When the men left for Azerbaijan, their wives, children, and parents found their own lives suspended in a temporal vacuum, while waiting and taking care of the houses. They were waiting not only for their loved ones to return from abroad, but also to receive enough money to pay off the debts that were causing so much pressure and anxieties and that created the conditions that forced the men to leave the villages in the first place.

Facing the absence and waiting, the women in the neighborhoods shared the emotional burden together and helped each other as much as they could. Back alone in their houses, however, it was the recourse to the Zbirka dova, and reading or listening to the Qur'an that became the prevalent sources of therapy in the face of mounting concerns for their husbands' good fortune and success, and their own well-being and sanity. Malika's anxieties became progressively debilitating and her migraines lasted up to three days at a time, making her increasingly reliant on her teenage daughters and neighbors.

Often, when the phone was silent for several days, or when she couldn't leave her bed, she reached out for her own old Zbirka dova and recited a dova that was "better than any pills." "We did the same during the war," she often said, and her female neighbors nodded. Sometimes they added their own war stories of praying dova to protect themselves and their families, whether before leaving the house as the danger of shelling was omnipresent, or while they were waiting for their husbands, brothers, sons, and grandsons to return from the front line.

ANALOGICAL ORIENTATIONS

The spontaneous comment "we did the same during the war" exemplifies the everyday historical work among villagers in which the past "offers itself up"

(Jackson 2007: 83). My friends and interlocutors were reaching for proximate analogies back to the (violent) past in order to make sense of their current predicaments (Knight 2015, Stewart 2017). Indeed, in situations that bear affective resonances, relationships and analogies between different temporal orientations and historical layers are created in the present through everyday historical work. Yet in such situations villagers were not doing so to recall the traumatic memories of the war as such. On the contrary, these stories and narratives that circulate among the women, neighbors, and villages are instances and potentialities of everyday historical work "that can guide moral action in the present" (Stewart 2017: 133–34; also Lambek 1996).

In the Zvijezda highlands, the act of performing dova entwines such affective resonances, which are as rich in ideas and images as a historical narrative, and constitutes a horizon of historical-cum-religious experience in the present. Put differently, mediating between different temporal layers and orientations, the act of dova becomes a "vehicle *for*" navigating the past and the future in the present (Lambek 1996: 241).

"OLD ANXIETIES": *SIHIR*

Performing dova is a mode of vital exchange with the divine whereby one's anxieties, uncertainties, loss of vitality, but also medical efficacy are addressed immediately and prospectively. In the Zvijezda highlands, it is common to perform dova in situations of unexpected individual or family anxieties, illnesses, ruptures, or misfortune.

The most frequent instances debated in the villages are prolonged illness, cows or sheep falling barren and being unable to produce milk, and cases in which a series of unfortunate events affect a household such as blackouts, or paintings or hangings falling from the walls.

"Misfortune talk" was common during my fieldwork. The widely shared diagnosis of such situations was that they were attributable to *sihir* (sorcery) or a *džin* (jinn). Such malevolent attacks are countervailed by a temporal shift to the intensified practice of piety. The shift in the rhythms of piety includes performance of the obligatory five daily prayers and the nonobligatory dova, and visiting a healer like Sadeta (Bringa 1995: 178–82; El Guindi 2008; Jašarević 2012b).[2]

The IC-BiH has long had a negative attitude to such practices and convictions. During the Yugoslav period, this theme was also repeatedly discussed in the *Glasnik Islamske Zajednice* and condemned by the leading Bosnian Islamic ulema (e.g., Hodžić 1967), not only as un-Islamic but also as antimodern. In the Zvijezda highlands, local imams as well as villagers who adhere to a more scriptural conception of Islam dismissed such practices and convictions as backward and unfounded, if not irrational and deviant, arguing that one's regular pious conduct as embodied in the namaz was more effective.[3]

More vocal villagers did not hesitate to say in public that "these folk are stupid—namaz is more worthwhile if performed regularly," whenever someone mentioned sihir or misfortune and the need to visit healers and get amulets for protection (*zapis*) from any malevolent attack. In such cases, the critical villagers vigorously distanced themselves from practices which they considered as old-fashioned and peasant-like. Unlike the religious establishment, however, they did not classify such practices as un-Islamic. These contrasting articulations of what is proper Muslim conduct and what is not are not clear-cut dichotomies but rather ambiguous and constantly negotiated.

This became even more apparent when it came to personal crises, ailments or any contemporary anxieties. In such moments, the very same critical interlocutors had no problems reciting dova for good luck (hajr-dova) and to restore nafaka, or seeking assistance from an Islamic healer. So whereas sihir belongs to the old times and "deviant beliefs"—to use the language of the ulema—the aftermath of the disintegration of socialist Yugoslavia and the 1992–95 war engendered new anxieties and misfortunes. In such situations, the act of dova, performed by villagers themselves or by a healer on their behalf, continues to guide moral action in the present.

NEW ANXIETIES: IN THE WAITING ROOM AMONG THE FORGOTTEN

The postsocialist, postwar years have brought about a vast spectrum of new anxieties. Larisa Jašarević (2012b) documents an exhaustive array that parallels the forms of anxieties I encountered in the Zvijezda highlands and among the people who visit the Islamic healer Sadeta in the Sarajevo suburbs. She observes that sitting in the waiting room of a therapist are

> a teenage girl who secretly suffered sexual violence and came on the insistence of her high school teacher, women and men with marital grievances, or survivors of car accidents or the 1990s concentration camps. There are students with test anxieties, and young people who are shy or listless, unemployed or struggling with school, heartbroken, or dependent upon parents who indulge them but can scarcely afford to. We find among *strava* [the practice of healing studied by Jašarević] clients people who are in mourning, patients released from hospitals, or those lately of psychiatric wards who are schizophrenic, epileptic, homicidal, suicidal, or suffer panic disorders. Then there are the bankrupt, the indebted, the impoverished masses, and the few who are newly rich. (Jašarević 2012b: 924)

The emergence of new anxieties and disorders, Jašarević crucially contends, cannot be separated from the emergence of the new postsocialist economy and medical market. The newly emerged healing practices and their claims to efficacy need to be positioned vis-à-vis their "competition with psycho-pharmaceutical treatments of anxiety" (Jašarević 2012b: 924).

If "misfortune talk" is associated with "old anxieties" in the Zvijezda highlands, "health talk" now articulates new anxieties. It has become a common conversational theme over coffee to openly discuss the new anxieties and people's health issues, such as Malika's migraines and insomnia due to Zakir's absence. Regular coffee visits among the neighbors thus often resembled diagnostic or therapeutic gatherings during which villagers shared practical advice about various forms of healing. Telephone numbers of healers were retyped time and again from one mobile phone to another. Facebook profiles of individual healers were recommended to other Facebook friends. Printed collections of prayer books, CDs, and DVDs with recitations of healing dove circulated between the houses, while the villagers tried to navigate this new terrain of postsocialist, postwar ailments, disorders, and treatments. This emerging medical pluralism in postsocialist, postwar Bosnia has opened up a field of possibilities for Bosnians of all walks of life to switch between them when dealing with new anxieties here and now, depending on one's piety, financial situation, or level of desperation (Jašarević 2017).

How do these new anxieties unfold in everyday life? Adil, now in his early fifties, once told me after we returned from the municipal medical center where he went regularly to check his blood pressure that "whenever I sit in the waiting room I see so many people around me and hear about their problems, I can see that their problems are the consequences of the war. Don't forget, every year of the war aged us by at least three years. All these problems with the pancreas, depression, blood pressure and diabetes are consequences of the war. Yes, it's great that the state is taking care of the families of the war martyrs and war heroes but what about these ordinary people who continue to suffer from the war? They are forgotten."

Adil's comment adds another layer to the reconfigured hierarchies of the privileged and the suffering of the forgotten. One of the forgotten villagers who started experimenting with the newly emerged medical pluralism was Najm, who is working with an amalgam of biomedical and religious curatives. For Najm, it has become vital to regularly visit an Islamic healer in the town of Zenica, a hundred kilometers away, while also visiting his local doctor in the municipal medical center as well as seeing a physiotherapist. Now in his mid-forties, Najm has experienced a prolonged pain in his right hip that has at times left him paralyzed. His wife Amira blames the war and the time he spent in trenches in the hills defending the village for causing his long-lasting medical conditions.

Yet Najm has become increasingly anxious not only because of the enduring pain but also because he faced difficulties in accessing health services and receiving any solutions for his problems and pain. He knew that if he had good "personal connections" (veze/štela), he would have perhaps been able to reach a medical specialist at the Sarajevo hospital. Despite many attempts, he has not been successful in reaching anyone. The situation was exacerbated by the fact that in 2002 Najm lost his job in the local sawmill. Since then he has been able to make money only from small-scale farming, and mainly from selling dairy products in Sarajevo, driving his old Volkswagen there every Saturday morning at 5 a.m. Although everyone in his family was helping, Najm was largely responsible for running the small family business and for delivering the dairy products to Sarajevo regularly. Any further paralysis threatened the family's precarious source of income, a concern that made him even more anxious and at times paralyzed him. Thus for Najm, as for the great majority of Bosnians today, living in precarity constitutes a pervasive source of anxiety that also becomes part of people's bodies (Jašarević 2017).

The discourses and practices of dova have become for villagers a potent idiom of meaning making and action for seeking immediate divine interventions to restore vitality and well-being in situations in which one's life trajectory has ruptured, stuck, and been kept on hold. Since Najm's economic struggle and uncertainty have intersected with health issues, a few years ago Najm, along with his wife and mother, all started regularly performing dova for hajr in an attempt to further Najm's nafaka and well-being. As they often said when discussing their predicament with me, and with other villagers, "that's something we also did during the war when Najm was in the trenches up in the hills." Just as Aiša did for her husband during the war, and Malika did for her husband abroad, Najm, his wife Amira, and his mother were reaching for historical analogies in the past that would effectively orient moral action in the present.

Prospective Orientations: Dreaming

As I was writing these lines in 2017, many Bosnians on social media were reporting and debating the words of Sadik Ahmetović, a leading SDA politician, which he made in public. Ahmetović told journalists that he had prayed *istikhara* (dream incubation prayer) in order to decide which companies would receive a lucrative contract to build a new motorway in the country.[4] Unsurprisingly to many observers, the winning companies had close links to the SDA.

Although it is true, as the media reported, that this was yet another case of how nepotistic political parties are in Bosnia and Herzegovina today, Ahmetović's reference in the speech to istikhara, a widely used form of divination in Islam, should not be dismissed. His reference to istikhara needs to be taken seriously, as it shows how the realms of the divine and miraculous are often entwined with the political realm rather than occupying separate domains of thought and action. These entwinements can resurface in unexpected moments and alliances.

Around the world, dreams and dream visions play a significant role in Muslim lives and politics.[5] Istikhara is a form of prayer that Muslims in Bosnia perform to make decisions about their future. Put differently, it helps them to address the quandaries of their lives. Istikhara is a nonobligatory prayer that involves reciting particular verses from the Qur'an before going to bed. The revealed vision that comes to them in their dream then guides their social action. Indeed, as we saw in the case of Sadeta, her dreams are received from God.

Dreams offer clues to the contingencies and ruptures of everyday life. In her seminal work on Islamic dreamscapes in Egypt, Amira Mittermaier (2011) writes about dream visions as a way for Muslims to conceive of parallel pathways of consciousness and imagination. Mittermaier describes istikhara as "seeking the best" in situations that involve taking decisions between two permissible (halal) alternatives (96). Istikhara prayer belongs to the repertoire of practices in which Muslims attempt to orient their actions, along with other future-oriented modes of reasoning and actions, such as hope or aspiration (Jansen 2015).

Over the years of my fieldwork, I encountered Muslims from diverse backgrounds who individually pray istikhara for a wide variety of reasons. Istikhara is invoked to assist in making personal decisions or when dealing with anxieties and uncertainties. In the Zvijezda highlands, women in particular regularly perform istikhara (see also Bringa 1995: 215). The most common impetus for praying istikhara is twofold. First, istikhara is invoked in making marriage choices. Second, villagers pray istikhara when seeking to resolve doubts or complex predicaments with the aim of achieving the right outcome, be it securing another microloan, buying a new appliance, or choosing which university program to enroll in. This was also the case for Malika, who prayed istikhara when Zakir was deciding whether or not to work abroad. The outcome of her dreams played an important role in his decision to go to Azerbaijan.

In villages, the dream visions invoked through istikhara are interpreted intuitively by the individuals themselves or by villagers experienced in deciphering dreams. This is preferable to following any of the popular dream interpretation manuals available in many Sarajevo bookshops. Yet the practice of dream interpretation in villages also generates frictions over appropriate religious conduct.

Several imams that I interviewed about dream interpretation were dismissive of such practices, arguing in a rather Freudian manner that praying istikhara is a way of deceiving oneself. They suggested that such dreams are an expression of one's wills and anxieties. One dreams, they contended, what one unconsciously wants to achieve. Again, this position was taken in particular by those imams who push for a scriptural stance toward Islam. But I also encountered local imams and dervish sheikhs who were open to listening to any dream narratives, and helped fellow villagers and urbanites to decipher their dreams. The sheikhs in particular encouraged dreaming as an important threshold of religious experience.

And that friction is what makes the practice of dreaming so contentious, be it in Bosnia or elsewhere in the Muslim world. It empowers and legitimatizes dream interpreters as sources of authority over established authorities of religious knowledge and practice (Mittermaier 2010). This is amplified as a third person can take on the role of medium. Indeed, istikhara prayer can be performed by a healer on behalf of others.

This is also the case of Sadeta, who prays istikhara for those who visit her. As we have already learned, she only became a healer in the early 1990s, after a series of very powerful dream visions that directed her on the way to becoming an Islamic healer. Unlike local imams or dervish sheikhs, she is a non-scriptural specialist guided mainly by her intuition, experience, and the dream visions themselves, as she has no formal religious training, and consults the dream manuals only rarely.

Dreaming a Better Society

It was not easy to arrange a meeting with Sadeta. The endless stream of visitors and phone calls, including villagers from the Zvijezda highlands, kept Sadeta busy. As someone who does not use a mobile phone, she felt obliged to remain by her landline as often as possible, and I usually succeeded in meeting with her only on regular prayer visits to the Gazi-Husrev Beg mosque in Sarajevo's Old Quarter. Sadeta patiently listens to anyone who calls or visits her. She deals with various forms of misfortune and with physical and mental ailments that articulate a range of new anxieties and disorders similar to those discussed earlier in this chapter. In such situations, the divinatory power of istikhara is not only therapeutic but also diagnostic, providing insight into how to turn a person's misfortune, ailments, and anxieties in the immediate present into fortune and well-being in the future.

Dreams are vehicles of historical consciousness, opening the gates of the past in the present, as well as horizons of possibilities that can guide moral action in the future (Stewart 2012). Amira Mittermaier (2011) suggests that dreams and dream visions are affected by political conditions but also have the capacity to articulate and challenge these conditions. Dream visions and dream stories "can open up critical spaces and possibilities" (2011: 2) and thus different temporal horizons for future-oriented action, including for example a revolution (Mittermaier 2019; see also Allan 2014).

In the Zvijezda highlands, the narratives accompanying villagers' dreams cannot be separated from the double rupture of postsocialist and postwar societal reconfigurations. The idiom of prayer, specifically istikhara, thus provided my interlocutors with a conceptual vocabulary to act as historical subjects and articulate and come to terms with the new sociopolitical configuration of postsocialist, postwar Bosnian society, both religious and secular. It is a vocabulary with which villagers can construct a narrative of their lives as a historical process between the past and the future.

Indeed, Sadeta described the years *after* the 1992–95 war as marked by increased activities of malevolent forces that led her fellow Bosnians to turn against one another, and which Sadeta has been called on to counteract. Such malevolent forces, she told me, are manipulated by individuals against one another, both because of existing forms of human envy, but also due to increasingly high levels of unemployment, indebtedness, and damaged interpersonal relations among spouses, neighbors, and their contemporaries. Facing such developments, Sadeta sees her capacity to dream for others, which was revealed to her when she was fifty-three as having a clear moral, political, and restorative purpose: not simply healing the wounds of the past but making damaged Bosnian society (*pokvareno družstvo*) better again. This resonates with Mittermaier's observation of how subversive and politically imaginative dreams can be to the established status quo.

Sadeta's diagnosis of the Bosnian polity mirrors similar disorders and troubles of everyday life that have emerged across the world as a result of the encounters of the post–Cold War global expansion of neoliberal capitalism with postcolonial, postsocialist and postrevolutionary societies (Comaroff and Comaroff 1999). In postsocialist, postwar Bosnia and Herzegovina the proliferation of numerous healers and fortune-tellers who offer services to assist people with new anxieties, alongside a growing interest in various forms of vernacular healing practices, indexes Bosnian encounters with such geopolitical and global economic shifts. The ways in which these are imagined, conceptualized, and articulated by healers like Sadeta and the visitors in her kitchen through various idioms of dova, even when referring to the istikhara, suggests that the dova, dream visions, and dream narratives are not a simple retreat to a timeless vernacular tradition of Islamic healing, which was hidden in a cupboard during the oppressive socialist era. Rather, these articulations reflect on historical experience of past and present predicaments in orienting a person's moral and even political actions prospectively.

Remembering

Having begun with the temporal orientations toward the present and the future, let me now move to the terrain of collective experiences of the past and how these are mediated by the idioms of dova. In the Zvijezda highlands, as indeed across Bosnia and Herzegovina, the 1992–95 war, and the memories of violence, suffering, and loss created a radical temporal rupture around which much of social and political life in the present is temporalized and organized.

As I have suggested, the Bosnian war constitutes a critical event (Das 1996), that is, a frame of reference and temporalization for both the stories of individual lives as well as the stories of competing ethnonational projects in the public sphere. Yet there is a disjuncture between "critical events" as lived frameworks of reference of past that "offers itself up" as potentiality (Jackson 2007: 83), and their appropriation in nationalist grand narratives and cosmologies in the present. This disjuncture is not uniquely Bosnian. In a similar vein, Michael Herzfeld (1991) described the disjuncture in modes of temporal reasoning between *monumental* and *social time* in the field of nationalistic cultural production.

Monumental time is the frame of the nation-state based on bureaucratic measures of history—generic, reductive, and supreme (Herzfeld 1991: 10). Or, as Michael Lambek puts it, nationalistic historiographies "put frames around [memory], they render remembering mechanical and impersonal; outside engaged experience and the give and take of social relations" (1996: 238). Social time is manifold, open-ended, affective, and embodied—it is the time frame of everyday experience and of ongoing hermeneutical engagement with the past in the present, in which grand (nationalized) historical narratives, local historical consciousness and experiences, and personal memories intersect.

Nation-state-driven historiographies, Herzfeld aptly documents, attempt to recast the past in terms of monolithic, chronological, and teleological present.

The techniques and practices for doing so can be a creation of a national monument, or the site of commemoration and associated "gatherings," that indeed mushroomed across Bosnia as a whole after the end of the war (e.g., Halilovich 2013, Jacobs 2017, Moll 2013). The commemorative practices of the Bosnian war that have become orchestrated as politically charged performances of ethnonational identities have gained prominence in Bosnian political life as well as in the scholarship of the postwar years.[6] Yet such perspectives, labeled as politics of memory (Hacking 1996), reduce the rich textures of everyday historical work and temporal reasoning to a single dimension, that of a public political teleological discourse on collective identity and memory.

The emphasis on commemorative discourses of the monumentalized past often runs against the grain of how everyday historical work operates. As Nicolas Argenti (2017) argues, the great majority of memory literature ignores the immanence of plural pasts in the present. As he puts it, "the immanence of the past in the present necessitates a shift from models of memory to a recognition of the presence of the past in everyday life" in multiple instantiations and potentialities (2017: 9). Put differently, remembering practices can be a form of everyday historical work in the present, but not every mode of everyday historical work is an act of remembering as it embraces "deeper time spans where the personal storage and retrieval of experience does not arise as a possibility" (Stewart 2016: 89). This leads me to the following questions: How are individual stories and experiences of the past entangled in collective narratives? And how do the idioms of dova become a form of everyday historical work? How do they reanimate the forms and practices of commemoration and remembering while remaining a part of religious experience as a flow of vital exchange with the divine?

In the Zvijezda highlands, the widely shared mode of engagement with the past, individual and collective, including the 1992–95 critical war events, is articulated through the idioms of dova for the souls of the dead (*dova za duše umrlih*), dova for martyrs (*šehidska dova*), and dova for rain (*dova za kišu*). Each of them follows its own temporal rhythms and choreography. Yet in the postwar years, the IC-BiH, Bosniak politicians, and local communities have invested much effort and money in raising the martyrs who died during the war into the nationalized cult of martyrdom (Bougarel 2007), and increasingly also of civilian casualties (Duranović and Karčić 2018).[7] Remembering the war martyrs has become an indispensable part of the highly nationalized commemorative politics in postwar Bosnia and Herzegovina. The politicized forms of remembering the martyrs, in turn, became part of the choreography of many religious gatherings as well.

The Srebrenica genocide during which over eight thousand male Bosnian Muslims were killed and their bodies subsequently dumped in mass graves in

"More than a commemorative site"—water well (*hajr česma*) for the good fortune of the souls of village soldiers who died during the war. By using the well daily, the living earn good deeds (sevap) on behalf of the dead.

1995 is a case in point. The Srebrenica commemoration, organized annually on July 11, is the largest Bosniak commemorative event of the war in Bosnia and Herzegovina today, during which the war atrocities are remembered and newly identified bodily remains receive an Islamic funeral (*dženaza*) (Wagner 2008). The process of creating the memorial site in Srebrenica-Potočari dates back to 2000. Writing about the process of a gradual "monumentalization" of the annual commemorative gathering of the Srebrenica massacre in public political and religious life, Lara Nettelfield and Sarah Wagner observe that the building of the memorial site encouraged "different facets of collective and individual commemoration" (2014: 41; Wagner 2008: 213–44). The orchestration of the event has been for many years an assemblage of Islamic practices, including daily prayers, the prayer for the dead, and the funeral for newly identified bodies; the date has entered the religious calendar (takvim), and a special fatwa about the massacre was issued in 2015.[8] The event has become a platform for articulating the Bosniak nationalist leadership (as well as for anti-Bosniak counter narratives) (Wagner 2008: 221).

But it is important to recognize that the nationalized facet is just one of many. Moreover, since the election of the grand mufti of the IC-BiH Husein ef. Kavazović in 2012, the political dimension has been significantly down-played during the orchestration of the commemorative ceremony in favor of highlighting the fact that the site is "a final resting place for the victims; a place for prayer and religious ritual; and a place where people could learn about the past" (Nettelfield and Wagner: 41). Following this argument, the Srebrenica commemorative site where many Bosnians as well as foreigners of different walks of life come to engage with the violent past and pay their respect to the souls of the dead in multiple ways reanimates a dominant perspective on issues of Bosnian postwar politics of memory. This has been largely discussed as being solely in a fatal embrace with publicly articulated forms of ethnonationalism and identitarian politics. Yet at the level of social time, other facets of engagement with the past through prayers and rituals of care for the dead unfold.

The dove for the martyrs performed by the living are forms of moral practice (Lambek 1996), whereby stories of individual entanglements in critical events are articulated. Villagers refer to such practices as an act of "witnessing." Many villagers have been to the Srebrenica commemorative event at least once. For the villagers, attending the Srebrenica annual gathering is a matter of patriotism as much as an act of vital exchange with the divine that cannot be separated from villagers' religious experience. Participation in the Srebrenica commemorative events, including the Marš mira (the March of Peace), has become a way for an increasing number of Bosnian Muslims, who did not

Praying for the dead in the village landscape.

necessarily lose anyone in the massacre, to relate to this critical event in the present, through religious travel, commemoration, or prayers for the deceased martyrs. Over the years of my fieldwork in the highlands, the annual Srebrenica memorial services were widely and vigorously discussed by many villagers, within families, as well as during Friday sermons in the mosques, on the streets, and in local cafés and shops. For example, in 2009 I briefly visited the capital Sarajevo before the date of the Srebrenica massacre. Returning to the village, I traveled on a bus with a few known faces from the municipality. Listening to news and gossip without even asking about the upcoming Srebrenica commemorative events, I was told that "nothing happened. It's been raining all the time and will last until Sunday, after the funeral in Srebrenica is over. It's always been like that because the sky is crying as well." When I eventually arrived at the village where I was staying, I was given almost the same explanation: "The sky is crying—the rain is Allah's tears."

It was not just the weather that resonated and invoked the events of the past in the present. It was also an omnipresent silence. Indeed, on the commemorative day during my fieldwork, people stayed inside their homes, watching live broadcasts from Srebrenica and other documentaries and programs on television, and the sawmills did not run. While watching TV programs about Srebrenica and discussing them, villagers invoked their own recollections and memories of the critical events. Others left for Srebrenica, as the local branches of the IC-BiH and municipalities organize bus trips every year, usually free of charge. One of the recurring themes in daily conversations around the date was about "who had already been there," or stating that "I would like to attend at least once in my life."[9] To ask my friends and interlocutors whether going to Srebrenica was a pious or patriotic act would not make much sense. The recurring answer to my impertinent question, "why do you feel so strongly that you should go there?" was that "I want to pray there for the souls of the martyrs, and thus *witness* what happened." The way to do so is to venerate the site and perform a dova. Prayer for the souls of the martyrs as an act of witnessing the atrocities of the past in the present became a vehicle for mediating relationships with the past.

Praying-as-witnessing is a practice of taking care of the souls of the dead whereby one's vital exchange with the dead and the divine, and the relationship between life and afterlife, are established and cultivated over a long period. Praying-as-witnessing is an act of recognition that expands the bounds of reciprocity and care beyond one's kin networks and across various scales of intimacy to those who died such a violent aberrant death. This is an ethical practice with an accompanying vocabulary of long-term reciprocity and care that renders continuity in the face of rupture comprehensive and realistic. Indeed, the act of praying or reciting dova for the souls of the dead is understood as a form of exchange with God. Performing dova for the dead is an act of giving (*pokloniti*) on behalf of the dead to Allah in return for a good deed (*sevap*) (Bringa 1995, Softić 2016). The good deed, however, goes to the soul of the dead; the living only mediate such exchanges between the dead and God. Praying-as-witnessing, in other words, needs to be understood in a wider moral economy of mourning.

The ritualized congregational prayer for the dead—tevhid—is the prime locus of the practice of taking care of the souls of the dead for village Muslims in Central Bosnia. Tevhid is orchestrated by the family of the deceased at least five times following death: on the day of the funeral, on the seventh and fortieth days after the funeral, after six months, and again after a year (Bringa 1995: 188). In the Zvijezda highlands, tevhid is organized in the mosques and houses. There has also been an increasingly public presence of tevhid during commemorative gatherings of the 1992–95 war that have proliferated locally in villages and municipalities, as well as nationally, and transnationally in diasporas with other forms of collective mourning (Halilovich 2013; Nettelfield and Wagner 2014: 45; Wagner 2008: 206).

Although tevhid is pivotal in the ethics of care for the souls of the dead, there are also other forms of mediating and cultivating these relationships between the living and the dead. Villagers pray and recite dova for the dead individually or collectively in the mosques, at homes, and outdoors around the holy sites and graveyards. During the last ten days of Ramadan it is mainly the Qur'anic *surah* (chapter) *Jasin* that villagers pray for the souls of the dead during the evening prayers in the mosques. In several villages along the Krivaja river in the highlands, the surah Jasin is prayed collectively for the dead every Thursday and Sunday evening respectively in the local mosques. The surah Jasin is not prayed on these occasions for a specific deceased person but rather for the souls of all dead of the respective *džemat* (local congregation), extending again the scale of care and intimacy beyond the immediate kinship networks. Praying *Fatiha* (the opening chapter of the Qur'an) on the graves situated at the outskirts of villages whenever villagers pass them on their way to the forest or the fields is another frequently performed act of care for the dead in the course of everyday life.

The Graves of the Martyrs

A gravestone, Engseng Ho (2006: 3) writes, "is a sign whose silent presence marks an absence." The graves of the martyrs and of the good people (*dobri ljudi*) who performed miracles (*keramet*) sit silently in the landscape across the

Zvijezda highlands. Villagers take care of their souls regularly by visiting, tending to, and praying at the graves. The significance of the martyrs' and good people's graves lies in their closeness to the divine. The closeness gives the martyrs and the good people the ability to mediate between God and the living (Bringa 1995: 173–74). The figure of a martyr (*šehid*) in a white robe, or a holy person (*dobri* or *evlija*) in a green robe often appears in many of the dream visions of villagers, Islamic healers, sheikhs, and some local imams as a guide through their night dreams visions and daylight dream narratives.

The category of "martyr" is elastic and inclusive. As Tone Bringa documented, it could be any Muslim "who had been innocently killed or had suffered a violent or tragic death" (174; also Škaljić 1966: 583). In the Zvijezda highlands, "šehitluci" refer to the sites of the usually unknown martyr graves from the Ottoman era or to the graves of the 1992–95 war martyrs. The 1992–95 war left behind thousands of martyr graves in village cemeteries, around local mosques, but also scattered in the landscape as its own memento and as a material remainder of the violent past (Bryant 2014). Nowadays, many Ottoman martyrs' graves sit silently in the meadows or forests, marking the absence of a person but in some cases also of any historical references or narrative; they cohabit the landscape with the shining white martyr graves from the Bosnian war (see Buturović 2015). The enduring omnipresence of šehitluci in the lived environment in the highlands has created a space "that would encourage different facets of collective and individual commemoration" (Nettelfield and Wagner 2014). Šehitluci thus act as a Bakhtinian chronotope (Bakhtin 1981)—a place in time and time in a place—that merges narratives, events and practices into a time-space where the everyday historical work takes place in the present.

Villagers' active engagement with venerating and praying at the sites, old and new, exemplifies the long-lasting significance of the ethical practice of dova as a way of taking care of martyrs' graves and their souls. It is the very elasticity of the category of "šehid" that enabled, both during and after the 1992–95 war, "Bosniak political, religious, and military leaders [to use] this word to refer to an expansive category of Muslim dead—from soldiers to civilians, men and women, heroes and victims" (Wagner 2008: 217). In making the historical transition to a new era, the practices of taking care of the souls of the dead, to invoke Heonik Kwon, placed the conflict within the dimension of a social order, social time, and the spectrum of everyday life (2008: 66). And in the course of everyday life it is the act of dova for the souls of the dead that has become an ethical practice for engaging with historical ruptures and transitions. The dova, in other words, as a mode of everyday historical work and religious experience, has encompassed the temporality of the recent violent past and ruptures rather than the other way around.

Landscape as a chronotope—šehitluci (Ottoman martyrs' graves).

Witnessing

"And at the end, one more prayer for Ottoman martyrs and for Bosniak martyrs," said the imam to the assembly of male Muslims who had gathered for one of the annual outdoor prayers for rain in the Zvijezda highlands. "You are witnessing," the imam continued, "by your prayers, by your presence here at this place, the history and continuity of Bosniaks in this region. You are witnessing and confirming our tradition, which has been sustained despite all the attempts to silence us."

The very place of outdoor prayers, which the imam intertwined in his speech with the martyrdom, suffering, and survival of the past, is nestled in the verdant foothills of the Zvijezda highlands. The prayer site has an enormous two-hundred-year-old lime tree instead of a mihrab in its center, facing in the direction of Mecca, and a cluster of old graves of unknown Ottoman soldiers to the rear (šehitluci). The old martyr graves are venerated by individual men and women, old and young, living in the vicinity, as well as farther afield, during the year. Those who venerate the martyr graves come to seek help and blessing, as well as to pray for the souls of the dead. There is a perpetual exchange of blessings and prayers around the šehitluci that maintains and cultivates vital relations between the living and the dead, and between the past and the present. In turn, as the imam's instruction about the act of praying-as-witnessing for the Ottoman and Bosnian martyrs illustrates, the critical events of the past have been absorbed into the flow of vital exchanges that take place at the holy sites in the present, and, again, it expands the bounds of reciprocity and care beyond one's kin networks and across varies scales of intimacy.

Praying for the Ottoman and Bosnian martyrs has become a part of many religious and political public gatherings in postwar Bosnia and Herzegovina during and in particular after the end of the war in 1995. In the Zvijezda highlands, praying-as-witnessing of the violent past formed the concluding part of all prayers for rain that I attended. Following the ritual calendar of rain prayers in the summer months, villagers not only collectively pray week after week for the fertility and prosperity of their bequeathed fields, houses and the living, but also commemorate and pray for the souls of the martyrs. The ritual calendar, as we saw in chapter 4, which is used to schedule the prayers for rain, counts Sundays or Tuesdays according to their respective weekly positions in relation to Jurjevdan (May 6) or Alidjun (August 2) during a given year. This calendar was modified after the 1992–1995 war. One fixed date—August 20—was added to the ritual calendar. The date marks the final collective dova gathering of the summer period in the region. This dova is orchestrated chiefly as the annual prayer for martyrs. The dova became central to the entire ritual calendar, and attracts the largest number of participants. Moreover, unlike the small-scale weekly prayers for rain orchestrated between Jurjevdan and Alidjun, the date of the final dova was moved from the local ritual calendar to Takvim—the religious calendar of the IC-BiH. The dova has thus been embedded in the postwar processes of a gradual "monumentalization" of the violent past in the present.

The closing collective gathering in the entire cycle of prayers for rain is referred to as šehidska dova and takes place in the village of Solun. The fixed date corresponds with the first officially recognized casualty in the municipality, and the funeral that took place in the village, dating back to August 20, 1992. By the end of the war in 1995, the number of martyrs buried in the verdant area (*harem*) around the local mosque rose to 140. The graveyard of martyrs in Solun is a commemorative site assembling the bodies of martyrs from various corners of the municipality, rather than indexing any mass atrocities of the Bosnian war such as Srebrenica, Koričanske Stijene, or Stupni Do. Unlike in the case of the Srebrenica commemorative complex, the bodies buried in Solun are not of formerly missing persons who have recently been identified. Nor has the annual gathering in Solun been accompanied by any new annual funerals. On the contrary, the bodies of the martyrs resting in the peaceful area around the mosque are of known individuals who were buried there during the war. The centrality of the gathering in the ritual calendar reflects its scale, choreography, and purpose. The shared reason for visiting the Šehidska dova is to

Annual prayer for martyrs in Solun—the final collective dova in the annual cycle of regional prayers for rain.

commemorate the war and take care of the souls of the martyrs, as well as the act of praying-as-witnessing to fill the void and silence indexed by the graves in the surrounding communities.

Creating a historical narrative of martyrdom is a laborious process. The poetics of martyrdom require both a constant reaffirmation through performances, and an attentive audience (Mittermaier 2015b: 588). The commemoration of the martyrs in Solun has been incorporated into the cycle of postwar nationalized commemorative gatherings that are orchestrated and managed by the IC-BiH, with the involvement of municipal and cantonal political establishments. Yet what renders the martyrs and the šehidska dova so powerful and central are not simply this-worldly affects generated by the politics of commemoration but rather affective resonances that can generate links between different layers of experience, different realms, and different temporal vectors, reaching as far back as the Ottoman past. Indeed, it is the capacity of the martyrs to converge their "otherworldly afterlife and their this-worldly social, political afterlife" (Mittermaier 2015b: 590), and thus to provide villagers, clergies, and politicians with a language to articulate and mediate between the past, present and future in locally intelligible idioms and moral practices.

Let me return to the participants in the event again. The Šehidska dova is probably the single-most important, emotionally charged, and arguably one of the biggest annual commemorative gatherings in the region that emerged after the war in the Zvijezda highlands. The gathering attracts hundreds and at times over a thousand Muslim travelers, men and women alike. The latter observation regarding participation of both female and male Muslims in a commemorative event has become characteristic for many similar events in postwar Bosnia and Herzegovina (Bringa and Henig 2017, Nettelfield and Wagner 2014, Sarač-Rujanac 2013, Wagner 2008, Wagner 2010). In the case of the outdoor prayers for rain, as well as in the case of funerals, women do not participate in the public prayers. Instead, women take part in orchestrating the tevhid—the congregational prayer for the dead. Yet, what the orchestration of Šehidska dova in Solun, or the Srebrenica annual commemorative service indicate is that the critical events of the war have transformed the relationship between gender and ritual practice. As Sarah Wagner points out, in the case of the Srebrenica massacre that deliberately targeted male Muslims, mothers, sisters, daughters, and wives often became the key participants in the funeral rituals when it came to burying their loved ones (see also Helms 2013). Similarly, the Šehidska dova, despite being incorporated into the ritual calendar of the prayers for rain that continue to be male-only gatherings, is not gender exclusive. Unlike the prayers for rain, however, its form of orchestration falls into the same aesthetic and affective registers as other postwar religious gatherings that haphazardly interweave religion and national politics of martyrdom together.

The gathering comprises individual prayers on the tombs, followed by a recitation of the Qur'an led by the local imams, and invited Islamic clerics and politicians delivering speeches, followed by collective midday namaz and prayers for martyrs. Yet such divergent forms of orchestration of the dova assembled within the ritual cycle, and diverse practices and gendered forms of inclusion in or exclusion from ritual action, were considered by my friends and interlocutors as instances of care for the dead in the pursuit of vital exchange between the living, the dead, and the divine. Furthermore, traveling to the site and praying on behalf of the martyr became an act of witnessing "a tradition that was sustained despite all attempts to silence it from history," as the imam suggested. If we leave the clearly evident nationalistic layer in the speech aside for a moment, we will be able to see the work of moral creativity and the actions of historical subjects engaging with historical junctures and ruptures, turning the acts of prayer into a way of engaging with history on the part of those who come and visit the places of the dead. But understanding the martyr's graves, and their position within the sacred landscape, would be impossible "without paying attention to the journey beyond it" as Engseng Ho suggests, and as I explore in the final chapter.

6

Blessing Falling from the Sky

One evening in 2014, I met Džafer over an iftar in Sarajevo. I enjoyed being invited to iftar as it always brought about unexpected encounters and gave me the opportunity to meet new people. It turned out that Džafer was originally from the outskirts of the Zvijezda highlands, where his parents still lived and where he regularly returned. "Did you hear about the dovište?" was one of his first questions to me. Since I had visited most of them, for the rest of the evening we could talk of nothing but the dovište. On that evening I became Džafer's interlocutor, feeding his spiritual hunger: What was the dovište like in the village where I lived? Was it different from the neighboring villages? What stories did the villagers tell about these sites? Were any *good people* associated with any of the dovište? Džafer never tired of asking these questions. As a seeker flirting with Sufism as well as other spiritual paths mediated via various online platforms that he would browse tirelessly for many hours every night, Džafer was particularly interested in the presence of the good people, or *evlija*, who might be linked to these sites in the local historical consciousness. For Džafer, dovište was a site that was instantly connected with the divine, where "*bereket* [blessing; divine grace] falls directly from the sky," as he told me. "We might not remember who exactly the *dobri* [good or holy people] were," he continued, "but their bereket is still there," as he was referring to the entire region of the Zvijezda highlands more broadly. It was therefore no coincidence, Džafer considered, that there were so many dovišta and so many graves of good people in

BiH compared with elsewhere in Europe, because BiH would play an important role when the Day of Judgment (*kijamet*) came.

The signs that the end times were coming were everywhere, he adamantly contended. Then, Džafer started listing them: the terrible floods that had hit BiH in the summer of 2014; several local earthquakes that occurred the same year; Muslims fighting other Muslims in the ongoing wars in the Middle East; the news about global warming; global economic turmoil; and the refugee crisis unfolding in the Mediterranean. Although Džafer's account echoed a common millennialist genre prevalent on many of the Islamic Internet forums and websites where he spent so much of his free time, his answer to the frenzy engendered by these virtual exchanges and discussions about the Day of Judgment was strikingly different. Unlike other participants on the online forums, who called for strict pious conduct as the only means of salvation, for Džafer the dovište, where divine grace fell directly from the sky, would become a space of refuge and protection for those who venerated these sites, prayed there, and took care of them.

Not everyone would agree with Džafer. A few years before our conversation, I was traveling by bus from Sarajevo to the Zvijezda highlands, when a billboard caught my attention. It was advertising the 499th Ajvatovica, allegedly the largest Muslim gathering in Europe. Neither the anniversary nor the advertisement itself intrigued me so much as the red graffiti visible from the bus window as we passed. Sprayed across the bottom of the billboard were the words "The biggest heretic religious feast." The second graffito was less wordy, yet the message was just as strong: the word *širk* (idolatry) had been sprayed across half of the billboard. I mentioned what I had seen to my village friends. They all quickly responded, "eh, *vehabije* [Wahhabis]!" The vernacular term "vehabije" emerged in the postwar years and refers to Muslims—Bosnian and foreign—who embrace the teaching of Salafism or other scriptural forms of Islamic teaching and practice and do not recognize the IC-BiH as their Islamic authority (see the sidebar in the introduction; see also Li 2019). The Salafi networks have entered public visibility and stirred controversies on many occasions since about 2000, and they have become vocal critics in social and print media, selected mosques, and elsewhere, of the centuries-long tradition of venerating the dovište to seek divine blessing mediated by the presence of the holy person buried there. Thus the practice of veneration and praying at the holy sites is not void of political entanglements and conflicting interpretations, as I discuss in this chapter.

The visitation of graves or other outdoor places of worship often becomes a site of contest and negotiation over boundaries of appropriate thought and practice in Islamic societies (Ho 2006: 10–11). Indeed, the two episodes illustrate the polysemic character of dovište. For Džafer, my village friends, and my other interlocutors, these are the sites where "blessing falls directly from the sky" and where villagers have entered through their veneration and prayers into vital exchange with the divine over a long period of time. They have done so despite various historical vicissitudes and attempts from religious as well as secular centers of power to mute such practices. The dovište and the forms of veneration it entails constitute a nexus that orients villagers in historical time and space, instructs them how to relate to the divine, and shapes villagers' self-construction and self-articulation of Muslimness in the course of history. For *vehabije*, the dovište represents an expression of un-Islamic idolatry, a set of wrong beliefs. But there is also the IC-BiH, local and national politicians, and numerous international Islamic actors, for whom the annual gatherings and venerations of dovište offer a platform for articulating their agendas and interests.

Although this chapter situates these two episodes within the context of the dynamics unfolding around the politics of holy sites in the Zvijezda highlands, the two episodes are also indicative of wider ambiguities and areas of contest over religious authority, authenticity, and historical consciousness in postsocialist, postwar Bosnian Muslim politics at large. The postsocialist liberation of religious life, heightened postwar ethnonational identity rhetoric, and the proliferation of international Islamic humanitarian organizations in the country have opened up public debates about the character of Bosnian Islam, about its geopolitical and georeligious orientations, and what it means to live a Muslim life. Special attention in these debates has been paid to discourses on renewed Bosniak traditions and to Muslim holy sites such as Ajvatovica, which was advertised on the defaced billboard. By tracking the local forms of visitation to the holy sites, and elucidating their polyvocality, this chapter addresses how villagers have responded to these transformations in the religious landscape in the postsocialist, postwar era.

The Journey

The engagement of the living with the graves of the holy people and martyrs, and with the dovište, cannot be fully understood without also understanding the journeys and histories of mobility behind it (Ho 2006). The dovište is not only a site fixed in a particular place. It is a node of encounter in the circuit of movement across time and space. People, miracles, sacred genealogies, and historical narratives dwell and flow in the orbit surrounding such sites. In the Zvijezda highlands, every dovište is intertwined with others through ritual calendars, through kinship and friendship relations forged between villages that are linked to the particular sites and cultivated over generations, and through personal histories of visitation and paying respect to other places in the region over a long period of time. Narratives of miracles (keramet), successful cures, and historical events associated with individual dovište are retold time and again. Very early on during my fieldwork, when I was conversing with Fadil, then in his seventies, about his religious socialization, he began with a reference to a particular dovišta. In 1955, when Fadil was ten years old, he started walking with his father to the dovište Karići to take part in the annual three-day *hatma dova*,[1] which was known regionally as little hajj (*mali hadž*), referring to the hajj in Mecca. Pointing in various directions with his index finger, Fadil then started listing other dovišta he regularly visited. In our conversation, Fadil was stringing one dovište after another into his narrative along the horizon of the Zvijezda highlands like the prayer beads that he always carried in his pocket, threaded together.

The discourses and practices surrounding the dovište thus encourage specific forms of travel to local or regional holy sites, recognized in the Islamic traditions as *ziyārat* (Eickelman and Piscatori 1990). In the highlands, this particular form of veneration is referred to by some villagers as *zijaret*, although the more common reference is the dova at a particular site. Villagers visit these sites individually or in smaller groups throughout the year whenever they seek blessings and divine intervention in their everyday life. Villagers travel in larger numbers across the highlands, along with urbanites and diasporic Bosnians living abroad, for annual gatherings scheduled according to the ritual calendar, and organized by the regional branches of the IC-BiH.

Although each individual site has its own story to tell, six distinct variables situate them in villagers' conceptual geography of dovište: scale (national-local); gender openness and restriction; historical trajectory between continuity and discontinuity (before, during, and after socialism); the degree of state involvement; presence or absence of commercial elements; and choreography, such as the inclusion of secular "folklore" elements into the ritual performances (Bringa and Henig 2017: 85). What all the sites share is the fact that they are the places where "blessing falls directly from the sky," and all dovišta thus mediate the relationship between villagers and the divine, villagers themselves, and the relationships between life and afterlife. Over the years, I frequently encountered references to the Karići dovište—the site of little hajj—that were similar to what Fadil told me early on during my fieldwork, underscoring its importance in the regional historical consciousness and in Muslim self-conceptions in the Zvijezda highlands

Karići Dovište

Dova na Karićima is the annual three-day zijaret during which Bosnian male Muslims—local and from farther afield—gather to recite the entire Qur'an (hatma dova) for Hajdar-dedo Karić, and pray for Allah, and the Ottoman and Bosnian martyrs at the place of the wooden mosque called Karići. The place is situated right at the top of the plateau at the intersection between Selačka, Budoželjska, and the Zvijezda highlands. Although there are no written historical records about Hajdar-dedo Karić, he remains alive through a vivid oral tradition, the annual dova, and Muslims' individual visits in search of blessing throughout the year. It is narrated that Hajdar-dedo Karić was one of the messengers of Islam who were brought to the Balkan peninsula during the early Islamization era. These narratives portray Hajdar-dedo Karić as a wise, knowledgeable Islamic scholar, effendi, the founder of the mosque through dream revelations, a dervish sheikh and a holy man (evlija and dobri) who performed keramet during his life. The very first tomb (mezar) next to the mosque, situated so as to face in the direction of Mecca, and with a small pit in the middle, is venerated not only during the three-day dova but during individual visits throughout the year. This kind of gravestone (nišan) was usually made for individuals who performed miracles during their lifetime. The rainwater caught in the pit is conceived as

Karići mosque—the place of *ibadet* (prayer) and mehabet (intimate conversation).

healing and is used to treat various kinds of illnesses, as well as for good luck, blessing, and fortune.

Many stories of divine power are associated with the site. During the Second World War, Četnik troops tried to burn down the wooden mosque but were unable to set it alight by any means. Another story relates that no Muslim community has dwelled on the plateau for the last 150 years, and that the mosque and pilgrimage site were used only during the annual gatherings and individual visits. The only residents living in relative proximity were a few Serbian households. The Orthodox families became very respectful caretakers for the mosque and even held the key in the past, although they did not participate in the zijaret as such. Even in the more distant villages I was repeatedly told one story. At the time when the Karići mosque was abandoned and visited only during the annual pilgrimage or individual visits, these Orthodox families despairingly struggled with bad crops as much as with illnesses of their livestock. While searching for help, they were told by an Orthodox cleric that there must be a sacred building near by their homes that they needed to take care of, and it was the Karići mosque. Eventually, the families did so and all the bad luck vanished.

During the period of socialist Yugoslavia, the Karići pilgrimage was neither sanctioned by the state nor banned by the IC-BiH. In 1993, during the Bosnian war, a VRS (Vojska Republike Srpske; the Army of Republika Srpska) army tank drove through the ancient wooden mosque. At the time, the region was barely accessible because of the many land mines scattered around the pilgrimage site during the war.[2] Local Muslims temporarily organized the annual gathering in a nearby provincial town mosque. After the war, the landscape was slowly demined, the wooden mosque was eventually rebuilt in 2002 with the timber from surrounding forest, and the three-day dova fully restored.

Although the restoration of the mosque was initiated by a group of local Bosnian Muslim patriots, the land and the mosque are officially owned and controlled by the IC-BiH. The IC-BiH is also responsible for organizing and setting the dates in July for the Karići annual gathering. The date is counted according to the old Julian calendar as the week of the eleventh Tuesday after Jurjevdan. The gathering begins with Friday's noon prayer and lasts until the Sunday midday prayer. Only male Muslims are allowed to attend the Karići gathering. The gathering involves reciting the entire Qur'an, singing *ilahija* (songs in praise of Allah), and other performances, such as singing verses from mevlud both in Turkish and Bosnian, tevhid for the Ottoman as well as Bosnian martyrs, and performing a collective devotional prayer, *kijam zikr*. The devotional prayer *kijam zikr* is performed by dervishes and led by a dervish sheikh. The devotional *zikr* prayer was also performed as part of the dova gathering under socialist

Yugoslavia; this is worth mentioning as all dervish orders in BiH had been officially banned in the 1950s by the IC-BiH itself, with the Yugoslav state's assistance, for being "devoid of cultural value" (Algar 1971: 196), and this ban lasted until 1989, following the postsocialist liberalization of religious life.

According to some Bosnian authors, the Karići pilgrimage has been an annual tradition for more than four hundred years (Muftić 2004; Mulahalilović 1989: 192–96). Some of those who associate the holy site with the ritual prayers for rain push the continuity of the practice even further back to pre-Islamic roots (Hadžijahić 1978). Be this as it may, the notion of undisrupted continuity of the Karići dova that belongs to the practice of journeying to dovište across the highlands plays an important role in Bosnian Muslims' historical consciousness throughout Central Bosnia.

Since the demise of the state socialist Yugoslav regime in the late 1980s, and in the postwar years in particular, the Muslim holy sites have become a nexus where debates often take place about continuity and discontinuity, about tradition and "new interpretations" of tradition.[3] Across the villages, this takes a form of frequent juxtaposing the Karići and the Ajvatovica sites. My friends and interlocutors often compared Karići and Ajvatovica, although the great majority had never traveled to Ajvatovica. Yet this juxtaposition and ensuing tensions are worth probing as they mirror how village Muslims make sense of the key transformations of Muslim holy sites and sacred landscape after socialism.

Ajvatovica

Let me now turn again to the story of the defaced billboard advertising the Ajvatovica pilgrimage. These days, the Ajvatovica gathering is presented by the IC-BiH as the largest Muslim pilgrimage in Europe, with a long history of continuity. This is done so despite Ajvatovica having been banned during the socialist period in 1947 and renewed only in 1990. Contrarily, according to the local Salafi circles, Ajvatovica is the largest heretic feast in BiH (Suljić 2013). So what renders Ajvatovica so contentious?

The Ajvatovica pilgrimage, near the town of Prusac, boasts legends and hagiographical accounts similar to those of the Karići site, dating back to the seventeenth century (and in some accounts to the fifteenth century), and involving another legendary messenger of Islam, an effendi, a dervish sheikh Ajvaz-dedo.[4] The stories say that Ajvaz-dedo was a holy person. When he came to Prusac, there was no proper water supply in the village. A spring was near the village, but the water was blocked by a rock. Ajvaz-dedo spent forty days praying to Allah, and on the fortieth day he dreamed about two billy goats colliding. When he awoke, the rock had split in half, freeing the water. Local villagers saw this as a miracle (keramet) and blessing (bereket), and, ever since, have traveled to the place where the rock split to perform prayers for Ajvaz-dedo and Allah.

Unlike the Karići gathering, Ajvatovica was officially banned during the socialist period, in 1947 (Mulahalilović 1989: 192–96). But again, the story is not so clear-cut. As Tone Bringa (in Bringa and Henig 2017: 91) writes,

> the story about what led to the ban has made the Ajvatovica procession in particular a powerful symbol of repression and defiance. In 1947 the procession was stopped by police before they reached Prusac. The police asked the participants at the head of the procession for official documentation for permission to proceed. They had no such documentation and refused to stop [. . .] the imam at the head of the procession was arrested a few days later. He received a six-year prison sentence. (For a detailed account of the event, see Hadžić 2005). However, like other banned religious activities, a lower-key and more secretive *dova* took place without the procession throughout Communist times. Prusac inhabitants and a small circle of trusted relatives and friends would continue to celebrate Ajvatovica out of sight of the public and the government's watchful eye, and dervishes would hold a *mevlud* and a *zikr* at the site (Hadžić 2005).

The "new" and increasingly more monumentalized Ajvatovica was created in 1990, following the postsocialist liberalization of religious conduct, supported by the IC-BiH, the SDA (led at the time by Alija Izetbegović), and various media, such as the weekly Islamic publication *Preporod.* In 1990, thousands of people attended the Ajvatovica. In the following year, 1991, it attracted even more Muslim travelers, this time also including women, and was accompanied by a cultural program (Perica 2002: 86). The program and changes in the choreography of the event need to be understood within a climate of increasingly competitive nationalisms of the time (Croat, Serb, and Bosnian Muslim or Bosniak) that became anchored in religious traditions, and instrumentalizing religious differences.[5] When the Bosnian war broke out in 1992, the gathering was interrupted again. However, since the region where the Ajvatovica pilgrimage site is located was controlled and defended during the war by the Bosnian army, Ajvatovica gained in public discourse the character of a holy land, expressing the continuity of a threatened Muslim community and its cultural heritage (Sarač-Rujanac 2013). In the postwar years, the celebrations continued with the expanded religious-cultural program and changed choreography that was introduced in 1991. Since then, Ajvatovica programs have spread to other cities in Bosnia and Herzegovina beyond Donji Vakuf and Prusac, and under the auspices of Program dana Ajvatovice there are "cultural, religious, and sports programs: in at least seven cities, including Sarajevo (Bringa and Henig 2017: 91).

The choreography of the "new" Ajvatovica has become part of the monumentalized Bosniak tradition of the postwar years as it has been promoted by the IC-BiH as well as many Bosniak politicians. The orchestration and choreography of the Days of Ajvatovica (Dani Ajvatovice) unfold as an assemblage of religious pilgrimage, political gathering, and social parade composed of various events, concerts, and lectures that are widely advertised and promoted on billboards across the Federation, as well as in televisions and newspaper advertisements. During my fieldwork, I was repeatedly told by male and female villagers alike that Ajvatovica used to be an all-male gathering; only after 1990 was it publicly promoted in the nationalized rhetoric as a gathering for all Muslims. Unlike Karići, for many of my interlocutors, the Ajvatovica pilgrimage was re-orchestrated and instrumentalized in Bosniak political discourse as a fertile national symbol in post-Yugoslav public debates on collective Bosnian Muslim identity.

Juxtapositions

Karići is an important historical anchor around which villagers can thread their individual and collective historical experiences. During my fieldwork in the highlands, I was often drawn into the conversations and memories of pilgrimage, expressing villagers' strong emotional attachment to Karići. Such conversations have a shared narrative form that characteristically starts with individual experiences, for instance, by noting the exact date villagers visited Karići for the first time and continues by recounting how all important historical dates are enfolded into their own life stories and travels to the dovište. The elderly Fadil, when asked how many times he had traveled to Karići, had a straightforward answer for me: "Only Allah knows, but as far as I remember I have never omitted, as my father never did," referring to inherited historical sensibility of obligation and care toward Karići that was cultivated in his family over generations. He also recalled specific years when he went to Karići, such as the year his father died, the year that the war in BiH broke out, and those years after the site was destroyed and later rebuilt. Younger villagers, born in the era of socialist Yugoslavia, told me other historical experiences. Men in their forties often said to me that they attended the pilgrimage for the first time only after the end of Yugoslav communism in 1990, many only after the 1990s war, when they realigned themselves with the renewed and liberalized Islamic tradition and discourses on Bosnian Muslim identity. A dervish sheikh from Herzegovina in his mid-fifties reminisced: "I visited Karići for the first time in 1981. I remember very vividly how I met old men in very old traditional clothes, fezzes wrapped in a golden cloth that they brought from hajj, and with beautifully decorated horses.

It was astonishing. They were so nice. Today it is different—these gatherings are one of the last expressions of living Bosnian Islam. It is not like Ajvatovica."

These narratives and ongoing conversations frequently juxtapose Karići and Ajvatovica. More generally, villagers are attempting to come to terms with profound transformations and monumentalization of numerous dovišta in the postsocialist, postwar years. Their accounts are often very passionate, as the narrators express pride and anger entwined with melancholy and nostalgia over the changing character of the Muslim sacred landscape. Media coverage of the Ajvatovica and the Karići events from recent years also favors the former; the latter received hardly any attention in the public sphere, and in the mass media in particular. Villagers and urbanites of various walks of life from the region also reflected on this fact and blamed the IC-BiH and its imams, as well as Bosniak politicians for overlooking Karići, and prioritizing and monumentalizing Ajvatovica. One of the villagers told me:

> Many of the [IC-BiH] representatives don't care when it comes to places like Karići. After the war, in 1997 when people wanted to return the dova back to Karići from the municipal mosque, the mufti was against it.[6] He said "I won't come—there are land mines." The old local imam, a real patriot, just said, "So what? We are going there anyway, and if you want to come, you are welcome." He at the end came, but it already demonstrated the attitude of the Islamska Zajednica [IC-BiH] toward Karići. Ajvatovica is more important for them. What do you expect, it's something that has already turned into an ideology. The previous grand Bosnian mufti [Mustafa ef. Cerić] said that the Ajvatovica is the biggest Muslim dovište in Europe. He didn't need to say anything like that. It was unnecessary and it also showed what was already at work at the time: nationalization.

What is unfolding in these narratives is a paradox. Although many villagers shared similar opinions, at the same time they were also proud that Karići had not been "sullied" yet by any novelties. Back in 2008, I was told by one Muslim traveler

> Today, Ajvatovica is like many other gatherings you can attend, all are just one big parade (*teferič*). Whereas Karići is the place where people come to pray and contemplate together (*ibadet*), to have a conversation (*mehabet*) but not a parade, and it has always been like this. Karići has had continuity! I tell you what, these Bosnian gatherings aren't what they used to be. Today, people say that they are going to a gathering, but they mean a parade (teferič). And Ajvatovica? Ehh, that's for tourists. Only Karići still continues in the way of traditional Muslims' gatherings as it used to be everywhere here. Even a few decades ago you could meet so many hajis in the Karići, the golden fezzes were just everywhere. Indeed, in the past people said, "Karići—this is our little hajj."

Narratives like this one succinctly articulate some of the competing and contradictory perceptions of how activities at the holy sites are orchestrated nowadays. The great majority of my friends and interlocutors critically reflected on the organization and choreography of the dovište. This runs to the heart of changing dynamics of power relations, shifting hierarchies, and the agency of various actors in the process of making dovište, and it magnifies the contradictions in changing postsocialist, postwar Bosnian Muslim politics. It particularly reveals how the various actors understand and validate what it means to be a Muslim or what constitutes genuine Bosnian Islamic tradition and practice, and how the long-lasting local Muslim practice of travel to the holy sites is controlled, authorized, negotiated, and contested.

In the case of Ajvatovica, it is mainly the change in its choreography that was often criticized. My village friends pointed out on various occasions that traditional Bosnian dove, such as that at Karići, used to be all male and that the IC-BiH should not have opened up the Ajvatovica gathering to women. This was also the reason some of my interlocutors cited for deciding never to conduct a pilgrimage to Ajvatovica. Another oft-repeated criticism was how Ajvatovica was turned into a widely advertised and expensive event with an opulent program. Because of its visibility, Ajvatovica opened the space for various Bosniak politicians as well as Muslim ulema to instrumentalize the event to promote themselves in the public sphere. Many local dervish communities also feel rather uneasy about the ways Ajvatovica is orchestrated, yet for different reasons. During pilgrimages over the past few years, folkloric groups from Turkey have been invited, sponsored either by Diyanet (Diyanet İşleri Başkanlığı; Turkish Directorate of Religious Affairs) or by TIKA (Türk İşbirliği ve Koordinasyon İdaresi Başkanlığı; Turkish Cooperation and Coordination Agency), to perform "classical Turkish Sufi music" alongside "whirling Turkish dervishes" as part of the construction and performance of "traditional Bosnian Islam" choreographed by the IC-BiH. By including such staged manifestations of "tradition" performed by Turkish folkloric groups, the IC-BiH silences the living tradition of Bosnian Sufism and makes it part of a distant and folklorized Ottoman past (for a similar case in Turkey, see Walton 2017). In more recent years, folkloric groups in the Ottoman army costumes took part on the stage as well. The increasingly visible presence of Turkish actors during such events indexes an increasingly assertive geopolitical role Turkey has pursued for over more than a decade in BiH and Southeast Europe at large (Merdjanova 2013, Öktem 2012). Drawing on the references to the Ottoman empire as well as on the discourse of quasi-kinship relatedness between Turkey and its "kin communities" (*akraba topluluklar*), in which the main connective tissues are Islam and shared Ottoman past, even the sites like Ajvatovica, local mosques, and other dovišta have become entangled in the neo-Ottoman realm of Turkey's geopolitical ambitions.

Karići is organized less ostentatiously than Ajvatovica. It attracts over a couple of thousand of pilgrims every year. Although it is perceived by the majority as a continuation of "traditional" and genuine Bosnian Muslim practice, the Karići dova has not been devoid of multiple tensions over the potentially competing meanings of the gathering. In summer 2009, a group of Diyanet representatives was invited by the local IC-BiH branch to attend the Karići pilgrimage. As part of its educational and humanitarian activities in Bosnia and Herzegovina, the group organized a summer Qur'anic school for children in mosques across the highlands. Some of the Turkish guests also took part in the Karići program by publicly reciting the Qur'an and mevlud. Eventually, in conjunction with the nighttime sermon, one of the guests gave a short speech during which he discussed the importance of Hajdar-dedo Karić and the even greater importance of the Ottoman Sultan Mehmed II, who conquered Bosnian lands more than five centuries ago and proselytized Islam in the region. The Turkish effendi emphasized how the sultan established intimate and enduring kinship ties (*porodične veze*) between Turkey and Bosnia and Herzegovina. This speech sharply contrasted with that of the local imam, who represented the IC-BiH and who only very briefly repeated a few historical facts about Hajdar-dedo Karić. During his talk, he did not speak of Hajdar-dedo Karić having brought Islam to the region or refer to Karići as a place connected to Sufism; instead, he characterized the Karići pilgrimage simply as a traditional gathering of Bosnian Muslims who had survived various aggressions in the past. This was not the only speech delivered by the imam in the public in a similar manner, and I found an echo of discontent among the audience.

My interlocutors contended that the imam detached himself from shared regional, long-standing historical narratives about Hajdar-dedo Karić and, as a result, departed from the local historically formed articulations and self-conceptions of what it means to be a Muslim. The great majority also rejected the Turkish guest speaker. Although he included Hajdar-dedo Karić firmly in his speech, he did so by embedding regional narratives into a grand narrative of postimperial Ottoman nostalgia in which Turkey was presented as the center, with Bosnia and Karići on a periphery that had been civilized and Islamized by the Ottomans. This statement also contradicted the attempts of the IC-BiH to present its large Muslim gatherings as being exclusively European. In a unanimous response to the entire orchestration of the pilgrimage, my Muslim interlocutors angrily disapproved: "Did they come to Turkify (*turčit*) us again?"

expressing sharp disappointment that the IC-BiH brought these Turkish guests and permitted them to intervene in the choreography of the Karići dova.

Another voice in this cacophony of discontent arose from local patriotic villagers who were engaged with the restoration of the damaged Karići mosque in early postwar years, and who were strongly attached to the story of Hajdar-dedo Karić. Yet they were largely excluded from organizing the event. These unfolding tensions illustrate that, despite the years of postsocialist liberalization, the IC-BiH is still trying to maintain a complete monopoly over the appropriation of the Bosnian sacred landscape and religious authority in its attempt to contain diverse and often competing interpretations of Islam and Muslim practice by various means, while silencing or excluding others from the orchestration of the dova.

Stinking Manure

According to Džafer, who we met at the beginning of this chapter, the Zvijezda highlands are a place of marvel due to the high number of dovište and a place where "blessing falls directly from the sky." Although Karići is the central dovište, it needs to be situated within this wider network of dovišta and the circuit of zijaret movement that intertwines them. Previous chapters discuss the long-lasting importance of local dovišta at the outskirts of villages to which villagers regularly travel in order to perform the prayers for rain, and according to the ritual calendar or their own individual circumstances, to seek blessing, prosperity, and well-being.

After 1945, the socialist Yugoslav state, with the assistance of the IC-BiH and its modernizing ethos at the time, imposed many restrictions on the use of dovišta, attempting to erase various religious practices such as prayers for rain. In the ensuing decades, nearly half of the sites ceased to exist in Central Bosnia, although numerous dovišta continued to be venerated despite the restrictions. It became common during my fieldwork to hear from older villagers, "Prayer for rain—it was the only place and moment where you could even meet people engaged with the [Communist] Party," as these events were usually organized with special approval under the official umbrella of traditional village parades (*teferič*) and gatherings. At the wake of postsocialist religious liberalization, and especially after the war ended in 1995, the organization of rain prayers gained significance again, and prayers at many sites have been revived, and in some cases incorporated into the process of monumentalization of Bosniak Islamic tradition and national collective identity.

For many villagers, who rely on their land and agricultural production due to widespread economic precarity, prayers for rain continue to be seen as significant fertility rituals that they use in order to schedule various agricultural activities. The IC-BiH and other actors view them differently. Local dervishes have actively participated in the rain prayers along with villagers and even assisted in some cases with their postsocialist revivals. For dervishes, an engagement with the dovište, and praying on these sites is also a form of historical practice. They link the proof and legitimacy of their own presence in the region with some of the dovišta that are associated in local historical consciousness with dervishes who came to proselytize Islam in the early Ottoman period. The toponyms of selected dovišta further confirm this narrative, as some of the sites are known in the vernacular as Sheikh's Tekke (Šejhova Tekija), Sheikh's Spring (Šejhova Voda), and Sheikh Feruh's Türbe (Šejh Feruhovo Turbe). Therefore, as was the case with the Karići site, by participating in the prayers for rain, many villagers also felt that they participated in continuing their spiritual tradition rooted in the region. Many imams, conversely, see these gatherings solely as a way of articulating the political identity of Bosnian Muslims, and debating, channeling, and authorizing the discourses on religious orthodoxy that have a long tradition among the urban ulema. This is often at odds with how villagers relate to the dova gatherings in their everyday historical work, and in their

Prayer for rain.

articulations of Muslimness through the practices of vital exchange with the divine at dovište—where blessing falls directly from the sky.

Over the years of my fieldwork I visited nearly all of the local prayers of rain, and became well acquainted with the imams who were responsible in organizing and leading the gatherings. After one of the prayers, I interviewed the imam who led the gathering, a cleric who had received religious training in a Gulf country. He was surprised that I was interested in these practices, and he ironically pointed out to me that "it would be better to abandon such heretical [*bogomil*] traditions." Then he added, with strong disapproval in his voice, "What a folk Islam! I don't understand why people still care." On a different occasion the imam used even more derogative language of "peasant Islam" (*seljački islam*), implying a moral hierarchy between his urban sensibilities, education, and manners, and villagers' rural practices. His opinions and comments were well-known to my friends and interlocutors. In response to his comments, villagers described the imam, apart from numerous swearwords, as a reformist. I was told that he was not born in the region and did not grow up there, and his regular income from the IC-BiH means he doesn't need to plough the soil, so he could hardly understand the importance of rain prayers. Other villagers often ironically commented that, for the reformist imams, "manure will always stink," thereby expressing the imams' detachment from village life. The reaction of one villager neatly and straightforwardly captures this ambiguity and the clashing conceptions of externally imposed scriptural reasoning and registers of Muslim conduct as they are shaped in regard to local historical consciousness: "He is not traditionalist but revolutionist. He is not interested in any tradition. If so, then it is the dead tradition contained in the books. He is from the outside, he does not understand what people care about and strive for here."

On another occasion, on which the prayer for rain was led by a local imam, the same villager who disapproved so strongly of the imam commented of the local cleric, "He is a good effendi, one of us, he does not pretend anything. The effendi is from here, not like those young imams today who don't respect our tradition, the tradition of Bosnian Muslims. Contrarily, they try to impose various foreign novelties from Turkey or Arabia where they studied. This is not good." These tensions are not simply a conflict between the "modernist" IC-BiH and parochial regional "traditionalists." The ways villagers apprehend and enact what constitutes "correct" Muslim practice or choreography of sacred spaces are often ambiguous, contradictory, and contested. In the villages where new mosques were built only recently, and often thanks to the aid of Islamic humanitarian organizations from the Gulf in the early postwar years (Benthall and Bellion-Jourdan 2003, H. Karčić 2010) and later from Turkey, the choreography of prayers for rain was also contested. In some cases, the prayers were relocated from the outdoor holy sites to the mosques, which has generated tensions in village politics, both secular and religious, and has often driven a wedge between neighbors.

During my visit to one village, I was quickly drawn into an ongoing dispute that consumed everyone for months over the relocation of the rain prayer from the outdoor holy site to the newly built village mosque: "We have a new mosque even with a balcony, so why should we climb to the hills forevermore? We should follow progress, we ought to be modern!" Here, the expression "being modern" refers to a similar rural/urban divide earlier articulated by the imam. Later, it was explained to me that the reference to "being modern" means "adjusting the tradition (*adet*) [of prayers for rain], not its abandonment." Nonetheless, on the day of the prayer for rain, approximately two hundred men of various ages assembled at the local holy site, about an hour's walk away, and the distance did not seem to deter anyone. Anthropologists of pilgrimage have long argued that movement and journeying are inseparable from actual pilgrimage sites (Coleman and Eade 2004). Indeed, here in the ongoing vital exchanges between villagers and the divine, it was the movement *to* the dovište that was as important as praying *at* the dovište.

The potential danger of tensions between villagers lies elsewhere. Throughout this chapter I have illustrated how dove and dovišta are to a great extent under the control of the IC-BiH, and any decision related to their orchestration needs to meet with the approval of the respective local IC-BiH branch (*medžilis*). In the village where a quarrel over the relocation of the gathering arose, the dispute had intensified because the newly appointed village imam, a representative of the IC-BiH, was a newcomer to the region. He had studied in Saudi Arabia, and his attitude toward prayers for rain was dismissive, meaning that he decided not to attend any of them. Some of the villagers did not hesitate to call him *vehabija*—the same term as they used to describe the vandals who sprayed the graffiti on the billboard advertising the Ajvatovica. And it was this imam's rather extreme attitude that eventually led to reconciliation of the two village factions, who became united in discontent against him and decided to invite another imam to the outdoor holy site. They invited one who did not question either the choreography or the practice of prayers, one for whom "manure does not stink."

Afterword

The Sultan Is Back

Visiting holy sites to pray for rain, well-being, and fortune, visiting a healer in moments of affliction, participating in the mourning for the dead, or giving alms to a needy neighbor rather than to the state-authorized religious institutions, are common sites of encounters and contestations over the meanings and conceptions of what it means to be Muslim and live a Muslim life across the Muslim world. But so are gardens, living rooms, cool shady spaces under the old trees in the meadows, or, increasingly, social media sites. Debates and disagreements are common in any religious tradition. Yet these are entangled in, and infused with, economic, social, and political predicaments emerging from particular historical junctures. And this is the nexus where everyday religious experiences and historical work intersect and Muslim lives are being renegotiated in Bosnia and Herzegovina today.

As we have seen throughout the preceding chapters, villagers' temporal orientations in making sense of the "hard-to-name period after 'the postwar'" (Nelson 2015: 40) as well as the postsocialist condition, emerge from within this nexus. Yet for many observers of the post-Yugoslav societies, and BiH in particular, any religious concerns continue to be rendered in the sphere of divisive ethnonational identity politics. This book offers another perspective on how villagers construe what it means to be Muslim and live a Muslim life. Of course it would be futile to ignore the ethnonational arguments. But these preoccupations, focused solely on the identitarian questions of *who I am* (and *who*

I am not), fail to address the fundamental question of *how to live* that dominates villagers' everyday concerns. As I document in the book, the pathways to addressing this question in villagers' everyday actions and conduct are multiple and uncertain, but they are all generated by human activities and interlocked through the rubric of *vital exchange*, which ultimately forge villagers' relationship with God over time. In so doing, I take the local religious sensibilities, practices, and conduct seriously as these unfold in a vast array of relations, situations, and scales in order to unpack how the politics and history unfold *within* and *as* the realm of religious experience.

The villager Raif, who we encountered at the very outset of this book, captured the sense of the affective and historical labor that villagers engage with in their everyday lives in the metaphor of "Bosnia being like a badly parked car." The "badly parked car" metaphor captured for Raif his own experiences with a series of critical historical events that have brought about an array of homogenizing processes, which he and other villagers had to negotiate. Whether these processes unfolded in the name of anti-religious secularism, religious nationalism, the spread of scriptural conceptions of Islam, or other forms of proselytizing "-isms," ranging from salafism to neoliberalism, they all brought about considerable transformations of Muslim lives in the Zvijezda highlands over the last century. Yet, as Raif himself added, "God willing [inshallah], everything will be fine," gesturing at how these experiences cannot be separated from other realms, and ultimately from God's grace and destiny.

Throughout the book I document the enduring vitality of such concerns among villagers and the creativity of cultural mediations between diverse temporal, political, and ethical realms as these reverberate in various guises, forms, materials, and genres. This includes not only villagers' engagement with recent critical events, and the ensuing economic precarity of their lives, but also increasingly clashing cosmogonies of Muslim lives in the Zvijezda highlands emerging from the current geopolitical entanglements that transcend the local postsocialist, postwar realm, as we saw in chapter 6. Let me therefore conclude this book by bringing the question of villagers' everyday historical work to a different temporal, geopolitical, and georeligious plane.

Around 1463, the troops of the Ottoman emperor, Sultan Mehmed II, conquered the Kingdom of Bosnia. It was the time of the kurban bajram (feast of sacrifice), and the troops were in the foothills of the Zvijezda highlands. To cross the river Krivaja, the troops built a bridge, and the place has carried its name ever since: Careva Ćuprija (Sultan's bridge). Here in the foothills, the troops also sacrificed rams to fulfil their religious duties. However, this was during the period of the first Islamizing encounter in the region, and there was no religious infrastructure to dictate where the collective prayer and the sacrifice could be carried out. Fortunately, one of the glades had a flattened stone that seemed particularly appropriate. The rams were brought and sacrificed there on the stone, and the soldiers followed with prayers. Since then the glade has been recognized in local toponymy as Kurban Kamen (the stone of sacrifice), and has become a place of annual collective gatherings of Muslims from the region to pray outdoors for rain at the end of May.

The act of sacrifice survives as a foundational myth, marking the beginning, and works as a narrative about the past in many cultures and societies in the past and present (Bloch 1992, Lambek 2007). For villagers who regularly attend the dovište, the legend and "the act of beginning" are lived and re-invoked in the present through acts of prayers as much as through embodied and sensual engagement with the place: through kneeling and sitting on the grass, touching the stone of sacrifice, or drinking cooling water from local springs in the surrounding forest. I learned about Kurban Kamen early on during my fieldwork in 2008. Villagers often asked me during our conversations if I had already visited Kurban Kamen and if I knew its history. The sense of pride among my friends was further cemented by the fact that the Bosnian Federal Television (Federalna Televizija) channel made a short documentary about it. I attended the annual gathering at the Kurban Kamen together with about two hundred Muslim pilgrims from the region in 2009. The orchestration of the event was indistinguishable from other outdoor gatherings I attended in the highlands over the years. Only after the gathering did I observe individual pilgrims coming and going to a rare corner of the glade where they recited the *fatiha* (the opening Qur'anic sura) in front of a fence. I discovered that the dovište complex also contained two Ottoman šehitluci—martyrs' graves—where villagers come and ask for blessing and fortune for the living, and for the souls of the dead, thus maintaining vital relations between the past and the future in the present.

In 2010 I received messages from my friends that the Turkish representatives of Diyanet (Directorate of Religious Affairs) had visited the dovište Kurban Kamen. There, they sacrificed a ram on the very stone of sacrifice that is part of the local cosmogonical story associated with the arrival of the Ottoman Sultan Mehmed II to the highlands more than five hundred years ago. When I returned to the highlands in 2012, in trying in find out what had actually taken place, I encountered various versions of the story. What all these versions have in common is that the story created for villagers a space for reflection on wider transformations of Muslim lives in postwar, postsocialist BiH. Indeed, for the villagers, they were not upset by the act as such. The act of sacrifice is a common practice performed on various occasions as we saw in chapter 3. The problem

Contested cosmogonies—Kurban Kamen.

lies in *where, how,* and *by whom* the sacrifice was performed and how it has been culturally mediated in everyday historical work. "They [the Turkish delegates] arrived here as Ottomans," villagers told me, adding "that's not acceptable."

The act of sacrifice, and the way it was orchestrated by the Turkish guests, was mediated by villagers' historical consciousness as an attempt to reenact the very "act of beginning" of the Ottoman presence abroad, in this case in the Bosnian lands as described in the village legend. The orchestration of the act of sacrifice was an inversion of hospitality, whereby the Turkish delegation acted as host rather than guest, and thereby challenging sovereignty of "spaces shaped by domestic privilege" (Shryock 2012: S21). Indeed, for villagers, this act was seen as interfering in the ways history is lived and experienced in the present. The act of sacrifice was exterior to the local everyday historical work whereby self-conceptions of what it means to be Muslim are constructed and mediated. It was an attempt to appropriate "the act of beginning," turning the status of outsiders and guests, and embedding it into a new (geopolitical) beginning and historical imagination of assertive new Turkey's foreign policy. The Diyanet delegation now represented a new *pax Ottomanica,* in which local ways of making history are hierarchically subordinate to the exterior forms of history and historical imagination, piety, and ways of being Muslim. For villagers, the mode of re-invoking the past and the historical beginning in the present belongs to the acts of "witnessing" as we saw in chapter 5. This is an instantiation of vital exchange between the divine and the living enacted through prayers, through which villagers are "witnessing" their own beginning and survival of their ways of life amid the past violent events, and thus exercising their agency as historical subjects. The act of sacrifice was of a different register of historical narratives and imagination. It was an imperial claim coming from outside, one that produces martyrs or subordinate servants. In the days that followed, these very same Turkish guests were distributing the books of the Qur'an to children and adults in the mosques, which triggered similar responses. As a response to these activities, some villagers asked, "do they think that we are illiterate peasants who can't even read and who need to be converted to Islam by the Sultan again?"

The historical analogy with the Sultan "offered itself up" (Jackson 2007: 83), and connected the events that took place a half-millennium back with the proselytizing encounter in the present. It expressed villagers' disapproval and anxiety over appropriation of the historical narratives and historical agency of Muslim lives in the Zvijezda highlands. What can we take from this story?

The various reenactments of the beginning during the gathering in 2009 and 2010 as performed by villagers, and later by the Turkish delegation, invite us to embark on our final historical meditation. The large-scale homogenizing projects—the transition from an "Ottoman order of things" to a post-Ottoman "national order of things" (Green 2010: 267), secular socialist and ethnonational postsocialist—are all embedded in the village landscape, in the local historical imagination and consciousness. They have left behind uncanny historical traces that continue to be contested and negotiated in villagers' aspirations and articulations of what it means to be Muslim and live a Muslim life in the Zvijezda highlands. A historical-ethnographic labor documenting and tracking the persistent features and durabilities of these homogenizing political ontologies (Stoler 2008), and their entwinements with grassroots counter-historicities embodied in villagers' actions, rituals, and repertoires of everyday historical work are vital exercises for developing a workable understanding of what living with the past entails, and how it shapes one's own prospective temporal orientations in the present.

Glossary

Ahiret	afterlife, the other world
Akšam namaz	evening prayer
Alidjun	celebration of fertility and harvest on August 2 (also Christian St. Elias's Day)
Bereket	blessing, divine grace
Bismillah	"In the name of God," the opening phrase in the Qur'an
Bula	female Muslim religious instructor
Dova (pl. *dove*)	nonobligatory prayer; a collective gathering, indoor or outdoor, for a nonobligatory prayer.
Dova za kišu	prayer for rain
Dovište (pl. *dovišta*)	outdoor site for individual and collective nonobligatory prayers
Dunjaluk	this world (as opposed to *ahiret*); these worldly matters
Dženaza	a Muslim funeral
Džin	jinn
Džuma	Friday sermon
Elhamdullilah	Praise be to Allah!
Evlija (also *dobri*)	a holy person
Ezan	call to prayer
Farz	Islamic obligatory practice (e.g., five daily prayers)
Hajr	the good, good luck, well-being
Hajr-dova	prayer for good luck and fortune

Halal	allowed, permissible according to the Islamic law; morally acceptable; forgiveness
Halalosum	an act of forgiveness
Haram	forbidden, prohibited according to the Islamic law
Hatma dova	recitation of the entire Qur'an, often on behalf of someone (the living or the dead)
Hodža	Islamic religious instructor, imam
Iftar	evening meal after breaking the fast during Ramadan
Ilahija	Islamic song of reverence; religious song
Inshallah	God willing; if God wills
Islamska Zajednica	Islamic Community of Bosnia and Herzegovina (IC-BiH)
Istikhara	a dream incubation prayer
Jacija	night prayer
Jurjevdan	celebration of fertility and spring on May 6 (also Christian St. George's Day)
Kabulosum	accepted; accepted from Allah
Keramet	miracle
Kijamet	the day of judgment
Komšiluk	neighborhood
Kuća	the house, house compound, household
Kurban	sacrifice, animal sacrifice, sacrificed meat
Kurban bajram	the feast of sacrifice
Mahala	residential quarter
Medžilis	regional branch of the Islamic Community
Mehabet	friendly conversation
Merhamet	mercy, good-heartedness
Mevlud	popular festive event including songs and poems honoring the birth of the Prophet Muhammad
Mezar	a grave
Moba	cooperative labor, mutual assistance
Nafaka	fortune, wealth
Namaz	obligatory daily prayers
Nišan	tombstone at a Muslim grave
Ramazanski bajram	the feast celebrating the end of Ramadan
Ramazanska vaktija	Ramadan prayer calendar
Sabah	obligatory morning prayer
Sadaka	alms, almsgiving
Šehid	Muslim martyr (a person who died heroically or innocently)
Šehidska dova	prayer for martyrs

Šehitluci	martyrs' graves, martyrs' cemetery
Sehur	morning meal before starting the fast during Ramadan
Sevap	a good deed
Sihir	sorcery
Širk	idolatry
Sofra	tablecloth, dining table, an act of commensality
Takvim	Islamic calendar
Teravija namaz	evening prayer during Ramadan
Tespih	prayer beads
Tevhid	prayers for the souls of the dead
Turbe	a mausoleum, a holy site for a holy person or a martyr
Utorkuša	Tuesday prayer for rain
Vakuf	an inalienable charitable endowment under Islamic law
Veze/Štela	setting up, maintaining connections to get things done; mediation or leverage of access to resources or services; a practice of informality
Vitre (also *sadekatul-fitr*)	obligatory almsgiving during Ramadan
Zakat	annual obligatory payment according to the Islamic law that purifies one's wealth
Zapis	a protective amulet against the attack of malevolent forces and jinns
Zijaret	religiously inspired journeying, visitation, and veneration of holy sites
Zikr	recitation and remembrance of the names of God

Notes

Introduction

1. All of the names of individuals in this book are pseudonyms.

2. A huge body of scholarship deals with the breakup of Yugoslavia and the Bosnian war. It would go beyond the scope of this book to engage fully with it. Here I refer only to key moments the reader might find helpful in contextualizing the arguments I will develop. For an excellent up-to-date overview see Baker 2015.

3. Stef Jansen's lucid summary provides a glimpse of the complex state architecture: "the two entities each had their own president, their own parliament and their own executive, consisting of over a dozen ministers each. The ten cantons in the Federation all had their own legislative assemblies and executives consisting of up to a dozen ministers [. . .] Judicial institutions were also dispersed across entities, the district and, within the Federation, across cantons. This list does not include municipal organs, local communes (MZs) or in-country and external institutions of foreign supervision" (Jansen 2015: 139).

4. The rate varies between 27 percent and 50 percent, depending on whether illegal work is factored in (Jansen 2015, Kurtović 2015).

5. Recent trends in anthropological writing about BiH have gradually moved toward a study of the reconfiguring of "normal lives" in postwar, postsocialist BiH. What has gained prominence in particular is the question of how notions of hope, citizenship and the state, care, and wellbeing unfold in everyday lives in the spatio-temporal configuration of post-Yugoslavia (see Bougarel, Helms, Duijzings 2007; Jansen, Brković, Čelebičić 2016).

6. Here I want to distinguish between the study of "Muslim identity" as being constructed in ethnonational terms in relation to non-Muslim others, and historical and religious studies of "Islam in Bosnia" and "Muslim lives". The latter build on the adjective "Bosnian" in terms of a center of religious and intellectual learning positioned within wider trans-regional networks of circulation and interaction, and "Muslim" in regard to one's religious experiences and sensibilities (Ahmed 2016, Bieber 2000, Rexhepi 2017).

7. Anthropological work on Muslim lives from the 1980s has also documented the pervasive continuity of religious practice and imagination in the course of everyday life in both rural and urban areas (Bringa 1995, Sorabji 1988).

8. For a critical diagnosis of these trends, see Asad 2003, Mahmood 2015, Wolf 1982.

9. On this historical genealogy, see, for example, Bieber 2000, Bringa 1995, Friedman 1996.

10. It is important to consider not only religious boundaries between Muslims and non-Muslims, but also socioeconomic hierarchies and how these have been cemented and/or crossed. As historical studies illustrate, in rural areas Muslim and non-Muslim peasants were equally exploited by the ruling aristocracy regardless of their "religious identity" (Bergholz 2016: 21–57; Irwin 1984: 438).

11. This position is in concordance with Gerald Creed (2011), who, based on his research of ritual revitalization in postsocialist Bulgaria, recently pointed out that scholarly privileging of ethnonational identities and their interactions in the Balkans has overlooked and devalued the importance of place identities, and the role of rituals and localized forms of knowledge and practice. As Creed observes, the exclusion of the latter while emphasizing the former "in analyses of this part of the world is an example of Balkanism par excellence" (2011: 168).

12. In the 1980s, the term *Islamic revival* gained prominence among scholars to describe the situation whereby Muslims in Yugoslavia began to actively articulate an orientation toward the Muslim world, that is, to the world outside of Yugoslavia, for inspiration and recognition. According to Cornellia Sorabji, this active attitude developed in response to the ideological position of "the official Muslim establishment, that Islam can cohabit happily with the state ideology of Socialism" (1988: 335). In this context, "the term 'Islamic Revival' is principally intended to describe a revival of active interest in Islam, rather than a conscious desire on the part of Bosnian Muslims to revive practices of the past" (331). This argument, however, is built on the assumption of a radical rupture and discontinuity from the past, which Sorabji links to the absence of Sharia values in the context of the secular state. Linking religious piety with scriptural and legalistic reasoning is however a relatively recent discourse that was promoted by Orientalist scholars and Islamic reformists alike (Ahmed 2016, Ernst 2005), including local reformists like Husein Dozo for example (Karić 2011). However, ways of being Muslim and modes of piety are manifold and cannot be reduced solely to the question of presence or absence of scriptural reasoning or performing piety in the public as "an active interest in Islam."

13. Anthropologists writing on Muslim lives have attested time and again to the enduring pervasiveness of such conceptions, described as the "circles of beneficence" (Rosen 2002), "seeking blessing and earning merit" (Bringa 1995, Softić 2016), "work for God" (Hart 2013), or, following the Maussian tradition, as an "economic theology" (Mittermaier 2013).

14. The unemployment rate among women was even higher. However, in the villages of my fieldwork, women rarely took on any employment in the past. This trend is now changing but is hampered by the lack of job opportunities.

Chapter 1. Houses in Flames

1. For similar entanglements across Eastern and Southeastern Europe, see for example Creed 2011, Duijzings 2013.

2. See Claude Lévi-Strauss and in particular Janet Carsten and Stephen Hugh-Jones (1995) on the house from a cross-cultural perspective.

3. By "ancestors" I refer here to the pervasive presence of patrilineal ideology.

4. Or as Annette Weiner (1992: 4) puts it, "the division of labor is not simply a dual gender construct, but encompasses the attention and effort that both women and men give to production and to those cosmologies that disguise the unresolvable tensions, problems, and paradoxes that make up social life."

5. The only exception to giving away bequeathed land that would not break the chain of continuity is to endow (*uvakufit*) one's property for the purpose of the common good. The conception of endowment is derived from the Islamic tradition of beneficence, and is known as *vakuf* (*waqf* in Arabic) (Singer 2008). This has been rarely practiced in the highlands. Moreover, in the interwar period (1918–39) and in particular after WWII religious property was nationalized and religious endowments confiscated (Zajimović 2010). That's also why the option of endowing one's property is steeped in mistrust and often discouraged by villagers.

6. These experiences of displacement and loss vary across villages and individual families as the fault line zigzagged across the highlands.

7. This also opens up a question about how the rural-urban dynamics and categorization play out nowadays in villages as a result of old/new socioeconomic hierarchies.

8. For the general context, see Pugh 2005. In the villages of my fieldwork, there were only a very few cases of houses built by families who now live in diaspora.

9. The traditional model of peasant households among the Slavs in Southeast Europe is known as *zadruga* (Barić 1967: 5–10; Bringa 1995: 42–54; Byrnes 1976; Filipović 1976; Halpern and Halpern 1972: 16–44; Halpern and Kideckel 1983; Hammel 1968; Hammel 1972; Kaser 1994; Mosely 1976; Wolf 1966: 38). This model has been highly idealized and nationalized by numerous historians and folklorists (Todorova 1989). For a more critical and dynamic understanding situated in particular social, political and historical junctures, see Kaser 1994, Brunnbauer 2003, Kertzer 1989.

10. See Andrei Simić's analysis of rural-urban dynamics during the early decades of socialist Yugoslavia (1974).

11. Verdery (1996: 65) argues that "socialism visibly reconfigured male and female household roles." Moreover, while the socialist regimes were drawing men out of villages into factories and industry, women have become "the bearers of a 'traditional' livelihood, since they were the ones who stayed at home in conditions from which state policies had excluded economic 'modernity'. [. . .] In women's centrality to life-cycle rituals and in their consumption styles ('traditional' clothing, food preparation, house décor, etc.) women reproduced this resistant localism more than did men" (70).

12. Indeed, as Gregory (1997: 88) points out, the act of erecting fences "transforms the meadow from being a natural good into a household good and the household that expends the labor will assert the property right."

13. For a comparative overview of the support networks in the postsocialist context, see Read and Thelen 2007.

14. On life in debt in BiH, see an excellent analysis by Larisa Jašarević (2017).

Chapter 2. Locked Doors

1. See Baskar 2012, Bougarel 1996, Halpern and Kideckel 2000, Hayden 2007, Helms 2010, Helms 2013, Jansen 2006, Maček 2009, Markowitz 2010, Sorabji 2008.

2. Indeed, numerous studies from Muslim societies point out that cultivating interpersonal relationships with one's neighbors is an important aspect of what it means to be a Muslim and live a Muslim life, though such sociality is not itself "Islamic" (Delaney 1991, Hart 2013, Marsden 2005). In his work on Islam in post-Soviet Uzbekistan, Johan Rasanayagam (2011: 18), determined three sources of Muslims' transcendent experiences. The first is revealed through the scriptural sources of the Qur'an and Sunna. The second is revealed through direct experience and observation of the world around us as a moral source in relation to which individuals might locate themselves as Muslim. And finally, the third emerges through sociality, that is, an individual's everyday involvement in interactions with fellow humans, in the neighborhood, village, market, or mosque. All of these, including sociality, form an embodied everyday experience that shapes the individual's own understandings and pursuit of a Muslim life.

3. If the average household of four to five had one cow, the surplus was minimal, and they were unable to make more than 100 KM a month. In Brdo, of the eighty-seven households, ten had two cows, and five households had three cows. In these cases, the households developed a link with an intermediary trader who came to the village weekly to buy the local dairy from them for the markets in Sarajevo and Visoko. The monthly income from selling dairy made 400–600 KM (2 KM for 1 kg soft cheese; 3 KM for 1 kg cream [*kajmak*]; 0.7 KM for 1 l milk). Paradoxically, although the cash generated through these petty entrepreneurial activities could have partially compensated for the lack of job opportunities, the families who actually owned more than one cow were already well-off.

4. As I discuss in chapter 3, *sadaka* refers to both voluntary charitable alms, but also more broadly to Muslims' conceptions of the ethics of giving.

5. On the intricate relationship between death and social order in relation to large-scale political ruptures, see Verdery 1999, Wagner 2008.

6. This trend is hardly surprising and was described widely in the older literature on the region as consequences of modernization (Du Boulay 1974), and in the case of former Yugoslavia also as a consequence of war displacements and population reshuffles (e.g., Čapo Žmegač 2007, Jansen 2005a, Jansen 2005b, Jansen 2008). However, less attention has been paid to the rural-urban dynamics as a consequence of postsocialist socioeconomic transformations in former socialist Yugoslavia, and indeed in post-socialist Southeast Europe at large (see Duijzings 2013). As Gerald Creed, based on his work in rural Bulgaria points out, "massive migration [. . .] ultimately removed a number of relations from the social field, which gradually simplified some village relations while complicating family relations that were now at a distance" (2011: 11).

7. Wagner draws on Adriana Petryna's (2002) work on trauma and suffering in the post-Chernobyl relief actions and programs during which Ukrainian citizens were stratified according to various criteria of suffering.

8. As I discuss in chapter 5, following Heonik Kwon's work on the aftermaths of the war in Vietnam, war suffering has been also appropriated by the statecraft, and in particular toward those who were killed during the war and uplifted to the status of national war heroes, in the Bosnian Muslim context martyrs (*šehidi*) (cf. Bougarel 2007). As Kwon writes: "This difference is conceived of a hierarchy of value from the perspective of the state [. . .] The state worships selfless heroes and altruistic martyrs, and in order to perform this worship, the system has to select regenerative death from the mass of war death based on a scale of virtue. The death that has done a meritorious service to the nation should be singled out and preserved for the future" (Kwon 2008: 25).

9. This observation is hardly surprising to scholars of postsocialism. This reconfiguration, however, is important to take into account when discussing komšiluk or sociality in proximity in post-Yugoslav space.

10. In the following chapter I discuss the emergence of a village moral economy articulated through the idioms of "halal exchange," whereby many of the rising inequalities are mitigated.

11. Similar programs have also been adopted in other parts of Bosnia and Herzegovina.

Chapter 3. Halal Exchange

1. Similarly, Amira Mittermaier documents the way practices of giving, their motivations, and their aspirations embrace "this-worldly parameters," "divine abundance" (*baraka*) and "the afterlife" (2013).

2. The general rate for zakat from any of the recognized categories of wealth, including gold, silver, revenue, property, and land, is 2.5 percent.

3. Unlike in other former socialist countries, no legal bill has been passed yet in BiH to restore the confiscated property of all churches and religious organizations (Zajimović 2010).

4. The infrastructures of Islamic charity were disrupted during the war. During that time, however, numerous international humanitarian organizations, including the faith-based ones, were active in the country (Benthall and Bellion-Jourdan 2003, Li 2019).

5. The Zekat office of IC-BiH (Ured Za Zekat, Islamska Zajednica u Bosni i Hercegovini), http://zekat.ba/index.php (last accessed Dec. 3, 2017). In 2013 it collected 10,191,735 KM (€5,210,915). The site works with many currencies, including AUD, CAD, CHF, EUR, GBP, and USD.

6. Vitre is calculated per household, currently 7 KM per person, so a household with five members gives 35 KM to the imam.

7. The numbers vary slightly from year to year, depending on villagers' success in finding work that coincides with the time of the feast. Nonetheless, the decrease has been by about a third.

8. In the postwar years historical inequalities between households resurfaced because subsistence farming requires resources, in particular land. Those households that control enough land regularly arrange barter exchange for various services, and also of young rams for hay from their meadows.

9. So, whereas for Weiner (1992) the "cosmological authentication" enables us to explore how hierarchies are established and objectified in social life through different forms of reciprocity and exchange, in this case, "cosmological authentication" works the other way round, as an active force to flatten hierarchies and inequalities engendered by the postwar socioeconomic inequalities.

10. As one of Mittermaier's (2014: 524) interlocutors puts it, "The poor don't need us; we need the poor. They're our gate to paradise," meaning "that the poor are better off than the wealthy because they will go to paradise without being questioned first" (see also Kochuyt 2009).

11. That Bilal and Nehrudin were brothers didn't make this arrangement automatically halal due to any assumed kin obligation.

12. Indeed, as Lambek (2015b: 221) puts it, "the incommensurability of ethical and economic value is precisely their distinctive constitutions with respect to commensurability."

13. Nowadays, a dowry mainly covers wedding-related expenses and furnishing a new household with white goods and utensils.

Chapter 4. Cosmological Time

1. The constitution of the IC-BiH states in the article 26 that its official calendars are both the lunar and the Gregorian. The official Islamic religious calendar (*takvim*) is issued by the IC-BiH every year in January and follows the Gregorian calendar. It is published either as a book, or as a wall calendar, with detailed prayer times, and the dates of religious feasts and important national dates of Bosnian Muslims' commemoration.

2. In his classic study of Bosnian Muslims in the west Bosnian highlands, Lockwood (1975: 85, 101) discusses a careful balance and synchronization of agricultural and pastoral periods. He shows how winter months contrast sharply with productive summer months, particularly at the level of social interactions. Although Lockwood (104–5) argues that Muslims in the highlands use Islamic as well as other calendars, he does not provide any systematic account. Similarly, Bringa (1995) discusses ritual calendars of Muslims in the rural context of central Bosnia. However, her primary locus of analysis is the actual conduct of religiously informed ritual actions, rather than culturally informed time-reckoning and temporalization as such.

3. Bismillah is the opening verse of the Qur'an.

4. In the Orthodox tradition, St. George is the patron saint of farm animals. The feast associated with St. George is widely spread throughout the Balkan peninsula (e.g., Sikimić and Hristov 2007). As Sobolev (2007) illustrates, the beginning of the spring-summer period that is related to St. George is often celebrated with an animal sacrifice (*kurban*) dedicated to the saint, although this wasn't the case in the Zvijezda highlands.

5. For more on St. Elias and Alidjun, see Safet HadžiMuhamedović's detailed study (2018).

6. I return to the history and politics of these sites in chapter 6. On the practice and significance of the Islamic prayers for rain in other rural Islamic contexts, see Abashin 2014, Basgöz 1967.

7. In some villages, the prayers of rain organized on Tuesdays are referred to as Tuesday's dova (*utorkuše*).

8. Women do not usually participate in the prayers for rain, although this has begun to change in recent years in villages where the outdoor gatherings were relocated to the local mosques (see ch. 6). Women, however, can and do venerate these sites individually throughout the year.

9. The focus on salāt has become one of the cornerstones of the anthropology of Islam in recent years (Mahmood 2005).

10. Similar moralizing arguments can be also found throughout the state socialist era of the 1970s and 1980s in the periodicals of the IC-BiH.

Chapter 5. Praying and Witnessing

1. As Amira Mittermaier writes, dream-visions and the miraculous often escape the anthropologist's gaze, yet "they offer much insight into the fragile processes of meaning-making in everyday life" (2015a: 112).

2. These conceptions, however, are not uniquely Muslim but widely shared irrespective of the religious tradition one draws on in Bosnia and Herzegovina (Bringa 1995, Jašarević 2012b).

3. Tone Bringa described a similar attitude on the part of the ulema in the 1980s (1995: 215).

4. See "Ahmetović: Klanjao sam istihare i vidio da će autoput graditi firme bliske vladajućim strankama," *Klix*, April 20, 2017, https://www.klix.ba/vijesti/bih/ahmetovic-klanjao-sam-istihare-i-vidio-da-ce-autoput-graditi-firme-bliske-vladajucim-strankama/170420064 (last accessed April 25, 2017).

5. See also Allan 2014, Crapanzano 1975, Edgar 2011, Ewing 1990, Lamoreaux 2002, Mittermaier 2011, Pandolfo 1997, Rothenberg 2004.

6. This dominant trend in the scholarship on the production of the past in postwar Bosnia and Herzegovina is unsurprising, as it can be found in other war-torn, post-conflict polities when it comes to questions about the ways people and polities produce knowledge about their violent pasts (Argenti and Schramm 2010).

7. This development is common across all communities in Bosnia and Herzegovina.

8. The fatwa is available at https://preporod.com/index.php/sve-vijesti/islamska-zajednica/vijesti-izbih/item/498-fetva-o-genocidu-nad-bosnjacima-u-srebrenici (last accessed February 7, 2020).

9. Muslims use this same argument when talking about the hajj.

Chapter 6. Blessing Falling from the Sky

1. A gathering during which an entire Qur'an is recited.

2. On land mines in postwar Bosnia and Herzegovina and their impact on local communities, see Henig 2012 and 2019.

3. As Vjekoslav Perica (2002) documented, this was the case for all religious communities across socialist Yugoslavia at the time.

4. In the Middle Ages, Prusac was an important town on the trading route between the Adriatic coast and Asia, and during the Ottoman era it also became an important center of Islamic learning (Bringa and Henig 2017: 90).

5. *Choreography* refers here to a configuration of actors and institutions, and the interplay between them in relation to the use and control over a (holy) site or shrine (see Barkan and Barkey 2014). The story of Ajvatovica (small Kaaba) was newly retold by a Bosniak intellectual, Husein Čepalo, in a short pamphlet published in 1991, *Ajvatovica: mala ćaba*.

6. During the war, the Karići gathering was relocated after the mosque was destroyed and the surrounding landscape heavily mined.

References

Abashin, Sergei. 2014. "A Prayer for Rain: Practicing Being Soviet and Muslim." *Journal of Islamic Studies* 25 (2): 178–200.

Ahmad, Attiya. 2017. *Everyday Conversions: Islam, Domestic Work, and South Asian Migrant Women in Kuwait.* Durham, NC: Duke University Press.

Ahmed, Shahab. 2016. *What Is Islam? The Importance of Being Islamic.* Princeton, NJ: Princeton University Press.

Alexander, Catherine. 2004. "Values, Relations and Changing Bodies: Industrial Privatisation in Kazakhstan." In *Property in Question: Appropriation, Recognition and Value Transformation in the Global Economy*, edited by C. Humphrey and K. Verdery, 251–73. Oxford: Berg.

Algar, Hamid. 1971. "Some Notes on the Naqshbandī Tarīqat in Bosnia." *Die Welt des Islams* 13 (3/4): 168–203.

Allan, Diana. 2014. *Refugees of the Revolution: Experiences of Palestine Exile.* Stanford, CA: Stanford University Press.

Amzi-Erdoğdular, Leyla. 2013. *Afterlife of Empire: Muslim-Ottoman Relations in Habsburg Bosnia-Herzegovina, 1878–1914.* PhD dissertation, Columbia University.

Anderson, Paul. 2011. "'The Piety of the Gift': Selfhood and Sociality in the Egyptian Mosque Movement." *Anthropological Theory* 11 (1): 3–21.

———. 2018. "'An Abundance of Meaning': Ramadan as an Enchantment of Society and Economy in Syria." *HAU: Journal of Ethnographic Theory* 8 (3): 610–24.

Archer, Rory. 2017. "The Moral Economy of Home Construction in Late Socialist Yugoslavia." *History and Anthropology* 29 (2): 141–62.

Argenti, Nicolas. 2017. "Introduction: The Presence of the Past in the Era of the Nation State." *Social Analysis* 61 (1): 1–25.

Argenti, Nicolas, and Katharina Schramm, eds. 2010. *Remembering Violence: Anthropological Perspectives on Intergenerational Transmission.* New York: Berghahn.

Armbrust, Walter. 2006. "Synchronizing Watches: The State, the Consumer, and Sacred Time in Ramadan Television." In *Religion, Media, and the Public Sphere*, edited by B. Meyer and A. Moors, 207–26. Bloomington: Indiana University Press.

Asad, Talal. 1986. *The Idea of an Anthropology of Islam*. Washington, DC: Georgetown University Press.

———. 2003. *Formations of the Secular: Christianity, Islam, Modernity.* Stanford, CA: Stanford University Press.

Bachelard, Gaston. 1969. *The Poetics of Space*. Translated by Maria Jolas. Boston: Beacon Press.

Baer, Marc, Ussama Makdisi, and Andrew Shryock. 2009. "Tolerance and Conversion in the Ottoman Empire: A Conversation." *Comparative Studies in Society and History* 51 (4): 927–40.

Baker, Catherine. 2015. *The Yugoslav Wars of the 1990s.* Basingstoke: Palgrave Macmillan.

Bakhtin, Mikhail M. 1981. *The Dialogic Imagination: Four Essays.* Translated by Caryl Emerson and Michael Holquist. Austin: University of Texas Press.

Bandak, Andreas. 2017. "The Social Life of Prayers—Introduction." *Religion* 47 (1): 1–18.

———. 2019. "Repetition and Uncanny Temporalities: Armenians and the Recurrence of Genocide in the Levant." *History and Anthropology* 30 (2): 190–211.

Barić, Lorraine. 1967. "Levels of Change in Yugoslav Kinship." In *Social Organization: Essays Presented to Raymond Firth*, edited by M. Freedman, 1–24. London: Frank Cass.

Barišić, Srdan. 2008. "Institucionalizacija Islamskih Zajednica Nakon Raspada SFR Jugoslavije." *Filozofija i Društvo* (2): 117–27.

Barkan, Elazar, and Karen Barkey, eds. 2014. *Choreographies of Shared Sacred Sites: Religion, Politics and Conflict Resolution*. New York: Columbia University Press.

Barraud, Cecile, et al. 1994. *Of Relations and the Dead: Four Societies Viewed from the Angle of Their Exchanges.* Translated by Stephen J. Suffern. Oxford: Berg.

Barth, Fredrik. 1969. "Introduction: Ethnic Groups and Boundaries." In *Ethnic Groups and Boundaries: The Social Organization of Culture Difference*, edited by F. Barth, 9–38. London: George Allen & Unwin.

Basgöz, Ilhan. 1967. "Rain-Making Ceremonies in Turkey and Seasonal Festivals." *Journal of the American Oriental Society* 87 (3): 304–6.

Baskar, Bojan. 2012. "*Komšiluk* and Taking Care of the Neighbour's Shrine in Bosnia-Herzegovina." In *Sharing Sacred Spaces in the Mediterranean: Christians, Muslims, and Jews at Shrines and Sanctuaries*, edited by D. Albera and M. Couroucli, 51–68. Bloomington: Indiana University Press.

Bear, Laura. 2015. *Navigating Austerity: Currents of Debt Along a South Asian River*. Stanford, CA: Stanford University Press.

Benthall, Jonathan. 1999. "Financial Worship: The Quranic Injunction of Almsgiving." *Journal of the Royal Anthropological Institute* 5 (1): 27–42.

Benthall, Jonathan, and Jérôme Bellion-Jourdan. 2003. *The Charitable Crescent: Politics of Aid in the Muslim World.* London: I. B. Tauris.

Berdahl, Daphne. 1999. *Where the World Ended: Re-Unification and Identity in the German Borderland.* Berkeley: University of California Press.

Bergholz, Max. 2016. *Violence as a Generative Force: Identity, Nationalism, and Memory in a Balkan Community.* Ithaca, NY: Cornell University Press.

Bernard, Sara. 2012. "Developing the Yugoslav *Gastarbeiter* Reintegration Policy: Political and Economic Aspects (1969–1974)." Working Paper No. 5. Centre for South East European Studies. Graz: University of Graz.

Bieber, Florian. 2000. "Muslim Identity in the Balkans before the Establishment of Nation States." *Nationalities Papers* 28 (1): 13–28.

Bloch, Maurice. 1992. *Prey into Hunter: The Politics of Religious Experience.* Cambridge: Cambridge University Press.

Bloch, Maurice, and Jonathan Parry, eds. 1982. *Death and the Regeneration of Life*. Cambridge: Cambridge University Press.

Bougarel, Xavier. 1996. *Bosnie: Anatomie d'un conflit.* Paris: La Découverte.

———. 2003. "Islam and Politics in the Post-Communist Balkans." In *New Approaches to Balkan Studies*, edited by D. Keridis and C. Perry, 345–60. Dulles, VA: Brassey's.

———. 2007. "Death and the Nationalist: Martydrom, War Memory and Veteran Identity among Bosnian Muslims." In Bougarel, Helms, and Duijzings, *New Bosnian Mosaic*, 167–91.

———. 2018. *Islam and Nationhood in Bosnia-Herzegovina: Surviving Empires.* Translated by Christopher Mobley. London: Bloomsbury.

Bougarel, Xavier, Elissa Helms, and Ger Duijzings, eds. 2007. *The New Bosnian Mosaic: Identities, Memories and Moral Claims in a Post-War Society.* Aldershot, UK: Ashgate.

Bourdieu, Pierre. 1977. *Outline of a Theory of Practice.* Translated by Richard Nice. Cambridge: Cambridge University Press.

Bowen, John R. 1989. "*Salāt* in Indonesia: The Social Meaning of an Islamic Ritual." *Man* 24 (4): 600–619.

———. 1992. "On Scriptural Essentialism and Ritual Variation: Muslim Sacrifice in Sumatra and Morocco." *American Ethnologist* 19 (4): 656–71.

Brenner, Suzanne April. 1998. *The Domestication of Desire: Women, Wealth and Modernity in Java.* Princeton, NJ: Princeton University Press.

Bringa, Tone. 1995. *Being Muslim the Bosnian Way. Identity and Community in a Central Bosnian Village.* Princeton, NJ: Princeton University Press.

———. 2016. "From Boundaries to Borders: Spatial Practices and State-Making: The Case of Bosnia-Herzegovina." In *Eurasian Borderlands: Spatializing Borders in the Aftermath of State Collapse*, edited by T. Bringa and H. Toje, 213–39. New York: Palgrave Macmillan.

Bringa, Tone, and David Henig. 2017. "Seeking Blessing and Earning Merit: Muslim Travelers in Bosnia-Herzegovina." In *Muslim Pilgrimage in Europe*, edited by I. Flaskerund, and R. Natvig, 83–97. London: Routledge.

Brisebarre, Anne-Marie. 1993. "The Sacrifice of *'Id al kabir*: Islam in the French Suburbs." *Anthropology Today* 9 (1): 9–12.

Brković, Čarna. 2015. "Management of Ambiguity: Favours and Flexibility in Bosnia and Herzegovina." *Social Anthropology* 23 (3): 268–82.

——. 2016. "Scaling Humanitarianism: Humanitarian Actions in a Bosnian Town." *Ethnos* 81 (1): 99–124.

——. 2017. *Managing Ambiguity: How Clientelism, Citizenship, and Power Shape Personhood in Bosnia and Herzegovina.* New York: Berghahn.

Brunnbauer, Ulf. 2003. "Decent or Territoriality: Inheritance and Family Forms in the Late Ottoman and Early Post-Ottoman Balkans." In *Distinct Inheritances: Property, Family and Community in a Changing Europe*, edited by H. Grandits and P. Heady, 181–206. Münster: Lit Verlag.

Bryant, Rebecca. 2010. *The Past in Pieces: Belonging in the New Cyprus*. Philadelphia: University of Pennsylvania Press.

——. 2014. "History's Remainders: Belonging, Temporality, and Unfinished Pasts." *American Ethnologist* 41 (4): 681–97.

——. 2016. "Introduction: Everyday Coexistence in the Post-Ottoman Space." In *Post-Ottoman Coexistence: Sharing Space in the Shadow of Conflict*, edited by R. Bryant, 1–38. New York: Berghahn.

Bryant, Rebecca, and Daniel Knight. 2019. *The Anthropology of the Future*. Cambridge: Cambridge University Press.

Buturović, Amila. 2015. *Carved in Stone, Etched in Memory: Death, Tombstones and Commemoration in Bosnian Islam since c. 1500.* London: Routledge.

Byrnes, Robert F., ed. 1976. *Communal Families in the Balkans: The Zadruga. Essays by Philip E. Mosely and Essays in His Honour*. London: University of Notre Dame Press.

Čapo Žmegač, Jasna. 2007. *Strangers Either Way: The Lives of Croatian Refugees in Their New Home*. Translated by Nina H. Antoljak and Mateusz M. Stanojević. New York: Bergham.

Carsten, Janet, and Stephen Hugh-Jones. 1995. Introduction to *About the House: Lévi-Strauss and Beyond*, edited by J. Carsten and S. Hugh-Jones, 1–46. Cambridge: Cambridge University Press.

Čepalo, Husein. 1991. *Ajvatovica: Mala ćaba*. Mala biblioteka.

Chari, Sharad, and Katherine Verdery. 2009. "Thinking between the Posts: Postcolonialism, Postsocialism, and Ethnography after the Cold War." *Comparative Studies in Society and History* 51 (1): 6–34.

Clayer, Nathalie, and Alexandre Popović. 1997. "Muslim Identity in the Balkans in the Post-Ottoman Period." *Comparative Studies of South Asia, Africa and the Middle East* 17 (1): 17–25.

Coleman, Simon, and John Eade, eds. 2004. *Reframing Pilgrimage: Cultures in Motion.* London: Routledge.

Comaroff, Jean, and John L. Comaroff. 1999. "Occult Economies and the Violence of Abstraction: Notes from the South African Postcolony." *American Ethnologist* 26 (2): 279–303.

Crapanzano, Vincent. 1975. "Saints, Jnun, and Dreams: An Essay in Moroccan Ethnopsychology." *Psychiatry* 38 (2): 145–59.

Creed, Gerald W. 2011. *Masquerade and Postsocialism: Ritual and Cultural Dispossession in Bulgaria.* Bloomington: Indiana University Press.

Das, Veena. 1996. *Critical Events: An Anthropological Perspective on Contemporary India.* Delhi: Oxford University Press.

———. 2007. *Life and Words: Violence and the Descent into the Ordinary.* Berkeley: University of California Press.

———. 2010. "Engaging the Life of the Other: Love and Everyday Life." In *Ordinary Ethics: Anthropology, Language, and Action*, edited by M. Lambek, 376–89. New York: Fordham University Press.

———. 2012. "Ordinary Ethics." In *A Companion to Moral Anthropology*, edited by D. Fassin, 133–49. Oxford: Wiley-Blackwell.

———. 2013. "Neighbors and Acts of Silent Kindness." *HAU: Journal of Ethnographic Theory* 3 (1): 217–20.

Davis, John. 1977. *People of the Mediterranean: An Essay in Comparative Social Anthropology.* London: Routledge.

Delaney, Carol. 1991. *The Seed and the Soil: Gender and Cosmology in Turkish Village Society.* Berkeley: University of California Press.

Donais, Timothy. 2005. *The Political Economy of Peacebuilding in post-Dayton Bosnia.* London: Routledge.

Dresch, Paul. 1998. "Mutual Deception: Totality, Exchange, and Islam in the Middle East." In *Marcel Mauss: A Centenary Tribute*, edited by W. James and N. Allen, 111–33. New York: Berghahn.

Du Boulay, Juliet. 1974. *Portrait of a Greek Mountain Village.* Oxford: Clarendon Press.

Duijzings, Ger. 2007. "Commemorating Srebrenica: Histories of Violence and the Politics of Memory in Eastern Bosnia." In Bougarel, Helms, and Duijzings, *New Bosnian Mosaic*, 141–67.

———. 2013. Introduction to *Global Villages: Rural and Urban Transformations in Contemporary Bulgaria*, edited by G. Duijzings, 1–31. London: Anthem Press.

Dunn, Elizabeth Cullen. 2004. *Privatizing Poland: Baby Food, Big Business, and the Remaking of Labor.* Ithaca, NY: Cornell University Press.

Duranović, Elvir. 2019. "Historijski kontekst davanja zekata u Bosni i Hercegovini do drugog svjetskog rata." In *Zekat na poljoprivredne proizvode, stoku i trgovačku robu*, 17–31. Sarajevo: el-Kalem.

Duranović, Elvir, and Hikmet Karčić. 2018. "Selektivni prikaz materijalnih oblika memorijalizacije odbrambeno-oslobodilačkog rata i zločina nad Bošnjacima na području općine Donji Vakuf 1992–1995." *Glasnik* 3–4: 269–82.

Duranović, Elvir, and Sumeja Ljevaković-Subašić, eds. 2018. *Islamska tradicija Bošnjaka na razmeđu stoljeća: Izazovi novih tumačenja islama.* Sarajevo: Dobra knjiga.

Edgar, Iain R. 2011. *The Dream in Islam: From Qur'anic Tradition to Jihadist Inspiration.* New York: Berghahn.

Edgar, Iain, and David Henig. 2010. "*Istikhara*: The Guidance and Practice of Islamic Dream Incubation through Ethnographic Comparison." *History and Anthropology* 21 (3): 251–62.

Eickelman, Dale F., and James Piscatori, eds. 1990. *Muslim Travellers: Pilgrimage, Migration, and the Religious Imagination.* Berkeley: University of California Press.

El Guindi, Fadwa. 2008. *By Noon Prayer: The Rhythm of Islam.* New York: Berg.

Ernst, Carl W. 2005. "Ideological and Technological Transformations of Contemporary Sufism." In *Muslim Networks from Hajj to Hip Hop*, edited by M. Cooke and B. B. Lawrence, 191–207. Chapel Hill: University of North Carolina Press.

Ewing, Katherine P. 1990. "The Dream of Spiritual Initiation and the Organisation of Self Representations among Pakistani Sufis." *American Ethnologist* 17 (1): 56–74.

Fabian, Johannes. 1983. *Time and the Other: How Anthropology Makes Its Objects.* New York: Columbia University Press.

Fernandez, James W., and Renate Lellep Fernandez. 1988. "Under One Roof: Household Formation and Cultural Ideals in an Asturian Mountain Village." *Journal of Family History* 13 (1): 123–42.

Feuchtwang, Stephan. 2011. *After the Event: The Transmission of Grievous Loss in Germany, China and Taiwan.* New York: Berghahn.

Fichter, Madigan Andrea. 2017. "Student Activists and Yugoslavia's Islamic Revival: Sarajevo, 1970–1975." In *Dropping Out of Socialism: The Creation of Alternative Spheres in the Soviet Bloc*, edited by J. Fürst and J. McLellan, 85–104. London: Lexington Books.

Filipović, Milenko. 1976. "Zadruga (*kućna zadruga*)." In Byrnes, *Communal Families in the Balkans*, 268–79.

Friedman, Francine. 1996. *The Bosnian Muslims: Denial of a Nation.* Boulder, CO: Westview.

Gaibazzi, Paolo. 2015. "The Quest for Luck: Fate, Fortune, Work and the Unexpected among Gambian Soninke Hustlers." *Critical African Studies* 7 (3): 227–42.

Gellner, Ernest. 1983. *Nations and Nationalism.* Oxford: Basil Blackwell.

Ghodsee, Kristen. 2010. *Muslim Lives in Eastern Europe: Gender, Ethnicity, and the Transformation of Islam in Postsocialist Bulgaria.* Princeton, NJ: Princeton University Press.

Gilbert, Andrew. 2006. "The Past in Parenthesis. (Non)Post-Socialism in Post-War Bosnia-Herzegovina." *Anthropology Today* 22 (4): 14–18.

———. 2016. "From Humanitarianism to Humanitarianization: Intimacy, Estrangement, and International Aid in Postwar Bosnia and Herzegovina." *American Ethnologist* 43 (4): 717–29.

Gilbert, Andrew, and Jasmin Mujanović. 2015. "Dayton at Twenty: Towards New Politics in Bosnia-Herzegovina." *Southeast European and Black Sea Studies* 15 (4): 605–10.

Gilsenan, Michael. 1982. *Recognising Islam: An Anthropologist's Introduction.* London: Crom Helm.

Grant, Bruce. 2011. "Shrines and Sovereigns: Life, Death, and Religion in Rural Azerbaijan." *Comparative Studies in Society and History* 53 (3): 654–81.

Green, Sarah. 2005. *Notes from the Balkans: Locating Marginality and Ambiguity on the Greek-Albanian Border.* Princeton, NJ: Princeton University Press.

———. 2010. "Performing Border in the Aegean." *Journal of Cultural Economy* 3 (2): 261–78.

Greenberg, Jessica. 2011. "On the Road to Normal: Negotiating Agency and State Sovereignty in Postsocialist Serbia." *American Anthropologist* 113 (1): 88–100.

Gregory, Chris. 1997. *Savage Money: The Anthropology and Politics of Commodity Exchange.* Amsterdam: Harwood Academic.

Gudeman, Stephen. 2016. *Anthropology and Economy.* Cambridge: Cambridge University Press.

Guyer, Jane I. 2017. "Aftermaths and Recuperations in Anthropology." *HAU: Journal of Ethnographic Theory* 7 (1): 81–103.

Hacking, Ian. 1996. "Memory Sciences, Memory Politics." In *Tense Past: Cultural Essays in Trauma and Memory*, edited by P. Antze and M. Lambek, 67–88. New York: Routledge.

Hadžić, Mulo. 2005. *Prusac i njegovo dovište.* Sarajevo: Centar za Promociju Civilnog Društva.

Hadžijahić, Muhamed. 1978. "Sinkretistički elementi u Islamu u Bosni i Hercegovini." *Prilozi za orijentalnu filologiu* 28–29: 301–8.

HadžiMuhamedović, Safet. 2018. *Waiting for Elijah: Time and Encounter in a Bosnian Landscape.* New York: Berghahn.

Hajdarpasic, Edin. 2015. *Whose Bosnia? Nationalism and Political Imagination in the Balkans, 1840–1914.* Ithaca, NY: Cornell University Press.

Halilovich, Hariz. 2013. *Places of Pain: Forced Displacement, Popular Memory and Trans-local Identities in Bosnian War-Torn Communities.* New York: Berghahn.

Haller, Dieter, and Cris Shore, eds. 2005. *Corruption: Anthropological Perspectives.* London: Pluto Press.

Halpern, Joel Martin, and Barbara Halpern. 1972. *A Serbian Village in Historical Perspective.* New York: Irvington.

Halpern, Joel Martin, and David A. Kideckel. 1983. "Anthropology of Eastern Europe." *Annual Review of Anthropology* 12: 377–402.

Halpern, Joel Martin, and David A. Kideckel, eds. 2000. *Neighbors at War: Anthropological Perspectives on Yugoslav Ethnicity, Culture, and History.* University Park: Pennsylvania State University Press.

Hammel, E. A. 1968. *Alternative Social Structures and Ritual Relations in the Balkans.* Englewood Cliffs, NJ: Prentice-Hall.

———. 1972. *The Zadruga as Process: In Household and Family in Past Time*, edited by P. Laslett and R. Wall, 335–73. Cambridge: Cambridge University Press.

Han, Clara. 2012. *Life in Debt: Times of Care and Violence in Neoliberal Chile.* Berkeley: University of California Press.

Hann, Chris. 1998. *Property Relations: Renewing the Anthropological Tradition.* New York: Cambridge University Press.

———, ed. 2003. *The Postsocialist Agrarian Question: Property Relations and the Rural Condition.* Münster: LIT Verlag.

Hart, Kimberly. 2013. *And Then We Work for God: Rural Sunni Islam in Western Turkey*. Stanford, CA: Stanford University Press.
Harvey, David. 2004. "The 'New' Imperialism: Accumulation by Dispossession." *Socialist Register* 40: 63–87.
Hayden, Robert M. 2007. "Moral Vision and Impaired Insight: The Imagining of Other Peoples' Communities in Bosnia." *Current Anthropology* 48 (1): 105–31.
———. 2013. *From Yugoslavia to the Western Balkans: Studies of a European Disunion, 1991–2011*. Leiden: Brill.
Helms, Elissa. 2010. "The Gender of Coffee: Women and Reconciliation Initiatives in Post-War Bosnia and Herzegovina." *Focaal: Journal of Global and Historical Anthropology* 57: 17–32.
———. 2013. *Innocence and Victimhood: Gender, Nation, and Women's Activism in Postwar Bosnia-Herzegovina*. Madison: University of Wisconsin Press.
Henig, David. 2012. "Iron in the Soil: Living with Military Waste in Bosnia-Herzegovina." *Anthropology Today* 28 (1): 21–23.
———. 2019. "Living on the Frontline: Indeterminacy, Value, and Military Waste in Postwar Bosnia-Herzegovina." *Anthropological Quarterly* 92 (1): 85–110.
Henig, David, and Nicolette Makovicky, eds. 2017. *Economies of Favour after Socialism*. Oxford: Oxford University Press.
Herzfeld, Michael. 1987. *Anthropology through the Looking-Glass: Critical Ethnography in the Margins of Europe*. Cambridge: Cambridge University Press.
———. 1991. *A Place in History: Social and Monumental Time in a Creatan Town*. Princeton, NJ: Princeton University Press.
Hirschon, Renee. 1978. "Open Body/Closed Space: The Transformation of Female Sexuality." In *Defining Females*, edited by S. Ardener, 66–88. London: Croom Helm.
Ho, Engseng. 2006. *The Graves of Tarim: Genealogy and Mobility across the Indian Ocean*. Berkeley: University of California Press.
Hodžić, Vehbija. 1967. "Sujeverje, ostaci mnogoboštva (širka)." *Glasnik* 30 (7–8): 302–9.
Hromadžić, Azra. 2015. *Citizens of an Empty Nation: Youth and State-Making in Postwar Bosnia-Herzegovina*. Philadelphia: University of Pennsylvania Press.
———. 2016. "Affective Labour: Work, Love and Care for the Elderly in Bihać." In Jansen, Brković, and Čelebičić, *Negotiating Social Relations in Bosnia and Herzegovina*, 79–93.
Humphrey, Caroline. 2002. *The Unmaking of Soviet Life: Everyday Economies After Socialism*. Ithaca, NY: Cornell University Press.
IC-BiH (Islamska Zajednica u Bosni i Hercegovini). *Glasnik Vrhovnog islamskog starješinstva u SFRJ*. 1973. 36 (3–4).
Irwin, Zachary T. 1984. "The Islamic Revival and the Muslims of Bosnia-Herzegovina." *East European Quarterly* 17 (4): 437–58.
Jackson, Michael. 2007. *Excursions*. Durham, NC: Duke University Press.
Jacobs, Janet. 2017. "The Memorial at Srebrenica: Gender and the Social Meanings of Collective Memory in Bosnia-Herzegovina." *Memory Studies* 10 (4): 1–17.

Jansen, Stef. 2005a. "National Numbers in Context: Maps and Stats in Representations of the Post-Yugoslav Wars." *Identities: Global Studies in Culture and Power* 12 (1): 45–68.

———. 2005b. "Who's Afraid of White Socks? Towards a Critical Understanding of Post-Yugoslav Urban Self-Perceptions." *Ethnologica Balkanica* 9: 151–67.

———. 2006. "The Privatisation of Home and Hope: Return, Reforms and the Foreign Intervention in Bosnia-Herzegovina." *Dialectical Anthropology* 30 (3): 177–99.

———. 2007. "Remembering with a Difference: Clashing Memories of Bosnian Conflict in Everyday Life." In Bougarel, Helms, and Duijzings, *New Bosnian Mosaic*, 193–208.

———. 2008. "Troubled Locations: Return, the Life Course, and Transformations of 'Home' in Bosnia-Herzegovina." In *Struggles for Home: Violence, Hope and the Movement of People*, edited by S. Jansen and S. Löfving, 43–64. New York: Berghahn.

———. 2011. "Refuchess: Locating Bosniac Repatriates after the War in Bosnia-Herzegovina." *Population, Space and Place* 17 (1): 140–52.

———. 2015. *Yearnings in the Meantime: "Normal Lives" and the State in a Sarajevo Apartment Complex*. New York: Berghahn.

Jansen, Stef, Čarna Brković, and Vanja Čelebičić, eds. 2016. *Negotiating Social Relations in Bosnia and Herzegovina: Semiperipheral Entanglements.* London: Routledge.

Jašarević,Larisa. 2012a. "Grave Matters and the Good Life: On a Finite Economy in Bosnia." *Cambridge Anthropology* 30 (1): 25–39.

———. 2012b. "Pouring Out Postsocialist Fears: Practical Metaphysics of a Therapy at a Distance." *Comparative Studies in Society and History* 54 (04): 914–41.

———. 2017. *Health and Wealth on the Bosnian Market: Intimate Debt*. Bloomington: Indiana University Press.

Johanneau, Cécile. 2016. "The Discretion of Witness: War Camp Memories between Politicisation and Civility." In Jansen, Brković, and Čelebičić, *Negotiating Social Relations in Bosnia and Herzegovina*, 31–45.

Kaneff, Deema. 2004. *Who Owns the Past? The Politics of Time in a "Model" Bulgarian Village.* New York: Berghahn.

Karčić, Fikret. 2015. *The Other European Muslims: A Bosnian Experience.* Sarajevo: Center for Advanced Studies.

Karčić, Harun. 2010. "Islamic Revival in Post-Socialist Bosnia and Herzegovina: International Actors and Activities." *Journal of Muslim Minority Affairs* 30 (4): 519–34.

Karić, Enes. 2011. *Contributions to Twentieth Century Islamic Thought in Bosnia and Herzegovina.* Translated by Saba Risaluddin. Sarajevo: el-Kalem.

Kaser, Karl. 1994. "The Balkan Joint Family: Redefining a Problem." *Social Science History* 18 (2): 243–69.

Keane, Webb. 2001. "Money Is No Object: Materiality, Desire, and Modernity in an Indonesian Society." In *The Empire of Things: Regimes of Value and Material Culture*, edited by F. R. Myers, 65–90. Santa Fe: School of American Research Press.

Kertzer, David I. 1989. "The Joint Family Household Revisited: Demographic Constraints and Household Complexity in the European Past." *Journal of Family History* 14 (1): 1–15.

Kideckel, David A. 2008. *Getting By in Postsocialist Romania: Labor, the Body, and Working-Class Culture.* Bloomington: Indiana University Press.

Kleist, Nauja, and Stef Jansen. 2016. "Introduction: Hope over Time—Crisis, Immobility and Future-Making." *History and Anthropology* 27 (4): 373–92.

Klepal, Jaroslav. 2018. "'The Only Thing I "Earned" in the Damned War Was PTSD.' Reconsidering Veteran Sociality and Politics in Bosnia and Herzegovina." *Southeast European and Black Sea Studies* 18 (4): 489–507.

Knight, Daniel M. 2015. *History, Time, and Economic Crisis in Central Greece.* New York: Palgrave Macmillan.

Kochuyt, Thierry. 2009. "God, Gifts and Poor People: On Charity in Islam." *Social Compass* 56 (1): 98–116.

Kopytoff, Igor. 1986. "The Cultural Biography of Things: Commodization as Process." In *The Social Life of Things: Commodities in Cultural Perspective*, edited by Arjun Appadurai, 64–91. Cambridge: Cambridge University Press.

Koutkova, Karla. 2016. "'The King Is Naked': Internationality, Informality and *Ko Fol* State-Building." In Jansen, Brković, and Čelebičić, *Negotiating Social Relations in Bosnia and Herzegovina*, 109–21.

Kurtović, Larisa. 2013. "Cataloguing Tradition in a Socialist Republic: Ethnology in Bosnia-Herzegovina 1945–1990." In *The Anthropological Field on the Margins of Europe, 1945–199*, edited by Aleksandar Bošković and Chris Hann, 305–39. Münster: LIT Verlag.

——. 2015. "'Who Sows Hunger, Reaps Rage': On Protest, Indignation and Redistributive Justice in Post-Dayton Bosnia-Herzegovina." *Southeast European and Black Sea Studies* 15 (4): 639–59.

Kurtović, Larisa, and Nelli Sargsyan. 2019. "After Utopia: Leftist Imaginaries and Activist Politics in the Postsocialist World." *History and Anthropology* 30 (1): 1–19.

Kwon, Heonik. 2008. *Ghosts of War in Vietnam.* Cambridge: Cambridge University Press.

Laidlaw, James. 2014. *The Subject of Virtue: An Anthropology of Ethics and Freedom.* Cambridge: Cambridge University Press.

Lambek, Michael. 1996. "The Past Imperfect: Remembering as Moral Practice." In *Tense Past: Cultural Essays in Trauma and Memory*, edited by P. Antze and M. Lambek, 235–54. London: Routledge.

——. 2002. *The Weight of the Past: Living with History in Mahajanga, Madagascar.* Basingstoke: Palgrave Macmillan.

——. 2007. "Sacrifice and the Problem of Beginning: Meditations from Sakalava Mythopraxis." *Journal of the Royal Anthropological Institute* 13 (1): 19–38.

——. 2015a. *The Ethical Condition: Essay on Action, Person and Value.* Chicago: University of Chicago Press.

——. 2015b. "Value and Virtue." In *The Ethical Condition: Essays on Action, Person, and Value*, 214–41. Chicago: University of Chicago Press.

———. 2015c. "The Value of (Perfomative) Acts." In *The Ethical Condition: Essays on Action, Person, and Value*, 282–301. Chicago: University of Chicago Press.

Lamoreaux, John C. 2002. *The Early Muslim Tradition of Dream Interpretation*. Albany: State University of New York Press.

Leutloff-Grandits, Carolin. 2006. *Claiming Ownership in Postwar Croatia: The Dynamics of Property Relations and Ethnic Conflict in the Knin Region*. Münster: Lit Verlag.

Li, Darryl. 2019. *The Universal Enemy: Jihad, Empire, and the Challenge of Solidarity*. Stanford, CA: Stanford University Press.

Lockwood, William G. 1975. *European Moslems: Economy and Ethnicity in Eastern Bosnia*. New York: Academic Press.

Lyon, Stephen M. 2004. *An Anthropological Analysis of Local Politics and Patronage in a Pakistani Village*. Lewiston, NY: Edwin Mellen Press.

Maček, Ivana. 2009. *Sarajevo under Siege: Anthropology in Wartime*. Philadelphia: University of Pennsylvania Press.

Mahmood, Saba. 2005. *Politics of Piety: The Islamic Revival and the Feminist Subject*. Princeton, NJ: Princeton University Press.

———. 2015. *Religious Difference in a Secular Age: A Minority Report*. Princeton, NJ: Princeton University Press.

Mair, Jonathan, and Nicholas H. A. Evans. 2015. "Ethics across Borders: Incommensurability and Affinity." *HAU: Journal of Ethnographic Theory* 5 (2): 201–25.

Makovicky, Nicolette, ed. 2014. *Neoliberalism, Personhood, and Postsocialism: Enterprising Selves in Changing Economies*. Abington, UK: Ashgate.

Markowitz, Fran. 2010. *Sarajevo: A Bosnian Kaleidoscope*. Urbana: University of Illinois Press.

Marsden, Magnus. 2005. *Living Islam: Muslim Religious Experience in Pakistan's North-West Frontier*. Cambridge: Cambridge University Press.

Marsden, Magnus, and Konstantinos Retsikas, eds. 2013. *Articulating Islam: Anthropological Approaches to Muslim Worlds*. Dordrecht: Springer.

Masquelier, Adeline. 2013. "Teatime: Boredom and the Temporalities of Young Men in Niger." *Africa* 83 (1): 470–91.

Maurer, Bill. 2005. *Mutual Life, Limited: Islamic Banking, Alternative Currencies, Lateral Reason*. Princeton, NJ: Princeton University Press.

Mauss, Marcel. 2003. *On Prayer*. New York: Durkheim/Berghahn.

———. 2016. *The Gift: Expanded Edition*. Translated by Jane I Guyer. Chicago: HAU Books.

McMahon, Patrice C. 2017. *The NGO Game: Post-Conflict Peacebuilding in the Balkans and Beyond*. Ithaca, NY: Cornell University Press.

Merdjanova, Ina. 2013. *Rediscovering the Umma: Muslims in the Balkans between Nationalism and Transnationalism*. Oxford: Oxford University Press.

Mesarič, Andreja. 2017. "'Islamic Cafés' and 'Sharia Dating': Muslim Youth, Spaces of Sociability, and Partner Relationships in Bosnia-Herzegovina." *Nationalities Papers* 45 (4): 581–97.

Mitchell, Timothy. 1991. "The Limits of the State: Beyond Statist Approaches and Their Critics." *The American Political Review* 85 (1): 77–96.

Mittermaier, Amira. 2010. "A Matter of Interpretation: Dreams, Islam, and Psychology in Egypt." In *After Pluralism: Reimagining Religious Engagement*, edited by C. Bender and P. E. Klassen, 178–200. New York: Columbia University Press.

———. 2011. *Dreams That Matter: Egyptian Landscapes of the Imagination*. Berkeley: California University Press.

———. 2013. "Trading with God: Islam, Calculation, Excess." In *A Companion to the Anthropology of Religion*, edited by J. Boddy and M. Lambek, 274–93. Oxford: Wiley Blackwell.

———. 2014. "Beyond Compassion: Islamic Voluntarism in Egypt." *American Ethnologist* 41 (3): 518–31.

———. 2015a. "Dreams and the Miraculous." In *A Companion to the Anthropology of the Middle East*, edited by S. Altorki, 107–24. Oxford: Blackwell.

———. 2015b. "Death and Martyrdom in the Arab Uprising: An Introduction." *Ethnos* 80 (5): 583–604.

———. 2019. *Giving to God: Islamic Charity in Revolutionary Times*. Berkley: University of California Press.

Moll, Nicolas. 2013. "Fragmented Memories in a Fragmented Country: Memory Competition and Political Identity-Building in Today's Bosnia and Herzegovina." *Nationalities Papers* 41 (6): 910–35.

Mosely, Philip E. 1976. "The Peasant Family: The Zadruga, or Communal Joint-Family in the Balkans, and Its Recent Evolution." In Byrnes, *Communal Families in the Balkans*, 19–30.

Muehlebach, Andrea. 2012. *The Moral Neoliberal: Welfare and Citizenship in Italy*. Chicago: University of Chicago Press.

Muftić, Azmir. 2004. *Bosanski jandžik*. Vareš: N.p.

Mujanović, Jasmin. 2018. *Hunger and Fury: The Crisis of Democracy in the Balkans*. London: Hurst.

Mulahalilović, Enver. 1989. *Vjerski običaji Muslimana u Bosni i Hercegovini*. Sarajevo: Starješinstvo Islamske Zajednice.

Munn, Nancy D. 1992. "The Cultural Anthropology of Time: A Critical Essay." *Annual Review of Anthropology* 21: 93–123.

Nelson, Diane. 2015. *Who Counts? The Mathematics of Death and Life after Genocide*. Durham, NC: Duke University Press.

Nettelfield, Lara J., and Sarah E. Wagner. 2014. *Srebrenica in the Aftermath of Genocide*. Cambridge: Cambridge University Press.

Öktem, Kerem. 2012. "Global Diyanet and Multiple Networks: Turkey's New Presence in the Balkans." *Journal of Muslims in Europe* 1 (1): 27–58.

Ortner, Sherry B. 2016. "Dark Anthropology and Its Others: Theory Since the Eighties." *HAU: Journal of Ethnographic Theory* 6 (1): 47–73.

Osella, Filippo, and Benjamin Soares, eds. 2010. *Islam, Politics, Anthropology*. Oxford: Wiley-Blackwell.

Osella, Filippo, and Daromir Rudnyckyj, eds. 2017. *Religion and the Morality of the Market: Anthropological Perspectives*. Cambridge: Cambridge University Press.

Özyurek, Esra. 2015. *Being German, Becoming Muslim: Race, Religion, and Conversion in the New Europe*. Princeton, NJ: Princeton University Press.

Palmié, Stephan, and Charles Stewart. 2016. "Introduction: For an Anthropology of History." *HAU: Journal of Ethnographic Theory* 6 (1): 207–36.

Pandolfo, Stefania. 1997. *Impasse of the Angels: Scenes from a Moroccan Space of Memory*. Chicago: University of Chicago Press.

Perica, Vjekoslav. 2002. *Balkan Idols: Religion and Nationalism in Yugoslav States*. Oxford: Oxford University Press.

Petrović, Tanja. 2017. "Nostalgia for Industrial Labor in Socialist Yugoslavia or Why the Post-Socialist Affect Matters." In *Nostalgia on the Move*, 14–29. Belgrade: Museum of Yugoslavia.

Petryna, Adriana. 2002. *Life Exposed: Biological Citizens after Chernobyl*. Princeton, NJ: Princeton University Press.

Pine, Frances. 2002. "Retreat to the Household? Gendered Domains in Postsocialist Poland." In *Postsocialism: Ideals, Ideologies, and Practices in Eurasia*, edited by C. Hann, 95–113. London: Routledge.

Pugh, Michael. 2005. "Transformation in the Political Economy of Bosnia since Dayton." *International Peacekeeping* 12 (3): 448–62.

Rasanayagam, Johan. 2011. *Islam in Post-Soviet Uzbekistan: The Morality of Experience*. Cambridge: Cambridge University Press.

Read, Rosie, and Tatjana Thelen. 2007. "Social Security and Care after Socialism: Reconfigurations of Public and Private." *Focaal: Journal of Global and Historical Anthropology* 50 (1): 3–18.

Rexhepi, Piro. 2017. "Unmapping Islam in Eastern Europe: Periodization and Muslim Subjectivities in the Balkans." In *Eastern Europe Unmapped: Beyond Borders and Peripheries*, edited by I. Kacandes and Y. Komska, 53–77. New York: Berghahn.

Ries, Nancy. 2009. "Potato Ontology: Surviving Postsocialism in Russia." *Cultural Anthropology* 24 (2): 181–212.

Robbins, Joel. 2007. "Continuity Thinking and the Problem of Christian Culture: Belief, Time, and the Anthropology of Christianity." *Current Anthropology* 48 (1): 5–38.

———. 2013. "Beyond the Suffering Subject: Toward an Anthropology of the Good." *Journal of the Royal Anthropological Institute* 19 (3): 447–62.

Rogers, Douglas. 2009. *The Old Faith and the Russian Land: A Historical Ethnography of Ethics in the Urals*. Ithaca, NY: Cornell University Press.

Rosen, Lawrence. 2002. "The Circle of Beneficience: Narrating Coherence in a World of Corruption." In *The Culture of Islam: Changing Aspects of Contemporary Muslim Life*, 3–20. Chicago: Chicago University Press.

Rothenberg, Celia E. 2004. *Spirits of Palestine: Gender, Society, and the Stories of Jinn*. Lanham, MD: Lexington.

Rudnyckyj, Daromir. 2010. *Spiritual Economies: Islam, Globalization, and the Afterlife of Development*. Ithaca, NY: Cornell.

———. 2014. Economy in Practice: Islamic Finance and the Problem of Market Reason. *American Ethnologist* 41 (1): 110–27.

Sanchez, Andrew. 2015. *Criminal Capital: Violence, Corruption and Class in Industrial India*. London: Routledge.

Sarač-Rujanac, Dženita. 2013. "Ajvatovica: A Bridge Between Tradition, National and Religious Identity." *History and Anthropology* 24 (1): 117–36.

Schielke, Samuli. 2009. "Being Good in Ramadan: Ambivalence, Fragmentation, and the Moral Self in the Lives of Young Egyptians." *Journal of the Royal Anthropological Institute* 15 (1): 24–40.

———. 2010. *Second Thoughts about the Anthropology of Islam, or How to Make Sense of Grand Schemes in Everyday Life*. Berlin: Zentrum Moderner Orient Working Papers.

———. 2015. *Egypt in the Future Tense: Hope, Frustration and Ambivalence Before and After 2011*. Bloomington: Indiana University Press.

Shryock, Andrew. 2012. "Breaking Hospitality Apart: Bad Hosts, Bad Guests, and the Problem of Sovereignty." *Journal of the Royal Anthropological Institute* 18 (S1): S20-S33.

———, ed. 2010. *Islamophobia/Islamophilia: Beyond the Politics of Enemy and Friend*. Bloomington: Indiana University Press.

Sikimić, Biljana, and Petko Hristov, eds. 2007. *Kurban in the Balkans*. Belgrade: Serbian Academy of Sciences and Arts.

Simić, Andrei. 1974. "Urbanization and Cultural Process in Yugoslavia." *Anthropological Quarterly* 47 (2): 211–27.

Singer, Amy. 2008. *Charity in Islamic Societies*. Cambridge: Cambridge University Press.

Škajlić, Abdulah. 1966. *Turcizmi u srpskohrvatskom jeziku*. Sarajevo: Svjetlost.

Sobolev, Andrey N. 2007. "On Balkan Names for the Sacrificial Animal on St George's Day." In *Kurban in the Balkans*, edited by B. Sikimić and P. Hristov, 15–32. Belgrade: Serbian Academy of Sciences and Arts.

Softić, Aiša. 2016. *Obećani čas: Običaji bosanskohercegovačkih muslimana vezani za smrt*. Sarajevo: Zemaljski muzej Bosne i Hercegovine.

Sorabji, Cornelia. 1988. "Islamic Revival and Marriage in Bosnia." *Journal of the Institute of Muslim Minority Affairs* 9 (2): 331–37.

———. 1989. *Muslim Identity and Islamic Faith in Sarajevo*. PhD dissertation, Department of Social Anthropology, University of Cambridge.

———. 1994. "Mixed Motives: Islam, Nationalism and *Mevluds* in an Unstable Yugoslavia." In *Muslim Women's Choices: Religous Belief and Social Reality*, edited by C. F. El-Solh and J. Mabro, 108–27. Oxford: Berg.

———. 2006. "Managing Memories in Post-War Sarajevo: Individuals, Bad Memories, and New Wars." *Journal of the Royal Anthropological Institute* 12 (1): 1–18.

——. 2008. "Bosnian Neighbourhoods Revisited: Tolerance, Commitment and *Komšiluk* in Sarajevo." In *On the Margins of Religion*, edited by Frances Pine and João de Pina-Cabral, 97–112. New York: Berghahn.

Stewart, Charles. 2012. *Dreaming and Historical Consciousness in Island Greece*. Cambridge, MA: Harvard University Press.

——. 2016. "Historicity and Anthropology." *Annual Review of Anthropology* 45 (1): 79–94.

——. 2017. "Uncanny History: Temporal Topology in the Post-Ottoman World." *Social Analysis* 61 (1): 129–42.

Stoler, Ann Laura. 2008. "Imperial Debris: Reflections on Ruins and Ruination." *Cultural Anthropology* 23 (2): 191–219.

Suljić, Safet. 2013. *Ajvatovica—Bogumilska ostavština i novotarska tradicija*. Et-Taqwa Web Publishing.

Sutton, David, and Michael Hernandez. 2007. "Voices in the Kitchen: Cooking Tools as Inalienable Possessions." *Oral History* 35 (2): 67–76.

Tambar, Kabir. 2011. "Iterations of Lament: Anachronism and Affect in a Shi'i Islamic Revival in Turkey." *American Ethnologist* 38 (3): 484–500.

Thelen, Tatjana. 2011. "Shortage, Fuzzy Property and Other Dead Ends in the Anthropological Analysis of (Post)Socialism." *Critique of Anthropology* 31 (1): 43–61.

Thiranagama, Sharika, and Tobias Kelly. 2012. *Traitors: Suspicion, Intimacy, and the Ethics of State-Building*. Philadelphia: University of Pennsylvania Press.

Todorova, Maria. 1989. "Myth-Making in European Family History: The Zadruga Revisited." *East European Politics and Societies* 4 (1): 30–76.

Trouillot, Michel-Rolph. 1995. *Silencing the Past: Power and the Production of History*. Boston: Beacon.

UNDP Report. 2009. *The Ties that Bind: Social Capital in Bosnia and Herzegovina*. Sarajevo: United Nations Development Programme.

Verdery, Katherine. 1999. *The Political Lives of Dead Bodies: Reburial and Postsocialist Change*. New York: Columbia University Press.

——. 2003. *The Vanishing Hectare: Property and Value in Postsocialist Transylvania*. Ithaca, NY: Cornell University Press.

——, ed. 1996. *What Was Socialism, and What Comes Next?* Princeton, NJ: Princeton University Press.

Verdery, Katherine, and Caroline Humphrey, eds. 2004. *Property in Question: Value Transformation in the Global Economy*. Oxford: Berg.

Wagner, Sarah. 2008. *To Know Where He Lies: DNA Technology and the Search for Srebrenica's Missing*. Berkeley: University of California Press.

——. 2010. "Tabulating Loss, Entombing Memory: The Srebrenica-Potočari Memorial Centre." In *Memory, Mourning, Landscape*, edited by E. Anderson, A. Maddrell, K. McLoughlin, and A. Vincent, 61–78. Amsterdam: Rodopi.

Walton, Jeremy F. 2017. *Muslim Civil Society and the Politics of Religious Freedom in Turkey*. Oxford: Oxford University Press.

Walton, Jeremy F., and Piro Rexhepi. 2019. "On Institutional Pluralization and the Political Genealogies of Post-Yugoslav Islam." *Religion and Society: Advances in Research* 10: 151–67.

Weiner, Annette B. 1992. *Inalienable Possessions: The Paradox of Keeping-While-Giving*. Berkeley: University of California Press.

Werbner, Pnina. 1990. "Economic Rationality and Hierarchical Gift Economies: Value and Ranking among British Pakistanis." *Man* 25 (2): 266–85.

Wolf, Eric R. 1966. *Peasants.* Englewood Cliffs, NJ: Prentice Hall.

——. 1982. *Europe and the People without History.* Berkeley: University of California Press.

Woods, Michael. 2011. *Rural.* London: Routledge.

Zajimović, Senaid. 2010. *Vakufi u Bosni i Hercegoviny: historijat, trenutno stanje i perspektive*. Sarajevo: Islamska zajednica u BiH.

Index

DAVID HENIG is an associate professor in the Department of Cultural Anthropology at Utrecht University.

INTERPRETATIONS OF CULTURE IN THE NEW MILLENNIUM

Peruvian Street Lives: Culture, Power, and Economy among Market Women of Cuzco *Linda J. Seligmann*
The Napo Runa of Amazonian Ecuador *Michael Uzendoski*
Made-from-Bone: Trickster Myths, Music, and History from the Amazon *Jonathan D. Hill*
Ritual Encounters: Otavalan Modern and Mythic Community *Michelle Wibbelsman*
Finding Cholita *Billie Jean Isbell*
East African Hip Hop: Youth Culture and Globalization *Mwenda Ntarangwi*
Sarajevo: A Bosnian Kaleidoscope *Fran Markowitz*
Becoming Mapuche: Person and Ritual in Indigenous Chile *Magnus Course*
Kings for Three Days: The Play of Race and Gender in an Afro-Ecuadorian Festival *Jean Muteba Rahier*
Maya Market Women: Power and Tradition in San Juan Chamelco, Guatemala *S. Ashley Kistler*
Victims and Warriors: Violence, History, and Memory in Amazonia *Casey High*
Embodied Protests: Emotions and Women's Health in Bolivia *Maria Tapias*
Street Life under a Roof: Youth Homelessness in South Africa *Emily Margaretten*
Reinventing Chinese Tradition: The Cultural Politics of Late Socialism *Ka-ming Wu*
Cape Verde, Let's Go: Creole Rappers and Citizenship in Portugal *Derek Pardue*
The Street Is My Pulpit: Hip Hop and Christianity in Kenya *Mwenda Ntarangwi*
Cultural Heritage in Mali in the Neoliberal Era *Rosa De Jorio*
Somalis Abroad: Clan and Everyday Life in Finland *Stephanie R. Bjork*
Hierarchies of Care: Girls, Motherhood, and Inequality in Peru *Krista E. Van Vleet*
Remaking Muslim Lives: Everyday Islam in Postwar Bosnia and Herzegovina *David Henig*

The University of Illinois Press
is a founding member of the
Association of University Presses.

University of Illinois Press
1325 South Oak Street
Champaign, IL 61820-6903
www.press.uillinois.edu